The Song of Songs is a spiritual  on
of that king and queen of the h   he
Church. But this pleasure is wra   be
more ardently desired and may be   e).

The reception of this book into the canon cannot be accounted for but on the
ground that it represents allegorically the reciprocal love of Christ and his
people.... Jesus loves the Church, by loving every single member of the
Church; and manifests his love to the Church, by a special manifestation
made to every member of the Church. The Song was given to illustrate that
love; and hence it must be interpreted by looking at the manifestations of the
love of Jesus to every believer, and at the corresponding exercises of every
believer towards Jesus (George Burrows).

There can be no parties mentioned, besides Christ and his Bride, to whom
this Song can agree. ... the doctrines which this Song yieldeth for all
conditions, and which for believers' use are to be drawn from it, are the
same plain, solid spiritual truths which are drawn from other scriptures,
wherein Christ's love to his church and people, and their exercises are set
down (James Durham).

When the saints shall see Christ's glory and exaltation in heaven, it will
indeed possess their hearts with the greater admiration and adoring respect;
it will not awe them into any separation, but will serve only to heighten their
surprise and joy when they find Christ condescending to admit them to such
intimate access, and so fully and freely communicating himself to them. So
that if we choose Christ for our friend and portion, we shall hereafter be so
received to him that there shall be nothing to hinder the fullest enjoyment of
him to satisfy the utmost cravings of our souls. We may take our full swing
at gratifying our spiritual appetite after these holy pleasures. Christ will then
say, as in the Song of Solomon 5:1, 'Eat, O friends, drink, yea, drink
abundantly, O beloved.' And this shall be our entertainment to all eternity!
(Jonathan Edwards).

This divine poem sets forth in a most striking manner the mutual love, union,
and communion, which are between Christ and his church; also expresses
the several different frames, cases, and circumstances which attend believers
in this life; so that they can come into no state or condition, but here is
something in this song suited to their experience: which serves much to
recommend it to believers, and discovers the excellency of it (John Gill).

It is a song...or nuptial song, wherein, by the expressions of love between a
bridegroom and his bride, are set forth and illustrated the mutual affections

that pass between God and a distinguished remnant of mankind.... Christ and the church in general, Christ and particular believers, are here discoursing with abundance of mutual esteem and endearment (Matthew Henry).

This sense of the love of Christ, and the effect of it in communion with him, by prayer and praises, is divinely set forth in the Book of Canticles. The church therein is represented as the spouse of Christ; and, as a faithful spouse, she is always either solicitous about his love, or rejoicing in it.

In brief, this whole book is taken up in the description of the communion that is between the Lord Christ and his saints (John Owen).

Other books of Solomon lie more obvious and open to common understanding; but, as none entered into the holy of holies but the high priest, so none can enter into the mystery of this Song of songs, but such as have more near communion with Christ. Songs, and especially marriage songs, serve to express men's own joys, and others' praises. So this book contains the mutual joys and mutual praises betwixt Christ and his church.

As in other places the Holy Ghost sets out the joys of heaven by a sweet banquet, so here he sets out the union that we have with Christ by the union of the husband with the wife.... This book is nothing else but a plain demonstration and setting forth of the love of Christ to his church, and of the love of the church to Christ (Richard Sibbes).

If, as you observe, the Song of Solomon describes the experience of the church, it shews the dark side as well as the bright side. No one part of it is the experience of every individual at any particular time. Some are in his banqueting house, others upon their beds. Some sit under his banner, supported by his arm; while others have a faint perception of him at a distance, with many a hill and mountain between. In one thing, however, they all agree, that he is the leading object of their desires, and that they have had such a discovery of his person, work, and love, as makes him precious to their hearts (John Newton).

The true believer who has lived near to his Master will find this book to be a mass, not of gold merely, for all God's Word is this, but a mass of diamonds sparkling with brightness; and all things thou canst conceive are not to be compared with it for its matchless worth. If I must prefer one book above another, I would prefer some books of the Bible for doctrine, some for experience, some for example, some for teaching, but let me prefer this book above all others for fellowship and communion. When the Christian is nearest to heaven, this is the book he takes with him (C. H. Spurgeon).

A Commentary on

THE SONG OF SONGS

Richard Brooks

Richard Brooks (signature)

Christian Focus

ISBN 1 85792 486X

© Richard Brooks
First published in 1999
by
Christian Focus Publications
Geanies House, Fearn,
Ross-shire, IV20 1TW, Great Britain

Cover design by Owen Daily

Contents

Introduction to the Song

This commentary takes a line. There was a time when this was the received line, at least among evangelical commentators, but those days have gone, even if occasional signs of their return or recovery may be seen in some quarters.

The line in question is this: the first and foremost reason why the Song of Songs was ever written and included in the canon of Scripture is as an exposition of the spiritual relationship between the Lord Jesus Christ and his church (or, to speak in more individual terms, Christ and the believer). That relationship is set forth in terms of a marriage. Speaking on one occasion of the entire Old Testament Scriptures, the Lord Jesus declared, 'these are they which testify of me' (John 5:39). In the gracious providence of God and under the glorious inspiration of the Holy Spirit of God we have been given this book, this song, to show us Christ in his glory and his beauty as the husband and bridegroom of his church, the beloved of the believer's soul.

There are those who are willing to see and speak of Christ in the Song, but for whom this is secondary. They argue that the chief intent and import of the book is to deal with human marriage and human sexuality, then add that for those with sufficient spiritual desire and insight it is possible to proceed to discover higher things here in terms of Christ and the church. Yet I am absolutely persuaded that such a view is completely upside down, topsy-turvy. It needs to be reversed, in this sense: the book begins at the highest level and in the richest dimension with Christ and the church, from which then may be drawn (in a secondary manner) teaching concerning human marriage.

It is not to be denied that we may learn from the Song at this human level. Ephesians 5 would be sufficient to show us that, since the apostle Paul sets all that he writes concerning husbands and wives in the framework of Christ's love to the church and the church's submission to Christ, and states, 'This is a great mystery, but I speak concerning Christ and the church' (Eph. 5:32). We may learn from the Song in such precious and delicate areas as the pleasures and perils of courtship, the blessedness of the wedding day, the ups and downs of married life, the dangers of indifference arising between husband and wife (when things get settled into a regular routine), and the purity and tenderness of sexual intimacy in marriage. Very important as these and related things are in their place, they are secondary (and very much so) in the Song.

The key point is that the Song of Songs is to be understood and interpreted spiritually. It will become apparent at several points in the commentary that there is a close connection between this Old Testament book and Psalm 45. Indeed it would not be an overstatement to say that this psalm is the key to unlocking the true meaning of the Song. Further, while some have objected to the Song's canonicity even (that is, its very place in Scripture), observing that the divine name is not mentioned in it and that nowhere is the book quoted from in the New Testament, Psalm 45 is full of the Lord's name and is most certainly quoted in the New Testament and applied to Christ. Referring to that psalm, Spurgeon has remarked: 'Some here see Solomon and Pharaoh's daughter only – they are short-sighted; others see both Solomon and Christ – they are cross-eyed; well-focussed spiritual eyes see here Jesus only, or if Solomon be present at all, it must be like those hazy shadows of passers-by which cross the face of the camera, and therefore are dimly traceable upon a photographic landscape'. Such words would serve equally well with reference to the Song of Songs.

This raises something else that needs to be touched on in this introduction. Since Solomon (under Holy Spirit inspiration) wrote the Song (see the commentary on 1:1), do he and his bride (the Shulamite) figure in the Song as real characters? Or, expressing that in a better way, is there what might be called a 'real life romance' going on in the background, involving the historical king Solomon and a maiden referred to as the Shulamite? I used to take that view, but am not so persuaded now of its necessity. In many ways, such would be a complication rather than an assistance. It would direct our efforts again and again into working out and tracing all the intricate details of the human storyline, and would deflect us from the main business. In a word, it would run the risk of taking us up more with Solomon and less with Christ. True, real places are mentioned (such as Sharon, Tirzah and Jerusalem), and Solomon and the Shulamite appear by name. May not all of this, however, rather be the vehicle that the Spirit of God has chosen for the setting forth of the central theme and focus of the book, namely Christ and his church? Let each student of Scripture be persuaded in his own mind.

As will be clear throughout the commentary, then, the two leading characters in the Song (the bridgegroom and the bride) are the Lord Jesus Christ and the church/individual believers. Regarding others who feature along the way, the virgins are interpreted as more mature believers, of like spiritual mind with the Shulamite in their devotion to Christ (see page 21); the daughters of Jerusalem are believers who are young in the faith (see page 32); and the watchmen are ministers of the gospel, those who have the care of souls (see page 77).

In the Hebrew Bible this book is the first of the five books known as the Megilloth (the others are Ruth, Lamentations, Ecclesiastes and Esther). These books (scrolls) were read in connection with the different feasts and fasts of the Jews. In the case of the Song, it was read at Passover time.

Without doubt, one of the greatest needs of the present generation church, along with a fresh grip upon the doctrines of the Word, is a fresh and experimental acquaintance with the love of Christ – to know what it is to belong to him and to be married to him, to appreciate the wonders of the grace of God, to be overwhelmed at the sheer fact of being a Christian, and to be moved to a loving esteem for the church of Christ. A serious and a joyful attention to the bridegroom/bride relationship here in the Song is able, quite uniquely, to supply this need.

It will be apparent immediately from its length that this is only a very modest treatment of the Song. Hopefully it will serve as an appetizer for those who use it to go on to something fuller. In this respect there are several helps available, among which the commentaries of James Durham, George Burrowes, Matthew Henry, John Gill and Thomas Robinson stand out. What tremendous cause we have for gratitude to God for those who have gone before us in the study of the Scriptures.

An outline of the book follows, and then we proceed with the actual commentary. Careful attention has been given to essential matters of exegesis (including meanings of words, tenses of verbs, and so on, as necessary), but things cannot be left there. At the end of the day my goal in writing is the glory of God, to the benefit of souls. That being so, exposition and application must have their place (even in a compact work like this one), and the Song must also be seen in its connection with the whole of Scripture. The unity of God's Word is a remarkable and wonderful thing.

May the Spirit of God be our teacher, according to the Lord Jesus Christ's own gracious promise: 'He will glorify me, for he will take of what is mine and declare it to you' (John 16:14).

Outline of the Song

1. A glorious theme (1:1-17)
Title and Introduction (1:1)
Desiring Christ (1:2-4)
Dark but lovely (1:5-7)
The beloved's response (1:8-11)
Shared affections (1:12-17)

2. Endless pleasures (2:1-17)
The rose and the lily (2:1-2)
The apple tree (2:3)
Banquet and banner (2:4)
Lovesick blues (2:5-7)
Spring fever (2:8-13)
Doves and foxes (2:14-15)
Possessing and possessed (2:16-17)

3. A dream and a wedding (3:1-11)
The beloved missing (3:1)
The beloved sought (3:2-3)
The beloved found (3:4-5)

*

A sight to behold (3:6)
The bride's true focus (3:7-10)
The big day (3:11)

4. The garden of the Lord (4:1-16)
She is beautiful (4:1-5)
The meeting place (4:6-7)
Declaring the bride's praises (4:8-11)
Christ's garden (4:12-15)
The north and south wind (4:16)

5. The altogether lovely one (5:1-16)
Christ in his garden (5:1)

*

Another bad night (5:2-8)
A leading question (5:9)
The glory of Christ (5:10-16)

6. The beauty of Christ's church (6:1-13)
Christ gathering lilies (6:1-3)
In praise of the bride (6:4-7)
The only one (6:8-10)
Nothing between (6:11-13)

7. The prince's daughter (7:1-13)
The bridegroom continues (7:1-5)
Precious moments (7:6-9a)
Devoted to Christ (7:9b-13)

8. Come, Lord Jesus! (8:1-14)
Bridegroom and brother (8:1-4)
Christ unchanging (8:5-7)
A sister and a vineyard (8:8-12)
A final word each (8:13-14)

Chapter 1

A GLORIOUS THEME

1:1. Title and Introduction

The song of songs, which is Solomon's. These words with which this book of Scripture opens are the expression of a Hebrew superlative. 'The song of songs' means the most excellent song, the outstanding song, the pre-eminent song. It carries the sense of the all-surpassing song, the most highly treasured and praiseworthy song, the unrivalled song. There is no song like it, none to compare with it, either among divinely inspired songs or songs of merely human composition. No other song comes near it. It stands alone. Let any who would despise, ignore or neglect this song take note!

With 'the song of songs', compare 'the holy of holies' (the literal rendering of Heb. 9:3, translated 'the Holiest of all', NKJV; 'the Most Holy Place', NIV); 'the heaven of heavens' (1 Kgs. 8:27); and 'King of kings and Lord of lords' (Rev. 19:16). Notice also 'a servant of servants' (Gen. 9:25). In each case the point of the superlative is the same. With regard to 'the song of songs', everything about it (its language, its poetry, its subject, its effect) surpasses every other song, and particularly every other love song, that has ever been written. The Jews called other songs 'holy', but 'the song of songs' they called 'the holy of holies'. They likened Proverbs to the outer court of the temple, Ecclesiastes to the holy place, and the Song of songs (or Song of Solomon) to the Most Holy Place.

It 'is Solomon's'. That is to be taken as a statement of authorship. Solomon wrote it. In this respect he was one of the 'holy men of God' who 'spoke as they were moved by the Holy Spirit' (2 Pet. 1:21). Solomon was the son of King David and his wife Bathsheba. He ruled Israel from 970-931 BC. A summary of his remarkable accomplishments is given in 1 Kings. 4:20ff, of which particular interest in the present context attaches to verse 32: 'He spoke three thousand proverbs, and his songs were one thousand and five.' In the providence of God all of those songs have been lost, except for this excelling one which has been divinely preserved (along with Psalms 72 and 127, unless they were written by David of Solomon). Maybe these ones alone were inspired by the Spirit of God; or, even if they all were, the others were not designed by God to be of edification to the church or to bring glory to his name as this one was. It is worth observing, in the face of those who deny Solomonic authorship, that there has been a general consent to it from both Jewish and Christian writers throughout the history of its interpretation. Moreover, the book exudes an acquaintance with various parts of the land of Israel, along with several other links and expressions which fit with Solomon's time.

We cannot affirm precisely when Solomon wrote the Song. It may have been in the earlier years of his reign, in the days of his close walking with God. Of that time 1 Kings 3:3 records, 'And Solomon loved the LORD, walking in the statutes of his father David' (though even then adds the caveat, 'except that he sacrificed and burned incense at the high places'). Or it may not have been until later on, after God's gracious recovering of him from his backslidings and his strayings, not least those caused by his many foreign wives.

It has been described in terms of being a song which only grace can teach and only experience can learn. Why? Chiefly because of its subject. This is no ordinary love song, of the sort which are two a penny. This Scripture song sets forth the mutual love, communion, fellowship and delight between the Lord Jesus Christ and the church – or, on the more personal level, the individual Christian believer. And it does so in terms of a marriage relationship. This is not itself unusual in the Bible (compare, for example, Psalm 45, Isaiah 54, Ephesians 5 and Revelation 19). The relationship between God and his covenant people, between the Messiah and his church, is often exhibited in Scripture under the figure of a marriage, with God/Christ being called the husband or bridegroom, and the believer/church being called the wife or bride. Here is displayed 'what is the width and length and depth and height' of the love of Christ, and what it means 'to know the love of Christ which passes knowledge', in order that we 'may be filled with all the fullness of God' (Eph. 3:18-19). Here we meet the one who 'loved the church and gave himself for it' (Eph. 5:25). Here we behold 'the Son of God, who loved me and gave himself for me' (Gal. 2:20).

The 'is' (the word is understood) in 'which is Solomon's' may also be taken in the sense of 'about' or 'concerning'. However, that does not make the song an exercise in self-praise by the king of Israel. The name Solomon means 'peace'. His name was also Jedidiah (2 Sam. 12:25), the name given to him by the prophet Nathan through the word of the Lord, and which means 'loved by the Lord'. Both names are 'typical' of the Lord Jesus Christ, and express the fact that 'a greater than Solomon is here' (Matt. 12:42). At point after point King Solomon is a type of Christ, though at every one of those points the antitype (Christ) exceeds the type (Solomon) – think, for example, of areas like wealth, wisdom, kingdom, authority, glory, prince of peace, and so on. We may put it this way: under the infallible and inerrant inspiration of the Holy Spirit, this Old Testament book was written by the earthly Solomon concerning the heavenly Solomon. It has been observed that, next to the Gospels, 'the song of songs' is the fullest of Christ and the sweetest to the Christian. Its 'motto' may be said to be 2:16a: 'My beloved is mine, and I am his'.

The construction of the book is along clear lines. The two chief characters (Solomon and the Shulamite, the bridegroom and the bride) take it in turns to speak to and of one another in the language of utter devotion. They are completely taken up with one another. They see everything they could ever desire in each other. Notice that Shulamite (the name given to the female

15

character in 6:13) is the feminine form of Solomon, and so a suitable name here for the Christian, and for the church as the bride of Christ. Which one is speaking at any given moment has to be established (in the words of the NKJV footnotes) 'according to the number, gender, and person of the Hebrew words'. That same footnote adds, 'Occasionally the identity is not certain'. The book proceeds with a combination of monologues and dialogues, and while there are different Hebrew words for 'song', that employed here is a general word for a joyful and celebratory song.

1:2-4. Desiring Christ

The bride is the first to speak, and in these three verses starts as she means to go on, addressing herself to her beloved in the language of passionate desire, and longing for that desire to be fulfilled. Here the believer's fellowship with Christ is set forth under three rich and poetic pictures:

> v.2: The kisses of his mouth: the enjoyment of Christ's love
> v.3: The fragrance of his perfumes: the excellence of Christ's name
> v.4: The privacy of his chambers: the intimacy of Christ's company.

These verses are something of a crystallisation of the whole book. It is striking that no names are mentioned – but then when two people are deeply in love, no names need to be mentioned. There can only be one 'him' and one 'her'! There is no one to compare with Christ, so far as the believer is concerned, no one who can match him or even hold a candle to him.

Let him kiss me with the kisses of his mouth (1:2). These are the words of one who knows already what it is to be loved by Christ, his love being the love which loves first and which then draws out our love after him. They express the desire for fresh tokens of Christ's love, and proceed with an acknowledgment that his love is the best love of all. A kiss can signify a number of things. It may express affection. It may be a pledge of peace in some societies or a token of reconciliation after difficulties or quarrelling ('kiss and make up'). It might be an expression of honour (kissing a monarch's hand). Most of all, however, it is an expression of genuine love. You do not kiss everyone you meet; and you certainly do not kiss everyone you do kiss upon the mouth (lips), for such kisses are to be for those for whom you entertain very special love – supremely in the marriage bond, between husband and wife. It is testified of Christ in 5:16, 'His mouth is most sweet', to which may be added, 'grace is poured upon your lips' (Ps. 45:2). The spiritual reference here is to those manifestations of Christ's love which only his dearest friends can receive or have any reason to expect (compare John 15:15 and 14:21). These kisses have been called pardons, promises and seals of everlasting love. They must be, for they are the kisses of him (the lovely and glorious one) to me (the poor and sinful one).

The root of the word is 'to join to each and to join together, particularly mouth to mouth'. This appeal to Christ and for Christ is the desire of the Christian church in all ages: for Christ to manifest himself to our souls, 'that I may know him' (Phil. 3:10). It is a constant desire for more of him, and an inability to be content or satisfied without him. If ever he appears to have withdrawn or departed, everything is gone. Where Christ is truly loved, he will be truly longed for. The heart of all gospel duty and obligation, as set out in Psalm 2:12, is to 'kiss the Son'; the heart of all gospel grace and comfort is the Son kissing us. 'Smother me with kisses' is one suggested translation, attempting to reflect the intensity of the language.

It may be that such language as this was the continual prayer of the Old Testament saints as they watched and waited for the promised coming of the Messiah in his incarnation, he who is 'the consolation of Israel' (Luke 2:25). The words of the Lord Jesus Christ to his own, recorded in the four Gospels, are very much 'the kisses of his mouth', as they are applied personally by himself to our hearts through his Holy Spirit. In this connection, notice the highly personal 'me' in 'let him kiss me'. Christ's kisses are for his church as a whole, but are also for each true member of his church, by name.

With her next breath, the Shulamite changes from 'him' to 'your': **for your love is better than wine.** For NKJV 'better', NIV has 'more delightful'. Just as 'kisses' is in the plural in the first part of verse 2, so now is 'loves', though the English translations fail to show this. The plural suggests the incomparableness, superabundance, immensities, ocean depths and overwhelming discoveries that already the Christian knows of Christ's love yet also has still to make. The love of Christ is to the believer the most desirable and enjoyable love of all. It is the 'love of every love the best'.

That is brought out in the comparison 'better than wine'. Wine is put here for all earthly pleasures, tastes, exhilarations and refreshments. When Queen Esther invited the king and Haman to the banquet, it was called 'the banquet of wine' (Esth. 5:6). There are several Old Testament references to wine, especially notable being, 'You have put gladness in my heart, more than in the season that their grain and wine increased' (Ps. 4:7). There are six references to wine in the Song (1:2, 4; 4:10; 5:1; 7:9; 8:2).

Why is Christ's love better than wine? Fundamentally, because it is Christ's own love. Arising from that, here are three further reasons.

First, it can be enjoyed without fear. Great dangers can attach to the drinking of wine: over-indulging, coming under its grip to your own and others' misery, even being killed by it. Christ's love, in contrast, brings only good and not harm, only blessing and not cursing, only joy and not sorrow, only pleasure and not regret.

Second, it brings lasting delight. Wine may stimulate and satisfy for a season, but its effect wears off and may leave a person in a worse state than he began. But the Lord Jesus Christ never fails to delight the souls of those he loves and who love him.

Third, it is absolutely pure. Wine might be good or bad, clear or full of dregs. Christ's love, however, is pure as can be. The plural 'loves' here amplifies this: there is Christ's covenant love, electing love, redeeming love, adopting love, preserving love, sanctifying love, glorifying love; the love that forgives, guides, provides and instructs; the love that disciplines and chastises for our good. And his 'loves' endure for ever. This the Christian enjoys!

It follows, of necessity, that it is only those to whom Christ's love is better than wine (who prefer his love to all the delights that life can offer, and who count spiritual joys to be the highest and most delightful of all) who may expect or will enjoy the kisses of his mouth.

Because of the fragrance of your good ointments, your name is ointment poured forth (1:3). NIV translates the first phrase, 'Pleasing is the fragrance of your perfumes'. A literal translation would be, 'for your ointments (have) a good (or, lovely) fragrance'. In oriental lands, perfumes, ointments and spices were and are used very widely. Because of the climate (so often hot, sticky and dusty) people wash several times a day, and after each wash pour upon themselves and rub into themselves all sorts of fragrant oils and such like. The richer or more royal the people, the more costly, fragrant and rare the perfumes. That gives the background to verse 3, which draws attention to the fragrance of Christ's ointments.

The Lord Jesus Christ is the Lord's Anointed One, the Messiah, of whom the psalmist declares, 'All your garments are scented with myrrh and aloes and cassia' (Ps. 45:8). On a number of significant occasions in the Gospels, fragrances are mentioned in connection with him. After his birth in Bethlehem (Matt. 2:11) he was brought the highly suggestive gifts of gold (for royalty: gold is associated consistently with kingship, and the Lord Jesus is King of kings), frankincense (for deity: frankincense appears regularly in Scripture in connection with the worship and service of God, and Jesus is God incarnate), and myrrh (for death: a classic use of myrrh was in preparing a body for burial, and the link between the birth at Bethlehem and the cross at Calvary is fundamental to the person and work of Christ as the Saviour of sinners). On a visit to Bethany, Mary, the sister of Lazarus whom Jesus raised from the dead, 'took a pound of very costly oil of spikenard, anointed the feet of Jesus, and wiped his feet with her hair. And the house was filled with the fragrance of the oil' (John 12:3). After Jesus' death and burial, 'the women who had come with him from Galilee ... observed the tomb and how his body was laid. Then they returned and prepared spices and fragrant oils' (Luke 23:55f). These they then brought to the tomb, having rested on the Sabbath.

The suitability of the reference to Christ's fragrance becomes clearer in the second line of verse 3: 'your name is ointment poured forth.' It recalls Ecclesiastes. 7:1: 'A good name is better than precious ointment.' This is the only occurrence in the Song of 'name', and, as so often in Scripture, it speaks of the true nature and being of the person in question – in this case, Jesus. Of course, he has many names. Immanuel, Wonderful Counsellor, Mighty God, Everlasting Father, Prince of Peace, Commander of the army of the Lord, Friend, Teacher, Lord, Lamb of God, Sun of Righteousness, the Bright and Morning Star, Prophet, Priest and King are just some of them. Yet the point of the use of the singular 'name' here is to emphasize the fragrance, the preciousness, the exquisiteness of the whole of Christ – all that he is in his person, work, offices and so on. In other words: the 'sum' of him, 'Christ ... all and in all' (Col. 3:11).

The name of Christ is not now like ointment sealed up, but ointment poured forth, which denotes both the freeness and the fullness of the communications of his grace and his Spirit. To him is given the Spirit without measure (John 3:34). He is anointed with the oil of gladness more than his companions (Ps.

45:7, quoted of Christ in Heb. 1:9). All of this is that out of his fullness we might all receive grace and more grace (John 1:16). To every true believer, Christ's name is 'the name high over all', the sweetest of all to a believer's ear, the most thrilling of all to the believer's heart.

In no way does the manner of expression in this verse suggest that the Christian's love to Christ is fanatical or unstable. It springs from a sensible and well-grounded appreciation of the excellency of his whole person and being. His 'fragrance' excels every other fragrance known to man, just as the holy anointing oil of the sanctuary was superior to all other perfume. Indeed verse 3b alludes to that very thing. The special anointing oil of Exodus 30:22ff, which the Lord commanded to be made for the anointing of the tabernacle, the ark and various other furniture and utensils appointed for the tabernacle, and the high priest and his sons, was typical of the richness, fullness and preciousness of the name of Christ, and the fragrance with which it ascended up to God.

There then follows, on the face of it, a puzzling statement: **therefore the virgins love you.** Who are these 'virgins' (NIV, maidens)? Where have they suddenly sprung from? They have been defined in various ways: unmarried young women of marriageable age, those who are chaste and faithful in their adherence to the bridegroom, young converts, believers in general, the pure in heart, or even angels who have never sinned, and so the list extends. A cross-reference to Revelation 14 may be appropriate and helpful, where there is also a mention of 'virgins'. 'These are the ones who follow the Lamb wherever he goes. These were redeemed from among men, being first-fruits to God and to the Lamb' (Rev. 14:4). In other words, like-minded believers, those who are of the same view as the Shulamite with respect to Christ. They are 'the pure in heart' (Matt. 5:8). They are marked by their chaste and devoted adherence to the bridegroom, the undividedness of their love and affection towards him, and the purity and holiness of their lives. The 'therefore' (NIV, 'no wonder') is very natural. How could his true church take any other view of Christ? Those to whom he remains 'despised and rejected' (Isa. 53:3) will not agree. But spiritual souls are in no doubt.

The NKJV of verse 4 divides things up into five parts: the Shulamite continues speaking, then the daughters of Jerusalem, then the Shulamite once more, followed by more from the daughters of Jerusalem, and then the return of the Shulamite in the closing words. There is no compelling reason, however, for ascribing the whole verse to anyone but the Shulamite, who then speaks the whole section from verses 2-7.

Lead me away! (1:4). These words (better translated 'draw me!') erupt after all that has just been said in the previous two verses. Verse 2 focussed upon the enjoyment of the love of Christ in all its effects upon the believer's heart. Verse 3 exhibited the richness of that love, not least as it is displayed in the excellence of Christ's name. Now what is the effect? The answer is, the language of 'let us get away together, the two of us, just on our own'. The Shulamite's desire is to be as close to her beloved as possible, and to have him completely to herself. She desires not only his kisses, but himself, and this is a desire never expressed in vain. Every glimpse the Christian gets of Christ's beauty, and every taste that is received of his love, increases spiritual affection, spiritual ardour and spiritual desire for more of him.

The Lord Jesus Christ is the magnet of redeemed souls. We love him who first loved us, and the soul who has been brought to know him and to regard him as the pre-eminent and (in the language later on of 5:16) the 'altogether lovely' one, cannot get enough of him. The same verb (draw) is also used in Jeremiah 31:3 and Hosea 11:4 to describe the power of love to draw the beloved to the one who is loved. 'Nearer, still nearer' is the believer's longing expressed here, enforced by the words, **We will run after you**. We cannot run after him unless he himself draws us, yet once he draws us it is our business to run. We run to him as sinners and we run after him as believers. We remain in need of the same drawings to Christ of divine power and love throughout our Christian lives, as we needed to bring us to him in the first place. Here is eager desire, fervent affection, vigorous pursuit – reminiscent of Jesus' own teaching about the need to take heaven by force or storm (Matt. 11:12). We may compare the language of Psalm 119:32 ('I will run in the way of your commandments, for you shall enlarge my heart'), and Psalm 63:8 ('My soul follows close behind you; your right hand upholds me').

There are degrees of communion with Christ (something which the Song continually teaches). None of these can be attained to or enjoyed without the divine drawing. What Peter refers to as growing 'in the grace and knowledge of our Lord and Saviour Jesus Christ' (2 Pet. 3:18) is the believer's desire. The language of this present verse 4 is very much that of making such progress, and doing so (or desiring to do so) with cheerfulness, vigour and strength. Here is a true taking pleasure in Christ.

Given what we have insisted all along concerning the Christian and the church, there should be found no difficulty in the swopping about of 'me' and 'we' in the Song, of which the present verse is a case in point. The Christian's personal experience of and longing for Christ, and the church's corporate experience of and longing for the same, is interchangeable in the Song. It is a matter both of keen individuality and resolved unity. Moreover, when Christ visits the church in a marked manner, individual believers are quickened, just as, when he manifests himself to a believer, the church is affected. We do not run after him alone.

What follows is really a 'before they call, I will answer' (Isa. 65:24), both immediately and abundantly. **The king has brought me into his chambers**. Again the background of the time of writing of the Song comes to the fore in aid of the spiritual dimension. With respect to oriental palaces, there was the court of the garden of the king's palace where feasts for many people would be held; there was the inner court of the king's house, where only invited guests were permitted to enter; and there were the king's own apartments or chambers, where he admitted only those whom he cherished most intimately and loved most warmly. Think of Psalm 27:5 and Psalm 91:1 in this connection. This is a reminder that the Lord Jesus invites his own not into some general court or vague and distant relationship, but into his very chambers, into the secret of his presence. Here is intended intimate fellowship, close enjoyment, intense mutual delight.

The title 'the king' is well applied to Christ. Indeed it belongs to him. He is the king by way of pre-eminence, 'King of kings and Lord of lords' (Rev. 19:16). He rules over his everlasting kingdom (Rev. 11:15). The Messianic reference of Psalm 2:8 declares that as the Mediator he has a kingdom given to him by the Father, one which he has purchased with his own blood and by the glorious and spiritual conquests of his grace.

It goes without saying that all of this being brought into the king's chambers is the provision of pure, free, divine grace; for how else could any 'who were dead in trespasses and sins' and 'by nature children of wrath' (Eph. 2:1,3) ever have such a royal invitation, access and welcome? Here, in this private and intimate place of fellowship and communion, Christ assures our hearts of his changeless love, he instructs us in the mysteries of his Word, he reveals to us some of his sublime glories, he listens to our cries, he renews our strength, he revives our drooping spirits, he restores our souls and he grants to us his Holy Spirit. Moreover, there we can tell him 'to his face' all that he means to us. All is mutual.

The thoughts of gladness and rejoicing are often linked in the Old Testament, and so it is here. **We will be glad and rejoice in you**. Both here and earlier in the verse ('we will run after you'), the focus is kept firmly upon Christ. In his chambers or out of them, in the secret place or away from it, how Christ's people are glad and rejoice in him! This is important, for our rejoicing is not a rejoicing in the chambers for their own sake (anymore than in the house of the Lord for its own sake); our rejoicing is in Christ, whose chambers and whose house they are. Such places without him would be desolate – as on occasions, to our cost, we may have found them to be, when he has withdrawn himself for a season and for a reason. Our joy is in the Lord. Our satisfaction is in God.

There is a redolence here of 1 Peter 1:8. Peter there, speaking in the previous verse of 'the revelation of Jesus Christ', continues, 'whom having not seen you love. Though now you do not see him, yet believing, you rejoice with joy inexpressible and full of glory'. Everything about Christ is a cause of gladness and rejoicing to the Christian: his person, his work; his offices, his promises; his blood, his righteousness; his power, his authority; his glories, his kingdom – everything. The list is endless.

We will remember your love more than wine. The verb 'remember' means to fix in the memory and (in its tense here) to bring to remembrance, and frequently to do so by way of praise. Not to remember Christ's love would be sheer folly and ingratitude. Wine is mentioned again, as in verse 2, and, as also in that verse, 'love' appears in the plural, 'loves'. The emphasis in this sentence is upon the excellence of the king's company, fellowship, gifts and blessings, as well as upon the greatness, the variety, the generosity and the abundance of it all. This remembering is not some cold mental exercise, therefore. It is a spiritual activity, assisted concretely by engaging in the means of grace which have been given and appointed to this end (such as public worship as well as private devotions, preaching and prayer, the Lord's Supper and Christian fellowship, and the careful and proper sanctifying of the Sabbath day). It will be very much to our spiritual comfort and edification, and will serve to keep before us both the sinfulness of sin (that we might avoid it the more) and the preciousness of Christ (that we might prize him the more). In both the 'we will be glad' and the 'we will remember', a holy resolution is declared.

25

Rightly do they love you. With these words this section closes. There is no need to refer 'they' to the daughters of Jerusalem. Their first appearance need not come until much later. Versions diverge in their translation here. AV has 'the upright love thee'. The word AV translates 'upright' only appears once more in the Song (at 7:9) where AV translates 'sweetly' and NIV, 'straight'. The word means level or straight, and appears in Isaiah 40:4 as such. If we choose 'the upright', the reference would be to the same as 'the virgins' (v.3), the point being that however others view Christ and whatever others think of him, those who are truly his own love him with a right mind and a sincere heart, and are all agreed in that, and share in the blessedness of communion with him. But the translation 'rightly' (NKJV – compare NIV, 'How right they are to adore you!') is not improper, and, if anything, makes a similar point more strikingly. With good reason do believers love him. How absolutely right, proper and justified it is to love Christ. How he is to be loved. Not to love him is robbery; to love others more than him is idolatry.

1:5-7. Dark but lovely

The Shulamite continues to speak here, though in verses 5 and 6 of herself rather than of her beloved. She addresses the daughters of Jerusalem, whose identity we shall consider at the end of this section. It appears they were looking at her with some disdain or suspicion because of her appearance.

The first thing she says of herself is **I am dark, but lovely** (1:5). NIV's 'dark am I' captures the Hebrew order and emphasis. Those who pursue the real-life interpretation of the Song see in this and the next verse the Shulamite as a rustic maiden ill-treated by her brothers, and made to work long and hard hours in the family vineyards. The result is that she becomes very sun-tanned and has neglected giving proper attention to her personal appearance.

How are we to understand the spiritual import of verse 5?

There are two possibilities. Either this is typical of the Christian's dual view of self (saved yet still a sinner), or there is a dialogue going on here, with the believer speaking and Christ interjecting. Both are worth exploring.

If we take this as the Christian's dual view of him/herself, we can identify straightaway with what is intended: conscious of sin, yet rejoicing in grace; dark in ourselves, yet made lovely in Christ; burdened with trial, yet enabled to persevere. 'Dark' may be translated 'black' – not necessarily 'as black as soot', as the saying goes, for the root of the word here is used of morning twilight or 'the morning grey'. 'Lovely' (AV, comely) makes the point that, notwithstanding her darkness, her beauty shines through.

The same contrast would then apply in the second part of the verse: **like the tents of Kedar, like the curtains of Solomon**. Kedar refers to a nomadic desert tribe descended from one of the sons of Ishmael. Their tents were made from black or dark-hair goatskin, and became blackened further by exposure to the sun. Mention is made of the tents of Kedar again in Psalm 120:5. In contrast, the curtains of Solomon (precious hangings like those of Exodus 26 and 36, and those which formed the tabernacle before the erection of the temple, 2 Sam. 7 and 1 Chr. 17) speak of richness, colour, value and beauty, and point to all that Christians have already become in Christ. The Christian has 'put on the Lord Jesus Christ' (Rom. 13:14). Think also of Isaiah 61:10: 'I will greatly rejoice in the LORD, my soul shall be joyful in my God; for he has clothed me with the garments of salvation, he has covered me with the robe of righteousness, as a bridegroom decks himself with ornaments, and as a bride adorns herself with jewels.'

There is a combination, then, of keenly felt unfitness and unworthiness on the one hand, and on the other, grateful and confident awareness of what we have become already in Christ. This is very much the believer's experience, being conscious of both. The choicer the saint, the more will this tension be known and acknowledged. Moreover, confession of sin ('I am dark') is part of the believer's rejoicing in all that Christ is and has done ('but lovely'). The blacker we are in our own eyes, the more precious is the Lord Jesus Christ to us. It is part of the mystery and reality of Christian experience and spiritual wisdom to understand that we are dark and lovely at the same time. We are not less dark in ourselves because we are lovely in Christ, nor are we less lovely in Christ because we are dark in ourselves. It is the glory of God's grace and Christ's work that those who are dark are ever made lovely. No language can ever set out fully just how dark we are by nature or how lovely we have been made (and are being made) through grace. He who knows all about us, loves us still.

However, the other possibility also presents us with a fruitful interpretation. The verse would run like this, the believer speaking first says, 'I am dark', then Christ interjects, 'but lovely' (i.e., lovely to me, lovely in my eyes); and then similarly the believers says of himself, 'like the tents of Kedar (dark)', and Christ interjects, 'but like the curtains of Solomon' (i.e., beautiful to me, exquisite in my estimation). This, too, is true to the believer's experience and is very wonderful: to know that despite all that we are with our sins, our shortfalls, our strayings, we are still lovely, precious and desirable to our beloved Lord Jesus, our bridegroom. Consider Psalm 45:11: 'So the King will greatly desire your beauty' (as well as verse 13 of that same psalm).

Continuing her address to the daughters of Jerusalem, the Shulamite says this: **Do not look upon me, because I am dark, because the sun has tanned me** (1:6). 'Stop staring at me' gives the sense of the opening phrase, and indicates the believer's unease at being the object of scrutiny by others, being all too aware of her own blemishes and imperfections. There are always those whose chief occupation in life it is to draw attention to all that Christians should be (and know very well that they should be) but are not. Here is the Christian not looking for attention, admiration or applause. The reference to being tanned by the sun is best understood as referring to the 'many dangers, toils

28

and snares' which the Christian and the church has to face while seeking to live godly for Christ Jesus in a hostile world (compare 2 Tim. 3:12), where our enemies will sometimes be of our own family and household (as the Lord Jesus Christ warns plainly in Matthew 10:36, quoting Micah 7:6). It is the effect of having to bear the burden and heat of the day. Yet even so, this is not the language of complaint on the believer's part.

My mother's sons were angry with me. This is the result. The Lord Jesus works this out in a passage like John 15:18ff. We should not expect our own case to differ from his in the matter of receiving hatred, misunderstanding and ill-treatment from the world which neither knows him nor desires him. This will come not only from the world identified clearly as the world, but from hypocritical professors of religion who have crept into the church as well, 'my mother's sons', those who may have their own form of godliness but deny and know nothing of its power (2 Tim. 3:5). The true Christian is under continual pressure to compromise, give in to temptation, cut corners, and fit in rather than stand out. Faithfulness to Christ, though essential, is costly. Even among our fellow Christians life will often be difficult and we shall feel very alone.

Hence, **they made me the keeper of the vineyards, but my own vineyard I have not kept**. The keeping of the vineyards was regarded as work for 'the poor of the land' (Jer. 52:16), while the promise of Isaiah 61:5 is that God's people would be free from that burden and drudgery and 'the sons of the foreigner' would do it for them, while themselves being freed to give themselves to being 'priests of the LORD' and 'the servants of our God' (Isa. 61:6).

This brings into view here in particular in verse 6 the neglect of maintaining personal communion and fellowship with the Lord Jesus Christ. The cause is not hard to find. The hardships, the temptations, the persecutions have all taken their toll, and drawn the believer away from the main thing, the chief work – the cultivation of the soul, the care that needs to be taken regarding a close walk with God. The believer was deflected. The church turned aside. How often has this happened! There may have been great zeal, much activity, a packed programme; but time with Christ himself has been overlooked. The first things of spiritual duty have been neglected. With the vineyard untended in this way, the weeds have grown and the fruit has not matured. This explains the question of verse 7 which the Shulamite puts to her beloved.

Tell me, O you whom I love, where you feed your flock, where you make it rest at noon (1:7). Why does she have to ask? Wouldn't you think she would know perfectly well? The fact that this question does ever have to get asked at all mirrors the experience which recurs at different points of the Song: our communion with Christ (unlike our union with him) is not a static thing. It comes and goes, it rises and falls, it ebbs and flows. Her 'you whom I love' is strictly 'you whom my soul loves', indicating the truth of the matter and how the believer really does regard Christ; but experience sometimes indicates a different story, or, at least, gives a different impression. The phrase is a circumlocution for 'beloved' (Neh. 13:26) or 'the dearly beloved of my soul' (Jer. 12:7). The Lord Jesus is to the believer our beloved, the dearly beloved of our souls, the one whom our soul loves (compare 1 Pet. 1:8 and John 21:17). He is all our desire and he captivates our whole being.

Made conscious again of her desire for Christ and her need of him, the believer appeals to him for renewed fellowship and spiritual communion together. The background picture in verse 7 changes from keeping vineyards to keeping sheep, but both pictures apply and there is nothing jagged about the change. The Lord Jesus is spoken of richly in Scripture in shepherd terms. He is 'the good shepherd' (John 10:11), who 'gives his life for the sheep'. He is 'that great shepherd' (Heb. 13:20), whom God 'brought up ... from the dead'. He is 'the Chief Shepherd' (1 Pet. 5:4), who will give to the faithful overseers of his flock 'the crown of glory that does not fade away'. He is the 'one shepherd'

(John 10:16), for there is no other shepherd to be compared with him. He is 'the Shepherd and Overseer of your souls' (1 Pet. 2:25), to whom once straying sheep have returned. His pastoral shepherd's manner is described exquisitely in Isaiah 40:11.

The verb 'feed' (NIV, graze) is used of both animals and people, and the same is true of 'rest' (or, lie down). 'Feed' here means to discharge the office of a shepherd. Note that the Hebrew does not have either 'your flock' or 'it', which (even if those words may be taken as understood) actually makes the believer's question to her beloved far more direct than the English versions imply: 'Tell me, O you whom my soul loves, where you feed, where you rest at noon'. Observe how the emphasis thus falls upon the repeated 'you', referring to the beloved. Where are you? Where can I find you? Where can I be with you? Where can I enjoy you? Where can my soul find refreshment? Where may I delight in you once more? Where are those 'green pastures' and 'still waters' (Ps. 23:2)? Where does the Lord Jesus 'stand and feed his flock in the strength of the LORD' (Mic. 5:4)? Where is there protection to be found in him? Noon (midday) in hot lands is a natural resting time from the heat in some suitable place of shade, or by some well or stream. The reference is appropriate here, given the burdens the believer is under and the straits she is in.

The verse ends with another question. **For why should I be as one who veils herself by the flocks of your companions?** The verb translated here 'veils' has been rendered variously, including AV's 'turneth aside', but NKJV appears correct. The question expresses the holy exercise of the true and sincere Christian not to appear unattached from Christ, not to drift or to wander, not to seem like a waif or stray, not to be giving in to the temptations or seductions of any who would seek to draw her from her beloved and his church, not to give any suggestion that she belongs to someone else rather than to Christ, not wishing to bring any reproach or dishonour upon his name. Here is a holy spiritual jealousy.

It is noteworthy that while the Shulamite had bemoaned to the daughters of Jerusalem her sins and her troubles, it is to Christ alone, her soul's best beloved, that she turns and looks for help and relief and refreshment. 'He restores my soul' (Ps. 23:3).

At this point we must address the question, who are the **daughters of Jerusalem**? They are mentioned in 1:5, 2:7, 3:5, 3:10, 5:8, 5:16, and 8:4 (along with 3:11, 'daughters of Zion'). They actually speak up for themselves in 5:9 and 6:1. Many suggestions have been offered regarding their identity. These include the following: professors of Christ in the church, yet who are not truly converted; weak Christians, babes in Christ, not understanding the depths of the bride's experience, as yet imperfectly instructed in the things of God but very willing to be taught; those who are near to the kingdom but do not as yet share with believers in the joys of true possession of Christ; companions of the believer, fellow believers, with whom Christians have been brought into association through conversion. In Luke 23:28, those described by Jesus as 'daughters of Jerusalem' are those who were literally the native women of Jerusalem.

In the Song it would be best to take them as babes in Christ, new believers, very young in the faith. Consequently, they are to be distinguished from 'the virgins' (verse 3, who delighted in Christ in a maturer way) and from the 'mother's sons' (verse 6, who despised Christ in a grievous way). They are not without some spiritual beginnings, spiritual interests and spiritual life, though they can only take milk and not meat as yet.

Why does the Shulamite address herself to them in the manner of verses 5-6? The answer is this. These daughters of Jerusalem aspire in measure after the experience of the Shulamite, in respect of the deeper things of Christ. She is therefore concerned for them, lest her darkness (remaining sin and impurity, and trials and persecutions for the faith) should put them off or cause them to stumble, and lest they fail to observe the loveliness that belongs to the believer by virtue of being in Christ, and the joy and blessedness that is her portion.

1:8-11. The beloved's response

The beloved answers, speaking for the first time, and does so in a manner of the most delightful gentleness, tenderness and encouragement. He is the speaker throughout the present section.

The fullest way of capturing the Hebrew of 1:8a would be to translate **If you do not know** as 'If you yourself do not know'. In other words, the challenge to the believer is precisely this: if you (of all people) do not know, then who will know? There are shades of the Saviour's words to Philip: 'Have I been with you so long, and yet you have not known me, Philip?' (John 14:9). How slow and foolish we are so much of the time to realise the unspeakable blessings and privileges that are ours in Christ. We are 'complete in him' (Col. 2:10). 'And of his fullness we have all received, and grace for grace' (John 1:16). Why should we be wondering where he is, when he has told us where to find him? Why are we weary and heavy laden, when he has given us rest for our souls? Why do we go around as if comfortless, when he has promised never to leave us or forsake us?

He calls her **O fairest among women**, or 'most beautiful'. It is a superlative, and provides an exquisite contrast with the Shulamite's anxious and self-deprecating view of herself back in verses 5-6. The Lord Jesus Christ sees a beauty in his bride, even if we do not. Indeed, the bride's beauty is one of the continual themes of the Song. Her very consciousness of her own shortfalls and defects constitutes a part of her beauty in his eyes; believers are fairest in Christ's eyes when they are blackest in their own. The mutual view is provided in Psalm 45:2. To him, she is 'fairest among women'; to her, he is 'fairer than the sons of men'.

The response continues with 1:8b: **follow in the footsteps of the flock, and feed your little goats beside the shepherds' tents.** The beginning can be rendered 'go yourself' or 'go out yourself'. Maybe we are to take it in the sense of the exhortation to 'imitate those who through faith and patience inherit the promises' (Heb. 6:12); or, from the same New Testament letter, the call in 13:13 to 'go forth to him, outside the camp, bearing his reproach'.

There is also here, by way of application, timeless counsel for the believer to discover Christ as she pursues faithfully the path of spiritual duty: sitting under the direction of Christ's choice ministers, whose holy and solemn task it is to feed the flock of God committed to their charge (compare Acts 20:28 and 1 Pet. 5:2); having regard to the ways of godly Christians who have journeyed to heaven before us along 'the old paths' and 'the good way' (Jer. 6:16), believing, praying, trusting, delighting and hoping, for we are not the first who have believed; and paying particular attention to commanding our households and training up the young in the way that they should go (parents directing their children, not the children having the upper hand).

All of this counsel, if truly taken to heart, will tend to the glory of Christ in his church, and the fulfilling of the promise of Psalm 22:30 that 'A posterity shall serve him'. Implicit in all of this is a proper emphasis upon the unity of Christ's people in every age; 'and there will be one flock and one shepherd' (John 10:16).

Moving into 1:9, we find the beloved continuing to express his delight in the one he loves. **I have compared you, my love** is how he begins. The word for 'love' can be rendered darling, dearest, friend or companion. This is the first of nine appearances of this word in the Song, always on the lips of the Lord Jesus, and usually in conjunction with some further explicit statement concerning her beauty. The stronger alternatives (love, darling) are more fitting here. What a way to be addressed by the Lord Jesus! His deep, devoted and amazing love for his people (his own, his bride) is difficult to put into words. His love is real, hearty, sincere, unchanging, strong and eternal. It is the love whereby he has created us, redeemed us, sanctifies us and glorifies us. He has loved his own from eternity, loves them through time, and will love them for ever.

Tying this blessed truth in again with verses 5-6, is it not especially necessary and especially welcome to have this assurance of his love when we are under an unusually heavy sense of our own sinfulness and unworthiness and lack of deserving? His love to us is a love to the loveless, in order to make us lovely. This should not be without vital effect upon us, stirring us up to such things as these: the avoidance of all known sin, a jealous watch against any rival in our affections towards him, bewaring of any coolness or distance creeping in to our relationship with him, and maintaining careful obedience to his commandments and wholehearted pleasure in promoting his interests and advancing his glory.

To what does he compare her? At first sight the comparison seems strange: **to my favourite foal among Pharaoh's chariots**. For 'foal', we can translate mare (NIV) or horse (cf. AV). The word is feminine. NKJV's 'favourite' is imported. As an expression of someone's beauty, it may not appear very usual to make such a comparison as this. To be told you look like a horse or remind someone of a mare could easily be taken the wrong way. So what are we to make of the comparison?

Evidently 'compare' here is never used in the Old Testament of literal physical likeness. Something larger than that is intended. We, in our day, might use the description 'horsey' to indicate lack of femininity, rather than the expression of it. However, it is very important to understand that in Solomon's day and in Solomon's world (which, of course, is when he wrote the Song) horses were viewed very differently from our own times. The comparison of verse 9 would have been a highly honouring and desirable compliment – a compliment of compliments, we might say – for horses were held in the highest esteem, and their noble looks and graceful lines were considered typical of true beauty. In the Ancient Near East, Egyptian horses (the sort referred to here in the mention of Pharaoh) were the choicest and most desirable of all. The royal horses would be the very best. We learn from 2 Chronicles 1:16 that 'Solomon had horses imported from Egypt'.

This still leaves us needing to know the point of the comparison in terms of what this is intended to teach about Christ and his church. Several points are worth making, all of them for our rich encouragement as Christians. Firstly, the horses harnessed to Pharaoh's chariots (or that Solomon had bought from Egypt for his own chariots) were of the purest breed and blood, a select company picked and singled out from others. The application of that to the church of Christ is plain. Think of the description of the church in 1 Peter 2:9 as 'a chosen generation, a royal priesthood, a holy nation, his own special people, that you may proclaim the praises of him who called you out of darkness into his marvellous light', and every reference you can find in Scripture to the wonders of God's electing, redeeming and calling grace.

Secondly, these mares would have been bought at a vast price by those merchants whose particular job it was to do the work for a king like Solomon. And are not Christians those who 'were not redeemed with corruptible things ... but with the precious blood of Christ, as of a lamb without blemish and without spot' (1 Pet. 1:18f)?

In the third place, these horses were the very delight of the king. He took great pleasure in them. The same is true of the way in which the Lord Jesus Christ views the Christian and the church. He has already used the endearing 'my love', and much more of the same, in even more ravishing language, is to follow as the Song continues.

Fourthly, these horses, though often wild to begin with, were brought under control and made submissive and obedient. They would be harnessed together and to the king's chariot, and in a peaceful, harmonious and docile manner would lead the king wherever he desired to go. So with believers: we are many, and we were disobedient, but now we have been made one and have been mastered by Christ and for Christ, and all our energies are to be engaged boldly, unitedly and tirelessly for him. Think, for example, of 1 Corinthians 12:13, Ephesians 4:3 or Philippians

1:27. The church of Christ is not to be like a company of untrained, unbroken and uncontrolled horses, some going one way and some going another, some responding in obedience and some taking their own stubborn and rebellious course, some doing the will of the Master and some doing whatever seems right in their own eyes (sadly, all too often the latter is the impression given in practice, but it ought not to be so).

One further feature of this interesting comparison comes out in 1:10. These horses would be very beautifully and richly adorned. It was the custom not only that the ladies adorned themselves with jewels, necklaces, chains and such things, but that the faces and necks of the horses would often be so adorned as well. This is what supplies the reference that now follows, where the thought of 'I have compared you, my love' is continued in these words: **Your cheeks are lovely with ornaments, your neck with chains of gold**. The word for 'ornaments' is used for round ornaments hanging down in front on both sides of a headband, and also interwoven in the braids of hair in the forehead; that for 'chains' denotes strings of pearls (or beads or other jewels) as a necklace.

The spiritual application is this. Christ gives great beauty and rich adornment to his people. What are the spiritual 'ornaments' (NIV, ear-rings) and spiritual 'chains of gold' (NIV, strings of jewels)? Surely they are the graces of the Holy Spirit, the distinguishing traits of Christian character. And what, in particular are these graces, these traits, given to believers by Christ himself? They are none other than the characteristics of likeness to himself, such as are set forth in passages like Matthew 5:1-12 (the Beatitudes), Galatians 5:22-25 (the fruit of the Spirit) or Colossians 3:12-17 (those things the Christian has put on, having put off the things mentioned in the previous verses).

The fact that the cheeks and neck are mentioned indicates that while these spiritual graces are worked internally upon our hearts, they are to be seen externally in our lives (compare Matt. 5:14-16 and the reaction of the Sanhedrin to Peter and John recorded in Acts 4:13 – 'they realised that they had been with Jesus'). This spiritual beauty and attractiveness, it must be underscored, is not of ourselves. It is given, it is imparted. True spiritual beauty is Christ in us, shining and displayed from us. Moreover, it 'is very precious in the sight of God' (1 Pet. 3:4).

The present section, with Christ speaking, concludes with 1:11. There is no need to attribute these verses (as some do) to the daughters of Jerusalem. The theme and language of verse 10 is continued. **We will make you ornaments of gold with studs of silver**. There is a significant change of pronoun: the 'I' of verse 9 now becomes a 'we'. This is a striking reminder that in the great work of our sanctification (as with our salvation itself) each person of the Godhead is involved – the Father, the Son and the Holy Spirit. This is covenant work. These beauties of holiness and insignia of royalty with which the Lord Jesus Christ adorns his church (compare Eph. 5:25-27) involve also the Holy Spirit who himself is given to the Son by the Father for this very object.

The sanctification of the church, the holiness of the believer, is never out of the divine hands. It is a comeliness or splendour which has been bestowed on us, for we were born both naked and polluted (compare Ezek. 16:8-14). This means that while the business of sanctification, if just left to us, would be far above our reach, its perfecting is infallibly sure and certain. That which is undertaken for us by God cannot fail. Whatever at present is wanting in us will be made up. All the ransomed church of God will be saved to sin no more. It is a classic illustration of the arm of the Lord's strength completing what the work of his goodness has begun. In terms of Psalm 50:2, 'Out of Zion, the perfection of beauty, God will shine forth'. Having brought his people from sin to grace (the greater distance), he will take us also from grace to glory (Ps. 84:11).

1:12-17. Shared affections

In this section, to the end of the first chapter, we have the Shulamite's response to what the beloved has just said (verses 12-14), followed by a further exchange of mutual delight (verse 15 and verses 16-17). The words of verses 12-14 exude the believer's delight in having Christ to herself, having desired him so earnestly.

While the king is at his table, the opening words of 1:12, provide the second reference so far to the king (the first was in v.4). The king, of course, is the same as the beloved of the next two verses – the Lord Jesus Christ. Our beloved is our king, who in all things has the pre-eminence (Col. 1:18). He is the king by virtue of his divine nature as the Son of God, and his mediatorial undertaking as the Son of Man. He is not merely a king, but is the King. The title sets forth his sovereignty, his majesty and his glory. How graciously and tenderly he condescends to us, that the King of kings should be the well-beloved of our souls!

A royal banquet has been suggested as the background scene here. This is possible (particularly in the light of what will come at 2:4), though 'at his table' has also been translated 'in his circle/in his own room/on his couch/among his own surroundings'. The root means 'surround'. It is sufficient to understand that the two are together, rejoicing in one another's company, taken up with each other. The Shulamite is not concerned chiefly here with the table, but with the king. This being so, the believer continues with a threefold reference to perfumes: spikenard (v.12), myrrh (v.13), henna (v.14).

She begins by saying **my spikenard sends forth its fragrance**. Spikenard (pure nard) is a scarce and expensive perfume extracted from a plant from the Himalayan region of India. Its fragrance has been described as exotic. When Mary of Bethany anointed the feet of Jesus with spikenard, 'the house was filled with the fragrance of the oil' (John 12:3).

The point to notice here in the Song is that it is while the king is at his table, with the Shulamite with him, that the fragrance of her spikenard wafts forth. In other words, communion and fellowship with the Lord Jesus Christ is not something the Christian merely prizes for its own sake. It has the effect (necessary for us, delightful to him) of reviving our spiritual graces and making them lively and fragrant – graces such as godly sorrow and true repentance for all our grievings of him, a tender conscience and a humble spirit, faith in Christ, love to Christ, joy in Christ, the hope of glory, desire to have him honoured, and anticipation of heaven (when our communion and fellowship with him will be at its height and remain so for ever). In his absence our graces wither, while in his presence they flourish. He kindles our affections into a lively glow.

A bundle of myrrh is my beloved to me, that lies all night between my breasts (1:13). So the believer continues, referring to Christ as 'my beloved'. It is a different word from that used by Christ of the Shulamite in verse 9. These verses are highly personal, being shot through with 'my', and all that 'my beloved is to me'. Myrrh is a resin/gum which comes from a species of South Arabian tree. It is familiar to us from the Scriptures, being an ingredient in the holy anointing oil used in the tabernacle (Exod. 30:22-33), and appearing in connection with the birth (Matt. 2:11) and the death (Mark 15:23; John 19:39) of the Lord Jesus Christ.

The import of 'between my breasts' is that in its solid (rather than its liquid) form people would sometimes wear it next to their body in a small sachet or pouch, while 'all night' signifies continuance. The imagery of this is very suggestive of the closeness, intimacy and permanence of the relationship between Christ and his own. It reminds us of how in the upper room 'there was leaning on Jesus' bosom one of his disciples, whom Jesus loved' (John 13:23), and of the apostle Paul's prayer for the Ephesian Christians 'that Christ may dwell in your hearts through faith' (Eph. 3:17).

This reference to the Lord Jesus Christ as 'a bundle of myrrh' is very suggestive when considered in the light of some other mentions of myrrh in Scripture. Two examples may suffice. It appears as a gift in Genesis 43:11, as well as in the already mentioned Matthew 2:11 – so Christ is God's 'indescribable gift' (2 Cor. 9:15). It was used in Esther 2:12 as part of the necessary preparations for the women to go in to the king – so it is in Christ, and in him alone, that we are made acceptable before God and have access into his presence.

The third of the fragrances appears in 1:14. **My beloved is to me a cluster of henna blooms in the vineyards of En Gedi.** Note the immediate re-appearing of 'my beloved (is) to me'. Henna (AV, camphire) is a common shrub in Palestine which produces fragrant blossoms (the reference here), and also whose leaves when crushed produce a dye of a bright orange-yellow colour. The mention of En Gedi is rather like the mention back in verse 9 of the mares of Pharaoh's chariots. Just as those were the finest and choicest horses, so the spices and perfumes produced from the plants of En Gedi were the finest perfumes. En Gedi itself has been described as 'the place of the wild goats', a lush oasis about halfway down the western shore of the Dead Sea.

The spiritual point here is this: the beloved having set forth the exquisiteness to him of the one he loves, she now seeks to respond in kind in making known what he is to her. He having loved her first, how very much she now loves him. It has been suggested that the word translated henna relates to a root which signifies atonement, propitiation, ransom, covering, including the covering of the ark (the mercy seat). This would make the description of Christ as 'a cluster of henna blooms' even more suggestive and appropriate. In him there dwells a divine treasure of grace and mercy, justice and holiness, truth and faithfulness. 'Christ is all and in all' (Col. 3:11).

Yet however lovely and fragrant is the spikenard, the myrrh and the henna, Christ is altogether lovelier and more fragrant still. He has furnished a table for his people here, while in the

41

wilderness, as well as a table in heaven. At his table he meets with us and sups with us (Ps. 23:5-6; Rev. 3:20).

The chapter closes with a delightful interchange between the two, in which the beloved, speaking first, addresses the one he loves in the most affectionate terms. **Behold, you are fair, my love! Behold, you are fair! You have dove's eyes** (1:15). In no way are the 'beholds' of this or the next verse redundant. 'Behold' is a word which calls for the giving of attention and/or admiration. It also sometimes strengthens a statement. The language here speaks for itself. The Lord Jesus Christ takes great pleasure in the work of his grace which makes his own so fair in his sight. This is rich encouragement for the humble believing soul.

Here is the first of what will be a number of references to doves in the course of the Song – a reference used by both speakers (compare 2:14 and 5:12). 'You have dove's eyes' is literally 'your eyes dove's'. Eyes are often considered to be features of beauty. It will be remembered that it was 'like a dove' that the Holy Spirit descended upon Jesus at his baptism (Matt. 3:16), and it is the character of the dove (or a dove-like character) that he desires to see in his people. For the significance of the dove, see the comments on the later verses.

Then, to show exactly how mutual this Christ and the believer, Christ and the church, relationship really is, the believer's opening words in 1:16 (**Behold, you are handsome**) are actually identical in Hebrew with those of the beloved just spoken (there is a change of gender from the feminine to the masculine). Love delights to return love. Whatever we have been made as believers is 'to the praise of the glory of his grace' (Eph. 1:6). There are those sweet seasons when Christ so opens his heart to us from the Scriptures and tells us all that we mean to him, permitting us to draw unusually near to him and to tell back to him in something of his own words all that he means to us, in responsive faith and love.

The word for 'handsome', while occurring fourteen times in

the Song, appears only on this one occasion in the masculine form directed to the beloved. The next word (**my beloved!**) is a different word from that used in verse 15, though expresses the same feeling. The praise of the beloved continues with **Yes, pleasant!** (fair, beautiful), referring to the delight and blessedness of Christ himself in every way (his person, his work and his offices); of the things concerning himself (his doctrines, his promises and his ordinances); and of all the communications of his love, grace, work, beauty and fullness to her soul. How attractive the Lord Jesus is to his people, and never more so than in those precious seasons when we are brought to an overwhelming realisation of his unchanging love towards us. This same appreciation of Christ and his beauty on the believer's part will erupt most magnificently in the second half of chapter 5.

Also our bed is green. The beams of our houses are cedar, and our rafters of fir. These words complete the chapter (1:16b-17). It seems best to take them as an expression of the believer's delight at the thought of being married to Christ. The bed (or couch) and the houses point very much in this direction. Domestic bliss would be an altogether inadequate way of intimating what is intended. Very striking is the repeated 'our', rather than 'mine' or 'yours', emphasising the joint interest of bridegroom and bride in each other. There is a recollection here of husband and wife being 'heirs together of the grace of life' (1 Pet. 3:7), and of believers being 'joint heirs with Christ' (Rom. 8:17).

Why should the bed be coloured green (NIV, verdant)? It may be that green is selected as symbolic of restfulness and fruitfulness. However the suggestion has been made that it is not so much the colour green itself that is the focus, but rather a canopy of leafy branches which gives shade and privacy to the couple as they desire 'to get away from it all' together. The whole language is suggestive of 'the two of us', Christ and the believer, in the secret of his presence, and such like. The plural forms for houses and rafters indicates how Christ and his own are not restricted for their fellowship to one particular place or another. This is the only occurrence of rafters in the Old Testament, though it receives this translation widely among the English versions.

The cedar will be the famous and magnificent cedar of Lebanon (a strong and durable wood which Solomon used in the building of the temple), and the fir will probably be some type of pine/cypress/juniper tree (possibly also used in the temple and certainly pleasing both to sight and to smell). Cross refer to Isaiah 60:13. Together these two trees, the cedar and the fir, consolidate the overall picture of the permanence and delightfulness of the fellowship and communion between Christ and his own.

If this is such a precious privilege and portion even now, what will it be when all is face to face in the Father's house in heaven? Since the Lord Jesus Christ regards us even now as so fair, and we consider him to be so handsome and pleasant, how shall we appear to one another when there is no longer any distance between? 'Your eyes will see the King in his beauty; they will see the land that is very far off' (Isa. 33:17).

Chapter 2

ENDLESS PLEASURES

This second chapter includes some of the most exquisite language (and some of the best known verses) of the entire Song, as the mutual love and delight of Christ and the believer for and in one another continues to be unfolded.

2:1-2. The rose and the lily

Although this commentary is based on the NKJV, we must depart from the translators' ascription of 2:1 to the Shulamite, believing firmly that both of the first two verses of the chapter proceed from the lips of the bridegroom, not the bride. He begins by describing himself in these terms: **I am the rose of Sharon, and the lily of the valleys** (2:1). He then proceeds to speak of his bride in this way: **Like a lily among thorns, so is my love among the daughters** (2:2). So in verse 1 Christ is speaking of himself, and in verse 2 he is speaking of his church.

This balances well. Christ himself is the 'I' of verse 1 who then proceeds to acknowledge and claim his bride as his own by the personal and possessive pronoun 'my' of verse 2. Or consider it this way: verse 1 shows all that Christ is to the church and verse 2 reveals all that the church means to Christ, in each case on his own testimony. The union of Christ and his people remains very much to the fore. In speaking of himself as he does, Christ owns the praises and honours that his bride has just given him in the previous chapter, and also stirs up her ardour and desire for him even more (as the potent effect of verses 1-2 in verses 3ff. makes plain). His words are full of grace and truth.

Of himself, he uses the pictures of a rose and a lily: a rose of Sharon and a lily of the valleys. The definite articles are not used. It should not be thought strange or problematic that Christ should so praise himself. If we were to engage in self-praise or self-advertisement, drawing attention to ourselves, that would be quite wrong. Yet it is thoroughly proper for the one 'who is over all, the eternally blessed God' (Rom. 9:5) to declare his own praise. There is no human language that can display his excellencies to any adequate (still less, any exhaustive) degree. He cannot be commended in a right manner and to a proper degree, until he is lifted up above all. Already in the Song so far the believer has sought to set forth Christ's praise, and will continue to do so right the way through the book. However, the glory and praise of our blessed Lord Jesus Christ, our Saviour and Bridegroom, will never fully be declared unless he describes himself.

Both separately and together the rose and the lily speak of Christ's unsurpassed excellence, his unparalleled condescension and his unrestricted accessibility or availability. It is worth working each of these out a little.

Firstly, there is Christ's unsurpassed excellence. Beauty and purity are the things to the fore here. For beauty and fragrance the rose, in all the multitude of its colours and varieties, is the chief of flowers. Whatever it is of Christ that we dwell upon at any particular time – his majesty, love, sacrifice, compassion, authority and so on – is beautiful and magnificent beyond compare.

Sharon (on the Mediterranean coast, south of Carmel) was a place of great fertility, where flocks and herds were kept and fruitful vines abounded. It was famous for its 'roses'. They were regarded as the best, rarest and most profuse of all. Some have argued that the flower intended here is a sweet-scented narcissus or a crimson anemone; others have advanced the claims of the iris, daffodil, crocus, or meadow-saffron, just to name a few. Evidently the word is derived from the Hebrew root 'to form bulbs'. Maybe we are not to understand it of what we know so well as our English rose, much as it is inviting to do so. In our English gardens 'rose of Sharon' is an alternative name for the hypericum calycinum, also known as Aaron's beard; it is an evergreen or semi-evergreen dwarf shrub, with large, bright yellow flowers from mid-summer to mid-autumn, and dark green leaves. It is very striking that the beloved says here not merely 'I am a rose' but 'I am a rose of Sharon'. No ordinary rose, no ordinary flower!

The lily seems to draw attention to Christ's purity. It has been said of him that he is a mingling of all perfections to make up one perfection. Peter describes Christ as 'a lamb without blemish and without spot' (1 Pet. 1:19), while the writer to the Hebrews says of him that he 'is holy, harmless, undefiled, separate from sinners' (Heb. 7:26).

Secondly, there is Christ's unparalleled condescension. He chooses here to liken himself to a rose and a lily. If the sun was to compare itself to a glow-worm, or an angel to an ant, that would be surprising enough. But here is the creator of the world (John 1:3), heaven's beloved one whom angels worship and adore (Heb. 1:6), the one before whom seraphim hide their faces (compare Isa. 6:2 with John 12:41), comparing himself to a rose and a lily. Is that not an amazing stoop? Consider it in the light of John 1:14 and Philippians 2:6-8. This is the one who forsook the thrones and the glories of heaven for a season, left behind the splendours of his Father's courts, to come down to this earth for our sakes and for our sins, to seek us, save us and take us for himself.

Thirdly, there is Christ's unrestricted accessibility or availability. The plain of Sharon was particularly rich in flowers. Its roses were not locked up in a private garden to gain access into which you had to pay an entry fee; nor were they only available to be looked at through specially constructed protective windows. They were there for all to see, to smell, to gather and to enjoy. The same is true of lilies of the valley, growing wild in the fields (though some identify these as water-lilies or lotuses). The application to Christ is clear. He is the Saviour of sinners. He is the rose and the lily, not to be looked at or admired from a distance, but to be plucked and enjoyed. He offers himself freely in the gospel, with invitations such as those recorded in Matthew 11:28 and John 4:13-14 and 6:35. Think as well of John 3:16 and Revelation 22:17.

It is noteworthy that when God announces, by way of prophecy, that 'the desert shall blossom as the rose; it shall blossom abundantly and rejoice', it is immediately said that 'the excellence of Carmel and Sharon shall be given to it' and 'They shall see the glory of the LORD' (Isa. 35:1-2). In contrast, when speaking of bringing desolation on the land, he announces that 'Sharon is like a wilderness' (Isa. 33:9).

Then in 2:2 Christ speaks of his church. One of the reasons why some interpreters of the Song find difficulty in ascribing verse 1 to Christ is this: how, they say, can he compare himself to a lily in verse 1 and then compare his church to a lily in verse 2? Yet where is the problem there? He is the 'I' of the first verse, who claims his own by the possessive pronoun 'my' in the second verse. Consider a similar example from the New Testament. In John 8:12 Christ calls himself 'the light of the world', while in Matthew 5:14 he calls his disciples 'the light of the world'. Yet that does not present a difficulty. The principle is this: the church is what she is, and believers are what they are, because the Lord Jesus Christ is who he is. He is the light, so they are the light, reflecting his light. He is the lily, so his people are lilies, for, being married to him, they bear his name.

The contrast between those who are Christ's and those who belong to the world is the difference between lilies and thorns. Once we were thorns, and now having been made a new creation in Christ we live and walk among thorns (the world), just as some of the most beautiful wild flowers in Bible lands would often be seen in the midst of a thorn bush or a thorn hedge. Yet however scratched and torn, battered and bruised we might end up, whatever hardships and troubles we might be exposed to, however lonely or discouraged we might feel, we are dear and precious to him. Observe his use of 'my love', just as in 1:15. Hence the language of verse 2. Attention has also been drawn to a linking of 'thorns' with an identical root meaning a crevice in the rock; in that case the believer's spiritual beauty is compared to a beautiful wild flower growing in the most unpromising setting of a rocky outcrop. Some have taken the flower here to be the white amaryllis, the woodbind or the honeysuckle.

It is important to underscore the strong implicit challenge here to Christ-likeness. It is conformity and likeness to Christ which constitutes the Christian's and the church's beauty. Christians are not to be private people. Rather we are to carry Christ with us wherever we go, in the sense of adorning the gospel we proclaim with attractive Christ-like lives. The reference at the end of verse 2, 'among the daughters', is not to God's children but rather to the daughters of men (mankind) among whom we live and move from day to day. This use of 'daughters' fits with such examples as daughters of Tyre, Edom, Babylon, and the like in several other Scriptures. Compare 'my mother's sons' of 1:6, and the language of Psalm 57:4 and Matthew 10:16.

The world will often be found to be a very thorny place; we shall frequently be misunderstood, spoken evil of, hated for Christ's sake, even turned out of jobs and homes on account of him. Ours it is, however, to 'shine as lights in the world, holding fast the word of life' (Phil. 2:15-16), owned by Christ, commending Christ, honouring Christ, counting all things loss for Christ. Whatever our surroundings, we are still to be like lilies. The purity, humility, meekness and gentleness of Christ are to be visible in us. Our charge is to magnify the grace of God towards us, and to manifest the grace of God within us.

In all of this, moreover, there is another thing which should capture our attention and our hope. We shall shortly be transplanted lilies, gathered lilies (6:2), taken out of this thorny wilderness into paradise, into heaven itself, 'to depart and be with Christ, which is far better' (Phil. 1:23). Then the difference between the lilies and the thorns will be seen clearly, once and for all. In the meantime, 'everyone who has this hope in him purifies himself, just as he is pure' (1 John 3:3).

2:3. The apple tree

It is the turn now of the believer to speak once again of her beloved, and the picture that is used of him is strikingly unusual. **Like an apple tree among the trees of the woods, so is my beloved among the sons** (2:3). Notice immediately the parallelism between this and the former verse. The bridegroom, Christ, speaks of his bride, the church, as 'my love among the daughters' – the standing out one, the special one, the unique one (v.2). The bride then speaks of the bridegroom as 'my beloved among the sons' (v.3), similarly: the outstanding one, the choicest one, the magnificent one.

As with the rose, so now with the apple tree, there has been some discussion on the matter of identity. What apple tree is intended? The citron and the apricot are among the leading suggestions. The citron was well known in the east, with its thick dark-green leaves for shelter, its white blossoms, and its deliciously refreshing and fragrant golden fruit. We may assert, however, that there are no absolutely compelling reasons which have been presented against an apple tree, ordinarily understood, even though it has been observed that there is no clear evidence that the apple as we know it was cultivated in the Ancient Near East. The leading English versions all translate 'apple tree'.

What the believer does here, having the king of the fruit trees in mind, and, most importantly, with Christ himself in view, is first to make a comparison and then to present a proof in support of it. The comparison is in the words already mentioned: 'like an apple tree among the trees of the woods'. The point is, that you would not expect to find an apple tree (or an apricot or a citron, if that is what the tree is) among the trees of the woods (NIV, forest), among (thinking in our English terms) the oak and the ash, the beech and the elm, the poplar and the cedar, or (if the root so indicates) in an uncultivated, rugged, mountainous terrain. You would expect to find an apple tree in a garden or in an orchard. That would be its more natural habitat. Just as the apple tree would stand out if it were found in unexpected surroundings, so the Lord Jesus Christ stands out from all other beloveds; 'so is my beloved among the sons' (NIV, young men). He stands alone. There is no one who can compare with him.

This the believer knows at first hand, for having made the comparison in verse 3a there is now presented the proof in 3b. **I sat down in his shade with great delight** (the literal word order is: 'in his shadow I delighted and I sat down'), **and his fruit was sweet to my taste** (or, palate). That is to say, I have not merely heard of this beloved or received from others second hand views or reports of his pre-eminence, preciousness and beauty; I know personally, for myself, from experience that all of this is true. I have myself sat in his shade. Indeed, I delight to do so, there is nothing I enjoy more. The Hebrew tense (piel) of 'I delighted' expresses intensity. Here is the believer's quietness and satisfaction of soul, a great contentment, that peace which the world can neither give nor take away. This is faith reposing and relying upon Christ. I have myself tasted his fruit, and how wonderfully sweet it is to the taste. The new and spiritual taste of the believer is the result of the divine work of regeneration.

From this luxuriant picture of a grand apple tree with its spreading boughs, welcome shade and exquisite fruit, is set forth another of the Song's magnificent 'portraits' of Christ. Taking the words of the comparison and the proof together we are taught of the majesty of Christ's appearance, the protection of his shade, and the sweetness of his fruit.

There is the majesty of Christ's appearance. While acknowledging again the sense in which the precise identity of the fruit tree mentioned here remains in measure an open question, it has been asserted that the term used comprehends all large round fruit not enclosed in a shell, and so the well-known (to us) apple of our English orchards certainly need not be excluded from our interpretation. The huge size to which such a tree will sometimes grow, outstripping the little bushes and the dwarf trees, and standing above them all, is a fitting picture for our glorious Lord Jesus. He is the pre-eminent one, altogether beyond compare. He is the one of whom the apostle Paul writes to the Colossians, 'For in him dwells all the fulness of the Godhead bodily; and you are complete in him, who is the head of all principality and power' (2:9-10), and 'in whom are hidden all the treasures of wisdom and knowledge' (2:3). He is 'Christ ... who is over all, the eternally blessed God' (Rom. 9:5). All 'power and riches and wisdom, and strength and honour and glory and blessing' belong to him (Rev. 5:12).

Not only largeness but loveliness is suggested as well. The apple blossom (with all its colour, brightness and fragrance) is highly suggestive of Christ, who (as 5:16 will assert) is 'altogether lovely'. He has captured our heart, our love, our all. How lovely Christ is to the eye of faith: undertaking our cause, taking our nature upon him, suffering, bleeding and dying in our place, rising again and entering heaven for us as our forerunner, great high priest, mediator and intercessor, with our names written upon his heart.

There is also in this picture in 2:3 the protection of his shade. A weary traveller (tired, thirsty, hungry, almost perishing in the heat) would relish a cool place to rest, some shady spot in which to find welcome protection from the heat. Such the apple tree would provide, and such, in the deeper and spiritual sense, Christ alone provides for the sinner: protection from the scorching heat of God's law that we have broken, God's punishment that we are under, God's wrath and condemnation that we must face. Christ alone is 'a refuge from the storm, a shade from the heat' (Isa. 25:4). None but he 'delivers us from the wrath to come' (1 Thess. 1:10). Only 'Christ also suffered once for sins, the just for the unjust, that he might bring us to God, being put to death in the flesh but made alive by the Spirit' (1 Pet. 3:18). Furthermore, only Christ's perfect work, only his all-availing shade, can deal with Satan's false charges, accusations and attempts to bring the Christian down. He is our shield and hiding place.

To complete the picture, there is the sweetness of his fruit. The weary traveller would desire not only protection but also refreshment, and the apple tree with its crisp, juicy, delicious fruit would do the job ideally. How much more does Christ refresh and bless the weary soul. His famous invitation in Matthew 11:28 assures of that, while Paul gathers the whole matter up by proclaiming, 'Blessed be the God and Father of our Lord Jesus Christ, who has blessed us with every spiritual blessing in the heavenly places in Christ' (Eph. 1:3). Nothing is left out of 'every spiritual blessing', whether for time or for eternity. The Lord Jesus Christ is the believer's apple tree.

2:4. Banquet and banner

Some familiar lines of Anne Ross Cousin, drawn from words of Samuel Rutherford, are these:

> Oh! I am my Beloved's
> And my Beloved's mine
> He brings a poor vile sinner
> Into his house of wine.

The 'prompt' for that is found in the verse of the Song we now proceed to. **He brought me to the banqueting house** (literally, house of wine) (2:4). What is in view with the banqueting house (NIV, banquet hall) is not the vineyard (where the grapes for the wine are grown), nor the downstairs cellars (where the bottles of wine are stored), but the actual grand hall of the palace (where the wine itself is drunk and enjoyed). The Shulamite's testimony here is that her beloved has brought her to the banqueting house. She is with him at the banquet, she is identified with him; he has brought her, taken her there.

This is full of the truth of the gospel, of which the whole of the Scripture speaks with united voice. There is here an even richer and fuller display of Christ's benefits than have already been intimated in verse 3, for pleasures are found in Christ's banqueting hall which exceed those under the apple tree. Further, there is an extension and expansion of spiritual enjoyment discernible in the sequence of 'his chambers' (1:4), 'his table'

(1:12), and now 'the banqueting house'. Here his bride enjoys his love which is 'better than wine' (1:2).

Through the gospel of God's grace, Christ has brought his church (notice the emphasis: 'he brought me') to his banqueting house. As a result of being saved by God's free, glorious and sovereign grace, those who once were nothing but poor and helpless sinners have now been brought to a banquet hall. The Christian's position and privilege is very much to the fore here: we have not been brought to some ordinary place or into some dingy back room, but to a house of wine, to a banquet hall, to a large and magnificent feast – the gospel feast, where everything is the best it can be. We are rich on account of Christ and rich in Christ!

At this feast is a pardon for sin which is a divine and royal pardon. Here is 'grace for grace' (John 1:16) and 'joy inexpressible and full of glory' (1 Pet. 1:8). Here is life 'more abundantly' (John 10:10). All the worldly honours and enjoyments which men spend so much time striving after are mere shadows and vanities compared with the excellencies and blessings that are the believer's in the gospel. And note the emphasis again: we have not invited ourselves, we have not somehow made ourselves worthy. If it was not for him, we should never have been acquainted with a single spiritual pleasure, yet through him we have been brought to drink of endless spiritual pleasures. Christ has invited us, Christ has brought us in, Christ has sat us down with himself, Christ has favoured us, Christ has owned us as his. All of this is a foretaste of the heavenly banquet, the heavenly feast.

Verse 4 continues, **and his banner over me was love**. Side by side with the banqueting house is the image of the banner. The two go together. The word for banner comes from a root meaning 'to cover', and so the force of the Shulamite's statement is that the king covers her with his love, he wraps his love over her and around her, identifying and owning her as his. This love is a conquering love, a protecting love, a possessive love. He who is 'the captain of (our) salvation' (Heb. 2:10, AV) has enlisted us under his banner. He has made us willing, and more than willing, in the day of his power (Ps. 110:3). The spiritual application is plain and fits like a glove with Paul's prayer for the Ephesians, 'that Christ may dwell in your hearts through faith; that you, being rooted and grounded in love, may be able to comprehend with all the saints what is the width and length and depth and height – to know the love of Christ which passes knowledge' (Eph. 3:17-19).

The banner of Christ's love over the believer (and the church) reminds us not only of whose we are (Christ's), but also of the sole basis of all his dealings with us (past, present and future), namely divine grace, mercy and love. In this love we were chosen and saved; in this love we are protected and sustained; in this love we shall be glorified and blessed for ever. Note the singular 'me' twice in this verse. It is intended as a reassuring reminder of the preciousness to Christ of each individual sinner whom he came from glory to purchase for his own, and then to take to be in glory with him (compare John 17:24).

2:5-7. Lovesick blues

What is the connection of verse 4 with verses 5-6, and what do those latter verses (which clearly belong together) mean? The connection is this: the overwhelming effect upon the believer of the felt experience of Christ's passionate and abundant love. Indeed verses 5-6 are very much experiential (or experimental) verses, touching the heights and depths of Christian experience.

The place to begin to understand these verses is at the end of 2:5, **for I am lovesick**. NIV has 'faint with love'. It could be translated 'sick with love' (that is, sick on account of or because of love). AV's 'sick of love' could give the wrong impression, in that in our current usage to be 'sick of' something implies weariness or boredom with it, which is certainly not what is intended here.

The believer's experience here can best be described as a

classic dose of the lovesick blues. This is not (as can be the case in a Christian's or the church's experience) a pining for Christ because of his absence or his withdrawing himself, maybe because we have grieved him, sinned against him, or wandered from him. Rather the lovesickness here is brought on by a surfeit of Christ. In verse 4 the believer was totally enraptured with Christ, possessed by him, wrapped in his love and herself in love with him, taken up with him, only having eyes for him, basking in the love of Christ. It was all blue skies with not a cloud in sight. In a vital sense, it was all too much to bear or to contain – which is precisely what accounts now for the apparent change in her language.

The Shulamite finds herself in need of being sustained and refreshed under this almost unbearably strong sense of the love of Christ. **Sustain me with cakes of raisins, refresh me with apples, for I am lovesick** (2:5). Some of the words here need closer attention. 'Sustain' is another intensive verbal form. AV has 'stay me' and NIV has 'strengthen me'. The translations 'prop up', 'support' or 'uphold' would also be appropriate. 'Refresh' is also a strong expression. AV has 'comfort', perhaps meant in the sense of revive. The verb could also carry the drift of to raise up from beneath for support, to furnish firm ground, to prepare a supporting couch or bed to lie on in order to recover from fatigue. 'Cakes of raisins' are grapes pressed together like cakes (compare 2 Sam. 6:19), and are not to be translated 'flagons' with AV (which presumably seeks to forge a connection with the house of wine in verse 4); and 'apples' remind us of the description given in verse 3 of Christ as the apple tree.

The believer is lovesick. However this surfeit of Christ, this passionate experience of 'the deep, deep love of Jesus', this weight of glory, does not lead to a desire for less of him ('I can't take any more – hold back') but rather to a longing for a still larger measure and experience of Christ and his love. The one whose love has brought her into this sick and fainting condition is the only one who can bring her out of it. The raisin cakes with which she would have Christ sustain her and the apples with which she would be refreshed are symbolic of the beloved himself and all that he gives – his virtues, his presence, his grace, his cordials, his merits, his promises, his doctrines and so on.

This assurance on the believer's part that the only remedy for lovesickness caused by a surfeit of Christ is still more of Christ is underscored in the next verse. **His left hand is under my head, and his right hand embraces me** (2:6). In other words, he comes to her and gives her what she asks him for. How the Lord Jesus loves to sustain and refresh a lovesick soul. His right hand supports and his left hand embraces. The verb signifies to enfold, to embrace lovingly. We rest in him absolutely at such a time, for the very last thing that assurance of the love of Christ can ever produce in the believer is pride or any sense of self-sufficiency; rather, its result will always be our humility and self-abasement, and the sense of 'why, O why, such love to me?'

The word picture here is of a husband's tender ministry to his wife. Just as a loving husband, if he sees his bride about to faint, hastens to her relief, embraces her in his arms, and holds her close to himself so that she is supported and comforted and does not fall – so the Christian's glorious bridegroom, observing our lovesick and fainting condition and hearing our earnest appeal to him, shows us and assures us still further of his tender, eternal and changeless love, comfort, sympathy and provision, and that he is all that we can and shall ever need. He cherishes us, revives us and comforts us when we are ready to faint or fall. He sustains us, upholds us and strengthens us when we are about to sink or collapse. 'He gives power to the weak, and to those who have no might he increases strength' (Isa. 40:29). 'A bruised reed he will not break, and smoking flax he will not quench' (Isa. 42:3). Is there not a hint here, too, of Romans 5:5?

We might well pause in the midst of these comments and ask: when have our souls been so overwhelmed with such communications, assurances and enjoyments of Christ's love that it has become almost beyond our strength to bear them? What do we really know of the believer's experience recorded here – anything at all? Surely we may learn from these verses that there is nothing to be experienced in all the earth which is quite like the love of Christ.

This section of the Song closes with a charge from the Shulamite to the daughters of Jerusalem upon this very subject of the mutual love between Christ and his church. **I charge you, O daughters of Jerusalem** (2:7). 'Charge' has the force of beg urgently. This is not some weak, sleepy, half-hearted request, but a serious and earnest plea on the believer's part. The charge is **by the gazelles or by the does of the field.** The gazelles and does are wild animals that roam the woods and fields freely, the former being members of the antelope family, the latter being female deer. It has been noted that gazelles are still common in Israel, and that three species of deer (red, fallow and roe) were known in biblical lands. Why they are brought in here is difficult to say. Maybe it is because of their attractiveness, docility and quietness, as well as their tendency to start up and take off at the least sound (compare the phrase 'a loving deer and a graceful doe', also in a husband and wife context, in Proverbs 5:19).

The nub of the Shulamite's desire expressed here, as she testifies to those who are witnesses to her joy in Christ, is that she and her beloved should not be disturbed. **Do not stir up nor awaken love until it pleases.** The verb is third person singular feminine, 'until she pleases'. It is a charge which incorporates a profitable lesson for the daughters of Jerusalem themselves (upon whom refer back to 1:5), as well as being in the personal interests of the Shulamite. She has happily lost herself in Christ, and wishes things to stay that way, with nothing arising to spoil. She wishes to go on enjoying him to the full, and is conscious that such tender moments as these can easily be harmed or interrupted. Consequently the 'until it/she pleases' does not contradict the charge, or give the daughters of Jerusalem leave to do the stirring up or awakening at some other time. What it does (true to the testimony of the Song as a whole) is to insert a realistic reminder that fellowship with Christ does not proceed from day to day at precisely the same temperature. There are days, and there are days.

Those who know Christ best are most anxious not to lose a single moment or opportunity of communion with him, and are concerned to keep themselves in the enjoyment of his love (compare Jude 21). To this end the heart must be guarded (Prov. 4:23), the devil must be resisted (Jas. 4:7), sin must be mortified (Col. 3:5) and heaven must be cherished (Col. 3:1-3).

A similar desire to that here in 2:7 is expressed by the Shulamite in 3:5 and 8:4 (see further on those verses).

2:8-13. Spring fever

The further we proceed through the Song, the more exquisite the poetic language becomes, and these verses break new ground for sheer beauty. The story so far is this, so far as chapter 2 is concerned. The believer has rejoiced in the person (v.3) and the work (v.4) of her beloved, the Lord Jesus Christ. She has been completely overwhelmed by his love, though with the effect of desiring more of him, not less (vs.5-6).

Such sublime and overpowering manifestations of the love of Christ to a soul cannot be borne without interruption. Consequently, in his love and in his wisdom, there are times (shorter or longer) when the Lord Jesus withdraws somewhat; times when the intensity of things between bride and groom is not so strong, even though deep and mutual love continues. After just such a season Christ now comes to his loved one again. The Shulamite continues to be the speaker throughout this section, and this is the believer's record of what transpired: his coming (vs.8-9) and his speaking (vs.10-13). Observe first the details as recorded.

The voice of my beloved! (2:8). There is no doubt whose voice it is. She 'rejoices greatly because of the bridegroom's voice' (John 3:29). When using the shepherd/sheep imagery

59

(instead of that of the bridegroom/bride) to describe the relationship between himself and his church, the Lord Jesus Christ says, 'My sheep hear my voice, and I know them, and they follow me' (John 10:27). There is immediate recognition, as there invariably is when the voice is heard of one who is particularly loved and desired.

Moreover, his approach is vigorous and not slow of pace, half-hearted or weary. **Behold, he comes leaping upon the mountains, skipping upon the hills.** The verbs 'leaping' and 'skipping' (NIV, bounding) signify not only speed but anticipation and pleasure, as well as the divine overcoming of all obstacles in the way, enabling him to come with perfect ease. He who came from heaven to earth in the first place, to 'save his people from their sins' (Matt. 1:21), comes again and again to those whom he loves. Just as it is the bride's delight to receive her bridegroom, so it is his joy to come to her and be welcomed by her. From of old, his 'delight was with the sons of men' (Prov. 8:31). This mutuality of Christian communion and fellowship is a frequent theme in Scripture, not least in a verse like Revelation 3:20: 'Behold, I stand at the door and knock. If anyone hears my voice and opens the door, I will come in to him and dine with him, and he with me.' It is in keeping both with that verse and the present verse from the Song (as well as with the whole of Scripture) that the coming of Christ which removes any distance between himself and his bride always has its first motion of love from his side.

The vigour and attractiveness of the Lord Jesus to the believer's soul is set forth in the words which follow next in the Song. **My beloved is like a gazelle or a young stag** (2:9). These are the masculine forms of the words used of the animals in verse 7. The gazelle (AV, roe) is a classic illustration of swiftness (compare 2 Samuel 2:18: 'And Asahel was as fleet of foot as a wild gazelle'; 1 Chronicles 12:8: 'as swift as gazelles on the mountains').

Behold, he stands behind our wall; he is looking through

the windows, gazing through the lattice. The beloved comes to the wall of the house where the Shulamite dwells, and two verbs are then used for his 'looking' and 'gazing'. The first, occurring only three times in the Old Testament, has the sense of a piercing, splitting or fixing kind of look. The second, here making its sole Old Testament appearance, can mean 'twinkle' or 'bloom', but here, evidently, when applied to seeing, indicates a quick darting forward of the glance of the eye. The mention of windows and lattice indicate that the openings would not be glazed, but rather comprise a wooden frame which one would look straight through. Christ standing behind the wall, looking through the windows and gazing through the lattice conveys the sense of his ever nearer approach, the varying degrees of his manifestations to the soul. From being further off, he comes closer; then, once at close quarters again and seen more clearly, he addresses precious and gracious words to his bride.

As soon as the beloved speaks, there follows a majestic description of the season of spring, reminiscent of those poetic lines about sweet lovers loving the spring. This is bracketed about in verse 10 and at the end of verse 13 with the Lord Jesus Christ's invitation to the believer, an invitation of a highly personal nature.

My beloved spoke, and said to me (2:10). Although what goes for the individual Christian so often applies just as much to the gathered church, nothing must ever be allowed to detract from the potently personal nature of the Christian life, walk and triumph of faith. In other words, 'Christ ... loved the church and gave himself for it' (Eph. 5:25) must always have side by side with it, 'the Son of God, who loved me and gave himself for me' (Gal. 2:20). This personal dimension is very much to the fore all the way through the Song. It is so here in verse 8 ('the voice of **my** beloved'), verse 9 ('**my** beloved'), and now also in verse 10 ('**My** beloved spoke, and said to **me**'). It will be seen again shortly in 2:16, which is virtually the motto text of this whole book of Scripture.

What did the beloved say? **Rise up, my love, my fair one, and come away.** Notice the double 'my' again, this time spoken from Christ to the believer. The invitation is to further mutual enjoyment of one another's company – the believer's communion and fellowship with Christ. 'My love' (NIV, my darling) has already occurred at 1:9 and 2:2, while 'my fair (or, beautiful) one' reminds us of 1:8 and 1:15. Christ's view of his bride is not subject to change. He is the constant and changeless beloved of our souls, and is far more desirous of our company than we are of his. This language of love is no whispering of sweet nothings in the ear. The Lord Jesus chooses his words carefully and means all that he says.

There then follows the description of spring, beginning: **For lo, the winter is past** (2:11). All that comes after, through verses 11-13, is a passionately and evocatively charged expansion of that introductory statement, with a six-fold contribution to the one total picture which may be set out in the following way for clarity:

> **the rain is over and gone.**
> **The flowers appear on the earth;**
> **the time of singing has come.**
> **and the voice of the turtle-dove is heard in our land (2:12).**
> **The fig tree puts forth her green figs,**
> **and the vines with the tender grapes give a good smell (2:13).**

A number of details require comment, though the magnificence of the overall picture must not be lost. This is the only occurrence of 'winter' in the Old Testament (v.11), very much the rainy season in Palestine. Once this was over, however, the whole of creation round about was clothed with the beauty of a new-born freshness. A literal translation of 2:11b would be, 'the rain has passed, it goes to itself.' The spring flowers appear, in all their loveliness and profusion.

It is the season of singing as well, the delights of sight and smell being joined by those of sound. There is no mention in the Hebrew of AV's 'birds', though birdsong is the most natural inference since human song is not a seasonal thing so is no more heard in spring than in winter, unless one thinks of renewed joy taking the form of an outburst of song at the approach of spring. The turtle-dove (v.12) is a migratory bird whose distinctive cooing call is one of the signs of spring. It is a different dove from the one mentioned back in 1:15 which (it is suggested) is the rock-dove which was a resident bird.

The green figs would be the premature unripe figs (around March time) which preceded the figs proper (August/September). Maybe for the tender grapes giving a good smell we should translate (literally) 'the vines give a fragrance by the blossom' (compare NIV's, 'the blossoming vines spread their fragrance'). Both fig trees and vines often stand as emblems of prosperity and fruitfulness.

This picture of being full of the joys of spring is as delightful as it is unmistakable. It ends with a repetition of the words of verse 10: **Rise up, my love, my fair one, and come away!** There is always a great earnestness on Christ's part, whatever may be the backwardness shown by his bride.

A word would be in order concerning the spiritual application of the whole section (vs.8-13) which we entitled Spring Fever. There is such a thing as the winter of the believer's soul, as well as wintry seasons in the experience of the church. Just as in the natural world as God has ordained things, spring follows winter, so it is in spiritual affairs. The dark, cold, barren times, when the very souls of Christ's people would shiver for want of him (not least on account of our sin, the influences of the world, and the superficiality of much of our Christian lives and experience), give way, in the purposes of grace, to the return of spring. What a difference that makes, when Christ fills the soul again, when he visits his church once more, when he pours out his Holy Spirit and grants tokens and assurances of his love, when he blesses his people with peace and adds to the church those who should be saved. He is the true 'dayspring from on high' (Luke 1:78) who visits us.

This can occur at various times. In the history of the church this is the experience in seasons of revival, while for the individual Christian this happens with conversion itself as well as at different stages of the Christian life after times of desolation, desertion, afflictions, sorrows, persecutions, backsliding and the like. The deathbeds of believers have sometimes been occasions of remarkable visitations of Christ to their souls, while the 'glorious appearing of our great God and Saviour Jesus Christ, who gave himself for us' (Tit. 2:13-14) will also be such a time. There will be no more winters then, only an everlasting spring in the perfect fragrances and eternal pleasures of heaven.

In all these connections, there is a reminder of the promise that 'weeping may endure for a night, but joy comes in the morning' (Ps. 30:5). All becomes delightful and fragrant again whenever Christ returns and makes himself known. It is like a different world.

2:14-15. Doves and foxes

This glorious visit of the beloved to the believer continues in these next two verses with a further highly personal word, comprising both an invitation (v.14) and an exhortation (v.15). The NKJV's attributing of verse 14 to the Shulamite and verse 15 to her brothers is to be rejected. It is Christ who speaks here still.

He uses a most endearing form of address: **O my dove** (2:14). Why this choice of word, not for the first time in the Song? Certainly it is not merely for poetry's sake. All the names, titles and descriptions given either to the church as a whole or to the believer as an individual in Scripture have a point, and that point invariably is to express an important truth about the church or the believer. So, for example, temple speaks of holiness, pillar speaks of stability, and sheep speaks of dependence and obedience. It is the same here with the dove. This address expresses the tender and affectionate nature of Jesus' love for us. More even than that, however, it expresses something by way of definition and description of what Christ's people as a whole and Christ's people one by one should be like.

Working this out a little, several characteristics are presented, such as beauty, chastity, helplessness, meekness and alluringness. There is beauty. The phrase appears in Psalm 68:13, 'the wings of a dove covered with silver, and her feathers with yellow gold', and this language is suggestive of the believer, washed in Christ's blood, clothed with Christ's righteousness, sanctified by his grace and his Holy Spirit, adorned with the beauty of holiness, having Christ's own beauty and comeliness put upon us, saved to be holy.

There is chastity and faithfulness. It is documented that the dove pairs with only one mate (even to the point of chastity that if a dove was to do anything other than this, the male would tear the offending male to pieces, and the female would do the same to the other female). To add to this, the mates mourn the loss of one another when one dies, and appear (as we should say) inconsolable and continue without mating again in a permanent widowhood. All of this reminds us that, as Christians, we are 'betrothed ... to one husband', 'presented ... as a chaste virgin to Christ' (2 Cor. 11:2). He is our beloved, our bridegroom; we are to be devoted exclusively to him, faithful to him, with no rival lovers and no one else and nothing else to take his place.

There is helplessness. Doves are unable to defend themselves against birds of prey. So we, of ourselves, are helpless and strengthless, and if we are to stand firm and endure to the end it must be the Lord himself being our helper, 'strong in the Lord and in the power of his might' (Eph. 6:10).

There is also meekness. This, along with quietness, gentleness, cleanliness and a gracious spirit, is indicated here also, and is exactly how we are to be, 'blameless and harmless, children of God without fault in the midst of a crooked and perverse generation, among whom you shine as lights in the world' (Phil. 2:15), putting on 'tender mercies, kindness, humbleness of mind, meekness, long-suffering; bearing with one

65

another, and forgiving one another (Col. 3:12f).

To complete the picture, there is alluringness. It has been observed of doves that they can allure wild doves into their dovecotes with them. So Christians, having been chosen, called and saved by grace, should be concerned to allure (gain, win) others to Christ, bearing the glad tidings of the gospel to them, and seeking to 'adorn the doctrine of God our Saviour in all things' (Tit. 2:10).

Christ's dove is pictured as being **in the clefts of the rock, in the secret places of the cliff** (or, in the secrecy of the steep place). Doves take refuge in such places and relish the protection offered there. So those who are loved of Christ (and are often timid and trembling souls) do not flaunt themselves or strut about but delight to be found close to Christ, in the secret of his presence, under the shadow of his wings, casting all their care upon him. They would be like John, the beloved disciple, 'leaning on Jesus' bosom' (John 13:23). The figure of the believer/church leaning upon Christ will appear at 8:5.

Let me see your countenance, let me hear your voice. With these words his address comes to the point. Bear in mind continually that mutual enjoyment is the key to the Song. The believer's enjoyment of Christ is only half the picture. The other part, required for mutuality, is Christ's own desire for and delight in his people, those whom the Father has given him (John 6:37). The reason for his invitation is revealed in the balancing statement at the end of verse 14: **for your voice is sweet, and your countenance is lovely**. The Lord Jesus desires to look upon us, to fill his gaze with us, and to hear the sound of our voice. The word here for 'voice' is the same as that used in verse 12 of the voice (the cooing) of the turtle-dove.

This remarkable invitation should be full of encouragement and comfort for every believer. When Christ so desires your fellowship, when he so graciously invites you to himself, when he coaxes you and draws you so tenderly to his presence, would you grieve him, would you disappoint him, would you turn away from him, would you forget him, would you keep yourself at a distance from him? Rather, should not his manner here humble us, draw and charm our hearts, and raise our spirits to desire him also? Christ desires to see his people trustful, cheerful and blessed in him; to see in us the exercise of faith and love; to enjoy our beauty which is but a reflection of his own. He regards it as lovely to see us and lovely to hear us (speaking of him, speaking to him, singing his praise, pouring out our hearts). The world may not think much of either the sight or the sound of the Christian or the church. Yet it would not be improper to say that the Lord Jesus Christ can never see too much of or hear too much from his own. If only his church always felt the same about him.

With the invitation comes an exhortation, though they are not formally separate or distinct, but intimately twinned together. **Catch us the foxes, the little foxes that spoil the vines, for our vines have tender grapes** (2:15). The point here is that notwithstanding Christ and the church's mutual desire for one another, so much, so easily, can spoil that communion and fellowship. Another of the Bible's descriptions of the church is that of the vineyard. The church of Christ is 'the vineyard of the LORD of hosts' (Isa. 5:7), which he has planted, and which he cultivates, watches over and waters every moment (Isa. 27:3). Individual believers may be thought of as the vines which make up that vineyard. Just as the foxes in view here would get over the walls or through the fences and ruin the vineyards and eat the grapes, so in our Christian lives and in our communion with the Lord the foxes – the little foxes – get in to hurt and destroy.

This is very much a straight charge to believers to examine their ways, search their hearts, mortify their corruptions and sinful appetites and passions – all those things, in a word, which are like foxes that destroy their graces and comforts, crush good beginnings, and hold back spiritual growth. Recall 1:6 and the dangers of neglecting the vineyard (which may be applied both to believers neglecting their own souls and to gospel ministers neglecting the souls of the congregation). Sin must be dealt with at its first risings. The devil must be resisted. No opportunity must be given for the flesh. Nothing is to be considered too small or insignificant in this connection – little foxes are mentioned, as well as foxes. Great damage may be caused by what we mistakenly consider to be small things that barely merit attention.

As well as this being a charge to avoid sin in our lives, it is surely also a call to avoid all false teaching or teachers and all suspect doctrine that will hinder the separateness, distinctiveness, beauty, purity and glory of the church of Christ, or which would grieve his Holy Spirit or cause God in any way to hide his face. Hence Christ's wording here, 'catch us/take for us'. He is thinking all the time of the effect upon mutual fellowship and communion. This matter is of the most serious common interest both to Christ and to his church.

There should be no sense of surprise to find verse 15 here. Against the lovely background of verse 14's invitation, this exhortation is given to his church by the Lord Jesus Christ in loving concern, in order to be a reminder of something which is so easily and so foolishly forgotten: communion with Christ is a tender plant. It is easily injured and marred, and that so often by the so-called little things (including the murmurings, the complainings, the idlings) that Christians often scarcely bother about. It is as if the bridegroom is saying to his bride: take care! be watchful! walk wisely! give thought! show sensitivity! keep awake!

NIV translates the last part of the verse, 'our vineyards that are in bloom'. This could indicate either actual blossom or 'in the first grapes' (just budding or sprouting and so very vulnerable to harm). Compare the similar wording back in verse 13. Either way, the emphasis is upon the delicate state of things and the ease with which hurt can be inflicted. Hence the need for great care and resolute action. The Lord Jesus Christ is exceedingly concerned over the condition of the work of grace in his bride, and the weaker or more fragile that state the more exercised he is. He would have his bride to be of the same mind with himself. The true believer's prayer continually will be Psalm 139:23-24.

2:16-17. Possessing and possessed

The words which come next, **My beloved is mine and I am his** (2:16), take us at once to the very heart of the Song. Compare this verse with 6:3 and 7:10. The literal rendering is striking and forceful: 'my beloved to me and I to him'. The believer is now speaking, and uses the language of possessing and being possessed – the intimate belonging of Christ and his people together, and their interest in one another. This is the language of full assurance, the believer's calling and election made sure (2 Pet. 1:10). The ground of this mutual relationship is the Father's gift or donation: as if to say, my beloved is mine and I am his, because before the foundation of the world God the Father gave me to God the Son, and gave God the Son to me. None can ever dispute the Father's right to give to the Son whomsoever he would choose, and none can ever take from the Son those whom it has pleased the Father to give to him in the everlasting covenant. The third person of the Godhead, the Holy Spirit, is not to be omitted from this transaction either, for he it is who makes all these things real to the believer (at a given moment in regeneration, and by a lifelong work in sanctification).

It is clear from the language of verse 16 thus far that this Christ/believer, Christ/church relationship is not only personal, spiritual and mutual, but is also firm, settled, loving and richly encouraging. There is the sense, too, in these words not only of 'Christ is everything to me' but also 'I have everything in him'; not only the possession of Christ but (with that) the fulness of Christ. Link this with 1 Corinthians 3:23, 'And you are Christ's, and Christ is God's'; and compare John 17:10: 'And all mine are yours, and yours are mine, and I am glorified in them.' The relationship is also to be enjoyed, hence the second part of the verse.

69

He feeds his flock among the lilies. NKJV's 'his flock' is an addition, not found in the Hebrew text. NIV's 'browses' is an alternative possibility for 'feeds'. The verb is common in the Old Testament for feeding animals and shepherding. Lilies have already featured at the beginning of this chapter, first with reference to Christ himself ('the lily of the valleys') and then with reference to his own people, by virtue of their union with him ('like a lily among thorns, so is my love among the daughters'). The imagery of Christ among the lilies (dwelling, walking, abiding, manifesting himself among his people) occurs again at 6:3 (see the comments on 6:2-3, and Christ gathering lilies which is mentioned there). There is a strong sense of Revelation 1-3, where the Lord Jesus Christ (risen, ascended and glorified) is pictured walking 'in the midst of the seven golden lampstands', those lampstands being his church. Just as he walks among the lampstands, so he feeds among the lilies. It is always important to observe and to learn from the unity and consistency of Scripture. Much light is shed thereby, and much profit gained.

The enjoyableness, on both sides, of this mutual relationship is very much to the fore here. Though Christ is in heaven and his church is on earth, yet how he delights to dwell among those who are his (Christ dwelling in our hearts through faith, Christ in the midst of his church gathered together, Christ present in the power of his Spirit and making his abode with us). We should wish for nothing more earnestly and enjoy nothing more satisfyingly than the presence of Christ, the knowledge of Christ, the love of Christ, the promises of Christ, the grace of Christ manifested to our minds and hearts and souls. It is both mysterious and sweet. Even all of this is not strictly all – for what will it be to behold the face of Christ in glory, and to be united to him in that holy and happy place for ever.

These considerations should have the effect of underscoring that exhortation in verse 15 concerning the foxes that spoil the vines, lest anything we do, think, say, leave undone and such like should grieve Christ, offend him, slight him or imply neglect of him. A true wife desires to bring pleasure and honour to her husband at all times, just as a true husband desires in all things to be a blessing and encouragement to his wife.

If in verse 16 the bride speaks to herself (and/or to others who will listen), in verse 17 she speaks directly to her beloved: **Until the day breaks and the shadows flee away** (2:17). The verb 'break' may be translated 'cools/breathes/blows', giving the sense of the day growing cool as the evening breeze is felt. What time is in view here? And while the next words, **Turn, my beloved, and be like a gazelle or a young stag,** are completely of a piece with the references to Christ in verses 8-9, what are we to make of **upon the mountains of Bether**?

Taking the latter first, for NKJV's 'upon the mountains of Bether', NIV has 'on the rugged hills' (NIV footnote, 'the hills of Bether'), and NKJV margin has 'separation' for Bether. AV margin offers 'division'. It seems that a specific geographical location is not to be looked for here. Certainly none presents itself very obviously. Another occurrence of the verbal root corresponding to Bether is Genesis 15:10, where the context is cutting or dividing an animal in a sacrificial ritual as part of God's covenant with Abram.

The meaning of the phrase here in verse 17 would seem to be the believer's earnest desire that anything and everything which causes separation or division between herself and her beloved would be removed by the appearing and overcoming of the beloved himself. It is a glad and willing response to his invitation to her in verses 10 and 13 to rise up and come away.

That being so, we are helped towards a right understanding of the first part of the verse concerning the day breaking and the shadows fleeing away. Just as the comfort of God's people throughout the Old Testament was the coming of the day-spring from on high (the first coming of the Messiah, the Lord Jesus Christ), so our great comfort, prospect and outlook (our assurance of hope as well as of faith) is that same Messiah's second coming.

On that day, when the day cools and the fresh evening breezes blow, all the shadows of our present state will flee away and a glorious and everlasting day will dawn – the day of the Lord, the day of Christ, the day of days.

Days of his presence on earth are precious indeed, but the eternal day of his presence in heaven will be precious beyond words. We are not yet in heaven, the place of unreserved and unhindered communion with Christ, the place of open vision and unbroken enjoyment. We are still on the earth, the place of faith and patience, the place of heaven-pointing and heaven-anticipating hope. Nonetheless: 'The night is far spent, the day is at hand' (Rom. 13:12). Our beloved is near. He is coming. His promise to his church is, 'Surely I am coming quickly'. His church's response to him is, 'Even so, come, Lord Jesus!' (Rev. 22:20).

On a similar note, with a similar longing, and in a similar confidence, the Song of Songs will end (8:14).

Chapter 3

A DREAM AND A WEDDING

Do you ever dream? There are good dreams and bad dreams; dreams you can remember when you awake in the morning and dreams you cannot recall. The first part of this third chapter of the Song (3:1-5) recounts a bad dream experienced by the bride. In fact, it was more a nightmare, and one which she could remember all too vividly. It is not formally stated in the text that this is a dream, but it is clearly implied that it occurred during sleep. There is to it a savour of Job 33:15: 'In a dream, in a vision of the night, when deep sleep falls upon men, when slumbering upon their beds ...'

She has just rejoiced in the language of full assurance (2:16), and has expressed her desire and longing for her beloved in the most passionate terms (2:17). But then, upon going to bed and falling asleep, she has the most terrible dream – terrible, because her beloved had gone, disappeared completely from her life. He was nowhere to be found, and her only thought and her alarming fear was 'I've lost him'. As the dream proceeds, she goes out into the city at night, looking for him, enquiring for him, and then eventually finds him, whereupon she takes him to her mother's house.

The five verses divide naturally into three parts.

3:1. The beloved missing
By night on my bed I sought the one I love (3:1). The bride describes her beloved in the dream as 'him whom my soul loves', just as in 1:7, when speaking of him there, it was 'you whom my soul loves'. Neither the 'him' nor the 'you' are in the Hebrew. So it is (literally) here: 'On my bed by night I sought whom my soul loves', there being no doubt, question or confusion about

his identity. It is pleasing and honouring to Christ to be so regarded and spoken of. 'By night' is strictly a plural, 'by nights'. NIV has 'all night long', which catches something of its force; or it could be something like 'night after night'. This is another reminder that true love to Christ is whole-souled, whole-hearted, whole-strengthed, absorbing all our affections, desires and energies. Moreover, even in a believer's darkest nights there remains some token of desire for him.

I sought him, but I did not find him. The double appearance here of the verb 'sought', in the space of so few words, underscores the agitation of the Shulamite, and her strenuous exercise in seeking to discover where and why her beloved had gone, and what had happened to him. Yet there was no immediate sign of him whatsoever. He has departed, and appears to have covered his tracks completely.

Pausing for a moment, sufficient clue has already been given to the very real and familiar problem of spiritual experience which is being described in this dream: desertion in the Christian life. It pictures that season (sometimes referred to as the dark night of the soul) when the Lord Jesus Christ seems altogether to have withdrawn his presence from us. Here, eloquently recorded, are those times when we continue to go through the motions of the Christian life, but have no felt sense or enjoyment of Christ in anything. All seems empty and barren, even though covenant bonds ('the one I love') remain firm. The friends of the bridegroom mourn when the bridegroom himself is taken away from them (Matt. 9:15). All of this is underscored by the believer's reference to 'my bed', when compared with her speaking of 'our bed' in 1:16. She seems to be completely on her own.

Our earlier remarks (see especially page 30; compare also pages 53f., 59, 68f.) about union and communion apply again here, so that there is no room for any misunderstanding. That is to say, although at such times we feel we have lost Christ, in reality we have not 'lost' him at all. Union with Christ is a permanent state of salvation, a settled condition of grace, a firm standing of justification, and is never subject to ins and outs or ebbs and flows. It rests not upon our feelings but upon his faithfulness to his covenant. Our communion with Christ, however, is a very tender and delicate plant. It is not uninterruptible. It is easily affected from within or from without, easily harmed and damaged, such that in strict terms of enjoying Christ and walking with Christ, he does not seem to be there any more. So we ask 'why?' and 'where is he?', because we still know him and regard him as the one our soul loves. It must not be thought that dark seasons and heavy spiritual frames are necessarily indicative of a Christless state.

3:2-3. The beloved sought

There is strong language through this whole section: 'I sought' (twice in v.1), 'I will rise ... I will seek ... I sought' (v.2), and 'Have you seen ...?' (v.3). This is earnest, careful, practical, thorough, methodical searching, as, in her continuing dream, the bride gets up out of bed and sets off to look for her missing beloved. There can be no more delay. Enough time has been lost and wasted already. It is a solid mark of a soul who is alive in Christ and who loves him that such a one cannot possibly be content for things to continue with him absent. It is a most precious mercy to be aroused afresh to seek him.

'I will rise now,' I said (3:2), announces the beginning of the task, **'and go about the city; in the streets and in the squares I will seek the one I love.'** In dreams one thing follows very quickly after another.

It needs to be asserted that we always desert Christ before he ever 'deserts' us. We do so when we leave aside close communion with him (in the means of grace, both public and private), when we stray away from the safe and clear paths of his Word that he has prescribed for his glory and our good, and when we exchange what we know to be the good will and pleasure of Christ for the deceitful and carnal imaginations and desires of our own hearts and passions, and forget that 'those who are Christ's have crucified the flesh with its passions and desires' (Gal. 5:24).

As a result, we have no one to blame but ourselves. Even so, if we know what is good for us we shall initiate a search. Is not that what it is always necessary to do if someone is lost? A search is made for them, and so the believer searches for Christ. No Christian, who has the least shred of spiritual health left about him or her, can rest content in such a state as is envisaged via this dream. There is the urgent need to get up and do something about things. No more time can be lost.

'The city', as a whole, and 'the streets and ... the squares (or, broad places)', in particular, reflect the detailed nature of this search. Every possible place is to be checked out in the examination and enquiry. Where might I have offended him? Where could the trouble have set in? What did I do or neglect to do which grieved Christ so much? Where might he have gone? These are some of the questions that press in upon the anxious soul.

At first the search gets nowhere. **I sought him, but I did not find him** is the initial sad result. Christ is not always found again immediately, in order that our earnestness in seeking him may be tested and proved. If this be thought of as a playing hard to get on his part, he would thereby chasten our former negligence of him, not quench any renewed diligence in seeking for him again. Yet the next verse begins most interestingly and perhaps more promisingly. **The watchmen who go about the city found me** (3:3). As before, the believer feels no need to name Christ: **to whom I said, 'Have you seen the one I love?'**. 'The one I love' will suffice, as if all the world should know immediately of whom she speaks. There can only be that one.

There is a reminder here of 1:7, 'where you feed ... where you rest'. The city is best understood of the church itself, the city of the living God, of which all who belong are 'fellow citizens with the saints and members of the household of God'

(Eph. 2:19; compare Ps. 87:3; Heb. 12:22-23; and also the picture in Rev. 1 of Christ walking in the midst of the seven golden lampstands, his church). The streets and squares of the city represent the means of grace, not least the public ordinances of the gospel – those provisions which the Lord Jesus has made for the very purpose of our finding him, knowing him and enjoying him.

The watchmen (in the dream, the city guards who would tour the cities during the night hours, keeping an eye out for any trouble, stopping and questioning any suspicious looking characters and assisting those in any need) are best understood, in spiritual terms, as those who watch over the believer's soul. They are 'those who rule over you, who have spoken the word of God to you, whose faith follow' (Heb. 13:7). They are those 'pastors and teachers' who are the gift of the risen, ascended, glorified Lord Jesus Christ to his church for the purposes set out in Ephesians 4:11-16. They are the stars in Christ's right hand, the angels of the churches (Rev. 1:20; 2:1). They guard the city and its citizens (the church and so the people of God), chiefly through the ministry of the Word and pastoral care in connection with that ministry. Theirs is the responsibility to take heed to themselves and to the flock among which the Holy Spirit has made them overseers; 'to shepherd the church of God which he purchased with his own blood' (Acts 20:28).

There is no substitute for Christ's own provisions. We neglect them at our peril. We are not intended to function without them. All earnest Christian souls will prize them and their ministries. It needs to be affirmed, however, that ministers must know, love and walk with Christ themselves if ever they are to be the least use in directing others where to find him. An unconverted minister (one who is himself ignorant of Christ), or a backsliding minister (one who has lost his love for Christ), can do no one any good, and is a danger to all.

3:4-5. The beloved found

Scarcely had I passed by them, when I found the one I love (3:4). A literal translation would be along the lines of, '(it was) a little while when I had passed from them until ...' The Lord Jesus Christ is never far away from the soul who seeks him. The Lord has not said to his people, 'Seek me in vain' (Isa. 45:19). Rather, he says, 'And you will seek me and find me, when you search for me with all your heart. I will be found by you, says the LORD ...' (Jer. 29:13-14). No true believer can be satisfied for long with an absent Saviour. It is a mark of grace in a soul that Christ must be found again as soon as possible, if he appears to have departed, and that the search will be continued resolutely whatever discouragements and setbacks are met along the way. Then what joy there is at the fresh discovery of his presence and the entering in again to fellowship with him. The bride here is enabled to go beyond the watchmen to the bridegroom himself. That is how it should be, for while we are grateful for the servants, the one we need most at all times is the master.

I held him and would not let him go. Seized, clutched, held tight to him would be a fuller capturing of the force of things implied here. The language is that of deep affection, of one who means business. It is a husband and wife picture. Having once lost him and now found him, she will not entertain the possibility of losing him again. Here is a holy passion and a pure jealousy of love. Surely that is most likely to be treasured carefully and held tightly which has already once been lost and then found again. It is well to remember here that ultimately, of course, it is Christ's hold of us, not our hold of Christ, that keeps us safe and enables us to endure to the end (compare John 6:37-40 and 10:27-30, as well as Jude 24-25). Yet how gracious it is of him to condescend to have us hold him in faith and love, that we would not let him go.

The verse continues: **until I had brought him to the house of my mother, and into the chamber of her who conceived me**. The interpretation of these words looks, at first sight, hard to come by, but we must not overcomplicate things needlessly. The truth is surely this: having found Christ again (or having been found of Christ again) the believer now wishes that he be magnified not only in her own heart but throughout the whole church and among her entire family, that all together may rejoice in him and his favours. Such a believer is a blessing to all. One indication of how dear and precious the Lord Jesus is to us is evidenced in our desire that others would find him dear and precious as we do, and that fellow believers would be revived and refreshed with his love (compare Paul's prayer for the Ephesian Christians in Eph. 3:14-21). The believer would have the whole church rejoice in a felt and present Lord Jesus Christ. There is no selfishness here. The good of the entire church is in view.

A word would be in place here upon the question, already touched upon, of why the one whom our soul loves should ever withdraw himself from us, so that (from our vantage point) he seems to have left us alone. For such, envisaged here in this dream, is very much the believer's experience. Indeed, the closer your walk with him has been, the greater your relish for spiritual things thus far, and the tenderer and more sensitive your conscience is for fear of grieving him, then the more desperate will this experience be of Christ (apparently) having gone from you. Maybe the reason why this dream recurred (the 'night after night' syndrome) and increased the believer's pain and anguish is that the more the bride feared she was no longer loved by her beloved, the more ardent became her longing for him and the less could she rest until she had found him again. Yet it is never without good reason on his part that he withdraws, and those reasons may be several. It is worth listing the most likely ones. They are these:

1. To cure us from laziness, idleness and slothfulness in seeking him and keeping up communion with him (warning us thereby of the danger of spiritual sleeping sickness), and to make us prize him and his closeness more than ever.

79

2. To wean our affection and satisfaction from the things of the world and to stir us up afresh to seek after him, kindling deeper longings for him.

3. To impress upon us the hatefulness of sin, creating a sense of our loss and danger in being without him, urging us to undertake an immediate inquiry into what it is that has caused Christ to depart, and making us realise (in this as in so many realms) that we only begin properly to appreciate the best blessings when we do not have them.

4. To show us more clearly than before all that Christ has suffered for us to have us for himself (for none will be so fired with love to the Saviour as those who have first been humbled sorely by desertion).

5. To prepare us for the joy of his returns to our souls, as well as (longer term) the future comforts and future joys of heaven itself, where desertions will be no more, for there 'we shall always be with the Lord' (1 Thess. 4:17).

It is alarming how quickly the shadows can fall in the Christian's experience. There is no time to speak of, sometimes, between the high experience at the end of chapter 2 and the low experience here at the beginning of chapter 3. Few children of God, who know their own hearts, are ignorant of this. One moment the believer is walking with Christ in the brilliant sunshine. The next you are seeking him alone in the dark. Yet it is part of his very faithfulness to us that he deals with us in this way and allows us to be troubled. It is for our benefit.

The section closes with precisely the same words as appeared in 2:7. **I charge you, O daughters of Jerusalem, by the gazelles or by the does of the field, do not stir up nor awaken love until it pleases** (3:5). However, this is no vain repetition. The bride addresses herself, as before, to the daughters of Jerusalem (see the earlier comments for their identification). These words have their own appropriateness coming at this point. Now that communion with Christ is so blessedly restored, it is wholly understandable that the believer hangs a 'do not disturb' notice upon the door so that nothing should now arise which would grieve him again, or which would hinder or spoil this new-found delight. Gazelles and does are timid creatures, easily frightened away; and while, of course, nothing like timidity is ever to be ascribed to Christ, very great care needs to be taken over the preserving and nourishing of our communion with him, lest he be provoked to withdraw again.

Another particular significance in these words at this point is that while in 2:7 the whole emphasis was upon personal and individual communion with Christ, here (as just noticed from the language used in verse 4b) the corporate aspect of the church is much in the picture also.

If only we were more taken up with Christ all the time, holding him and not letting him go, careful not to offend him or cause his withdrawing, prizing his company and fellowship as the choicest thing, and clinging more closely to him. It is impossible to overstate what the consequences of this would be, whether in our personal lives, family lives and relationships, or in the church. Zeal, prayer, faith, love, hope, holiness, mortification, heavenly mindedness, and much else besides, would all be quickened, and the gospel adorned with far greater beauty. The world itself would have to take notice.

* * * * *

This is an appropriate point at which to remark that it is not required of necessity that we discern in the Song (still less, impose upon it) a strict chronological scheme in terms of the narrative. At times such an arrangement is plainly visible in passing from one section to another (compare, for example, the movement from the ecstasy of 2:16-17 to the desolation of 3:1; or from the expressed desire of the believer to the beloved in 4:16 to his response in 5:1). At other times, however, such a progression is not so obviously the case, and the whole book rises above such a straightjacket. The present instance may be a case in point. That there is a clear division of chapter 3 into two parts (vs.1-5, vs.6-11) cannot be missed. A natural connection or chronological progression between the two, however, does not need to be forced.

The earlier part of the chapter records the Shulamite's dream of her absent beloved, and treats, as we saw, of the experience of spiritual desertion and the earnestness with which the true believer will seek the Lord Jesus Christ afresh at such a season. This second part of the chapter, to which now we come, takes us to the theme which is absolutely central to this whole book of Scripture, and its chief reason for being there at all: the marriage of the bridegroom and the bride, the wedding of the believer/church and Christ, pictured or represented in the persons of king Solomon and the Shulamite maiden.

If, for completeness, a connection is to be pressed between the two sections of this chapter, it would be along the following lines. After the separation (or the imagined separation) the two are now together again, with their fellowship restored, and everything is set for the marriage to take place. Or it may be understood in this way: if the whole of the Song up to this point (1:1-3:5) be viewed in terms of courtship and betrothal, there now comes the wedding. There is a choice emphasis in these further verses upon the believer/church being carried safely to glory, for while in one sense she is already married to Christ, in a fuller sense the marriage of the Lamb is yet to take place. All things should become clearer as we proceed.

3:6. A sight to behold

Who is this coming out of the wilderness ... (3:6). With these words begins a description of a wedding procession, and the language that is used throughout these verses plainly indicates a royal wedding, eastern style. Observers can see some way off in the distance something heading towards them. It would seem that this verse is spoken neither by the bridegroom nor the bride but by different ones among the bystanders, the waiting and watching crowds. We are familiar enough with the picture, not least on state occasions and royal weddings, when vast crowds line the processional route, trying to get into position for the best view. These onlookers here we take to be the daughters of Jerusalem, who are mentioned by name in verse 10 (and in v.11 as daughters of Zion). To them the charge of 3:5 was given, a charge which, it seems, stirred them up to take a fresh and fuller view of Christ and his church.

Who indeed is it who is coming out of the wilderness? The word 'this' is a feminine singular, so it cannot refer to the bridegroom. It could refer to the couch which will be mentioned shortly in verse 7, since that is a feminine noun, but the word here for 'who', with which the question begins, would be expected to refer to a person rather than an object. A similar phrase occurring at 8:5 refers, without any doubt, to the bride, and the same is true of 6:10. It would be proper to take the reference as such here also in 3:6. NKJV's 'wilderness' is to be preferred to NIV's 'desert'. The word signifies open country as distinct from cultivated land or a built-up area.

There is a deep truth here which will surface again in chapter 4 when the believer/church is pictured as 'a garden enclosed' (4:12). Christ's bride has been brought from one wilderness (that of sin and slavery) and is being brought through another wilderness (that of this world). This is pictured typically in the Old Testament in Israel coming up out of Egypt and through the wilderness and into the promised land of Canaan. She has been made acceptable to God, and is being prepared for heaven. The graces of God's Holy Spirit have been and are continually being plied upon her while she is 'being transformed ... from glory to glory' (2 Cor. 3:18). She is described in 8:5 as 'coming up from the wilderness, leaning upon her beloved'. See the later comments on that verse.

As the procession gradually comes a little nearer, those straining their eyes and watching closely so as not to miss anything see increasingly identifiable shapes and movements: **like pillars of smoke, perfumed with myrrh and frankincense, with all the merchant's fragrant powders?**, completes the question they are asking. The pillars (columns) of smoke will refer no doubt to incense being burned at the head of the procession, and ascending like pillars into the sky. The word appears to be related to the palm tree, with the sense conveyed by that tree of rising up straight and erect and spreading out.

Myrrh has already been commented upon in 1:13. It was a component part of the holy oil (Exod. 30:23), while frankincense, also mentioned here, was part of the holy incense (Exod. 30:34). A translation of the Hebrew for frankincense is given as 'white stuff', and is described as an amber resin, covered with a whitish surface dust, which comes from the bark of a species of tree which was abundant in India, south-west Arabia, and along the north-east coast of Africa. Like myrrh, frankincense was one of the gifts brought to the Lord Jesus Christ in Matthew 2:11. The final statement of the verse indicates a perfumer's special mixture of all manner of crushed perfumes. The word for merchant serves for a general denoting of travelling spice merchants who traded in various aromatics. The phrase is literally 'from all powders of the merchant'.

Putting together the pillars of smoke and the various perfumes, there may be an allusion here, first, to the pillar of cloud by which the Lord's people of old were led on their journey through the wilderness, and, second, to the fact that nothing can prevent the true church arriving safe (and perfumed, holy through and through) in glory to be presented to Christ and to be with him for ever.

It is already beyond doubt that this is no ordinary wedding procession, and no ordinary marriage. Nothing ever known or seen before can compare with it. There is a notable connection here with 1:5-6. There the daughters of Jerusalem were rather dubious about the Shulamite, and how she looked. Now they are full of admiration and astonishment concerning her, and are taken up increasingly with her beauty and privilege. The individual Christian and the gathered church is a thing of wonderment. When the Lord Jesus Christ returns at the end of the age, 'revealed from heaven with his mighty angels', he will 'be glorified in his saints and ... be admired among all those who believe' (2 Thess. 1:7, 10).

3:7-10. The bride's true focus

Behold, it is Solomon's couch (3:7). The daughters of Jerusalem have just been admiring the Shulamite, but she would far rather they admire her Solomon who here, as throughout the Song, stands as a type of the Lord Jesus Christ. So she leaps in swiftly at this point, as if to say, 'no more praises for me, let them rather be directed to him, from whom I have received everything and to whom I owe everything.' This is the consistent attitude and testimony of the true believer and the true church of Christ, as it was with John the Baptist, whose motto was 'He (Christ) must increase, but I (John) must decrease' (John 3:30). Let Christ be admired; let him be adored; let him be delighted in, 'that in all things he may have the pre-eminence' (Col. 1:18). So with an arresting and confident 'behold', the bride seeks to redirect the gaze and admiration of these onlookers.

The 'is' is added. Without it, the bride's insistence upon the need to focus upon her bridegroom is more striking: look! Solomon's couch! NIV has 'carriage'; 'bed' is also acceptable. It is a common word for a place to rest or sleep. The root is to stretch oneself out. It would be a sort of litter or travelling couch, maybe a glorified and expanded sedan chair. It is a different Hebrew word from that used of 'our bed' in 1:16. See further on 'palanquin' (v.9). It illustrates the happiness, restfulness and mutual husband and wife fellowship that believers have with Christ. The Shulamite knows full well that while things between herself and Solomon are 'ours', yet they all proceed from 'him' and depend upon him.

Solomon is mentioned by name here, the first time since 1:5

and the first of three times in the remainder of this chapter. Of these three occurrences here it is interesting to observe what might be called a gradation: he is Solomon (v.7), King Solomon (v.9), and 'King Solomon with the crown' (v.11).

It is important to understand that wedding processions in eastern lands were (and still are) rather different from our own. We are used to the bridegroom making his own way to the church or wherever the wedding is to take place, and waiting there for his bride, who arrives with her father who is to give her away. In the east, however, the bride and groom (either separately or together) would be escorted to the wedding with great pomp, ceremony and style. The procession might take several hours, moving slowly, and sometimes deliberately going the long way round so that as many people as possible can see it. As well as the burning of incense (v.6) and (if at night) the bearing of flaming torches, the procession would have an escort, or guard of honour. That is so here, and, since this is a royal wedding, the escort is one of the king's most select troops: **with sixty valiant men around it, of the valiant of Israel.**

Moreover, as the next verse reveals, they were ready for action, especially lest there be the possibility of ambush (for theft of jewellery, or for kidnap and then ransom, for example). **They all hold swords, being expert in war. Every man has his sword on his thigh because of fear in the night** (3:8). Here is evidenced both the stateliness of Christ (who will be designated 'King Solomon' in verse 11), and the security of his chosen one. See the care with which the heavenly bridegroom safeguards his bride, the one who shares his glory, to ensure her safe arrival at their marriage. Special care is invariably taken of royal personages, and of none more so than Christ's own bride. She is conveyed with all royal honours to their wedding. No expense is spared for her. No trouble is too much to be taken for her. No bodyguard is too extensive for her. No provision is too lavish to be made for her. No fears need possess her. Many are the dangers along the way to the wedding, often summed up in the classic threesome of the world, the flesh and the devil; but there is no danger whatsoever either of the bridegroom not being there or of the bride failing to turn up.

The bride of Christ is well attended. All the poetic details here serve to show that this is so: that the guards are valiant men (bold, courageous, steadfast, brave), the good number of them surrounding the bed between them, their arms and proficiency in the use of them, and their continual combat readiness. That sixty are mentioned has been described as a definite for an indefinite number, thereby indicating a complete sufficiency to cover any and every possible emergency between here and glory. Notice they are styled 'of the valiant of Israel'. Truly this regiment may be called the King's own. His bride is 'kept by the power of God through faith for salvation ready to be revealed in the last time' (1 Pet. 1:5). The church comprises 'those who are called, sanctified by God the Father, and preserved in Jesus Christ' (Jude 1). 'The angel of the LORD encamps all around those who fear him, and delivers them' (Ps. 34:7). It is the believer's security in Christ which accounts for the believer's serenity in Christ. None shall pluck them out of the Father's or the Son's hand. 'I and my Father are one', testifies Christ (John 10:30).

Of the wood of Lebanon Solomon the King made himself a palanquin (3:9). Here is a further reference to these travelling arrangements. This is the only appearance in the Old Testament of the word translated here 'palanquin'. (NIV has 'carriage', as in v.7, though the words are different; AV has 'bed' in v.7 and 'chariot' here). It is probably best understood, as mentioned above, of a portable sedan chair, or litter-bed. However, it is of such magnificence that it performs the function almost of a state coach.

It is underscored that Solomon made it for himself, and of what he made it: **he made its pillars of silver, its support of gold, its seat of purple** (3:10). Solomon was famous for an endless number of inventions, and is even described here as designing his own wedding carriage. The construction was of the choicest materials. The wood (cedar and cypress from Lebanon) was legendary as providing timber for building and construction work, including Solomon's temple, palace and various other buildings (see 1 Kgs. 5-7). Gold and silver were employed, indicative of his wealth, while the interior furnishings (cushions? coverings?) for reclining upon have been made of material in the royal colour purple. From the typical perspective, Solomon making the palanquin himself reminds us forcibly that all that Christ does he does in his own wisdom, by his own power and for his own glory, that his church may show forth his praise.

How are we to understand the detail added at the end of the verse: **its interior paved with love by the daughters of Jerusalem**? This is the solitary Old Testament occurrence of the verb translated here 'paved', though the related noun appears a number of times, twice used of 'live coals' and the other times translated 'pavement'. The suggestion 'mosaic' has been offered, the thought being of this interior of the palanquin catching and reflecting the light and giving the impression of being on fire. The point made in the statement is that this beautiful interior has been laid by the daughters of Jerusalem as a token or expression of their love for Solomon, thus reminding us of the great gospel truth that 'we love him because he first loved us' (1 John 4:19). AV's 'for the daughters of Jerusalem' cannot be sustained; that 'for' has to be taken as 'by' with NKJV/NIV, unless the 'from' of NIV margin be followed, giving a similar sense.

To say that, is probably to say enough. What verses 9 and 10 do is add to the total picture begun in verse 6, a picture which is intended to set forth the loving and abundant provision of Christ for his church, her royal state, her eternal security, her spiritual beauty, her safe conduct through this world to heaven, and (to be climaxed in a moment in v.11) her marriage to Christ. So while the unashamed position of this commentary all the way through is to set forth the union and communion of Christ and his church from the Song, believing that to be the first and fundamental thrust of this portion of Scripture, there is always the danger (which must be avoided) of going too far or getting carried away in a minutiae of interpretation. That can happen particularly in this section and has done so in various ways.

The fact that Solomon himself made the palanquin is taken by some to set forth the covenant of grace of which Christ himself is the Mediator. The wood is referred to the humanity of Christ, and the gold to his divinity. Or again, the gold is taken to speak of his divine glory, and the silver of the purity of his church. The fact that the furnishings are purple becomes linked to the blood of Christ. Since it is recorded that the interior (or midst, or middle) of the palanquin is 'paved with love', some are persuaded that it refers to the heart of Christ which is filled with and paved with love to poor sinners. In the earlier verses of the section, the pillars of smoke are taken for the devout affections of the believer's soul ascending heavenwards, and the perfuming with frankincense for the mediation and intercession of Christ, while some regard the valiant men as referring specifically to the angels or to ministers of the word.

It is safer, however, not to proceed down these paths in our interpretation of these few verses. This is not because we desire to be neglectful of such glorious Scripture doctrines as the covenant of grace, the two natures in the one person of Christ, his precious blood, the wonders of his love, or any other such things. Rather, we are on speculative and overimaginative ground to see them all worked out here (just as, in some other passages, for example, it is not necessary to apply a different and distinctive meaning to each and every perfume). We need great spiritual wisdom to know how far to take each part of the Song, not holding back when it would be cowardly to hold back, yet not surging forward carelessly either. Sometimes (though not always) we have to be content with more of an overview, even though the expositions of some of those commentators who take the detailed lines indicated above are exceedingly rich and satisfying, and full of what is ultimately glorious Scripture truth.

3:11. The big day

There is no journeying to heaven except with Christ. Which brings us to the verse which is really the very heart and hinge of the whole of the Song. The bystanders and onlookers, the daughters of Jerusalem, have been watching in rapt attention as king Solomon's wedding procession makes its way to Jerusalem. They have been taken up with the royal pair in their glorious chariot. The bride, as we have seen, has been insistent in taking their attention away from herself and fixing it firmly upon him, the king and bridegroom.

Go forth, O daughters of Jerusalem, and see King Solomon (3:11). Pictured in this verse is the wedding day itself, that day spoken of in Revelation 19:7 as 'the marriage of the Lamb'. Note that entire verse. 'Let us be glad and rejoice and give him glory, for the marriage of the Lamb has come, and his wife has made herself ready.' That day will be one of the most intense interest to the whole universe.

So often at weddings the focus is on the bride: how she will look, what she will wear, and so on. Most certainly the bride of Christ – the church – being the elect of God, chosen from eternity, bought by blood, born again of the Holy Spirit, will indeed be beautiful on her wedding day. This truth is set out in a number of Scriptures. She will be 'all glorious' (Ps. 45:13); 'radiant' (Isa. 60:5); 'a crown of glory in the hand of the LORD, and a royal diadem in the hand of your God' (Isa. 62:3); 'holy and without blemish' (Eph. 5:27); 'faultless' (Jude 24); 'ready', with all that word implies in terms of being absolutely fitted and meet to be married to Christ (Rev. 19:7). She who has 'been made a spectacle to the world, both to angels and men' (1 Cor. 4:9) will on that day be exquisite beyond words. Yet what will all this beauty, radiance, glory, and so on, be? Surely a reflection of the bridegroom's own glory. The bride, at her wedding, will be dressed in beauty not her own – but his. Hence the focus upon the bridegroom.

As this verse unfolds, the focus becomes even more specific: **with the crown with which his mother crowned him on the day of his espousals**. Historically, Solomon's mother was Bathsheba, the wife of King David. While she was not herself actually responsible for Solomon becoming king, nonetheless she helped secure the throne for him when his brother Adonijah was scheming to take it away. Evidently the use of nuptial crowns was a general practice in the ancient world. Among the Greeks and Romans these crowns tended to be chaplets of leaves or flowers, while among the Hebrews they were also sometimes of richer materials such as gold or silver, depending upon the wealth of the families involved. The word here for crown is found in 2 Samuel 12:30 of a royal crown taken from the head of the king defeated at Rabbah and placed instead upon David's head. 'Its weight was a talent of gold, with precious stones.' It appears also in Esther 8:15 as 'a great crown of gold' with which Mordecai went out from the king's presence, and in Job 19:9 where royalty is not in view.

In applying these words to Christ, of whom Solomon is the type, they do not mean, of course, that on his wedding day his earthly mother, Mary, will be stepping forward to crown him. So what is the reference, since on his head are many crowns (Rev. 19:12), thus setting forth his great and manifold glory? It is to the true church of Christ, the bride herself. In one of the strange symbolic visions in Revelation 12, the church is pictured as a woman giving birth to 'a male child who was to rule all nations with a rod of iron' (Rev. 12:5). That is a reference to the Lord Jesus Christ who, while he is very God of very God, from the bosom of the Father, is also declared in Scripture from the human side as coming from an earthly line, the line of David, to redeem men. Also in favour of the church interpretation are the words of Jesus in Mark 3:35 and parallels: 'For whoever does the will of God is my brother and my sister and mother'.

There is a strong sense in which the church actually is Christ's crown and glory as well as the sense in which she crowns and glorifies him. Even now, every conversion day of a sinner is a crowning day for Christ, so how much more will his wedding day be his crowning day, when all for whom he left heaven's glory, came to earth, shed his blood at Calvary and died are gathered into heaven with him, and all the ransomed church of God is saved to sin no more. Then – when he is crowned on the day of his espousals – 'He shall see the travail of his soul, and be satisfied' (Isa. 53:11). On that day he will appear in all his kingly glory.

In the light of this, it is no surprise to find the day of Christ's espousals described also as **the day of the gladness of his heart**. Maybe we think insufficiently of the things that give God pleasure, the things that delight and rejoice Christ's heart. One such is spelt out here: his wedding day! This is part of 'the joy that was set before him' (Heb. 12:2) which sustained him during the days of his humiliation, enabling him to endure the cross and despise the shame. We learn from Psalm 104:31 that the Lord rejoices in his works, so he will surely rejoice in the completion of redemption and the final 'bringing many sons to glory' (Heb. 2:10). The perspective of Isaiah 62:5 is also to the fore here: 'and as the bridegroom rejoices over the bride, so shall your God rejoice over you.' It is in no way improper to say that our heavenly bridegroom longs for that day. That being so, should not the bride long for it too? Reflect upon Isaiah 61:10:

> 'I will greatly rejoice in the LORD, my soul shall be joyful in my God; for he has clothed me with the garments of salvation, he has covered me with the robe of righteousness, as a bridegroom decks himself with ornaments, and as a bride adorns herself with her jewels.'

While Christ and his church are already married, in the sense of our union with him being a present and settled thing, yet many of his elect remain still to be saved, and so the wedding itself, in its public splendour and glory, has still to take place. What a day it will be!

Before leaving this chapter a gathering up note is needful upon Solomon as a type of Christ. This has been stated already, but is worth emphasising. We have Scriptural warrant to do so from Christ himself. He it is who, speaking of himself, announced 'and indeed a greater than Solomon is here' (Matt. 12:42).

Solomon was noted for his vast wealth, but it was all poor and perishing stuff compared with the riches, wealth and titles belonging to the Lord Jesus Christ, who is 'King of kings and Lord of lords' (Rev. 19:16). Solomon was noted for his wisdom, yet even that was as nothing compared with the one 'in whom are hidden all the treasures of wisdom and knowledge' (Col. 2:3). Solomon was famous for his works (buildings, inventions, writings, and all manner of skills), yet he who is the second person of the Godhead is the one in view when John 1:3 records, 'All things were made through him, and without him nothing was made that was made.'

Solomon's kingdom was remarkably extensive; 'he reigned over all the kings from the River to the land of the Philistines, as far as the border of Egypt' (2 Chron. 9:26). Yet the kingdom of the Lord Jesus Christ is an everlasting dominion which will never be destroyed (Dan. 7:13-14), and of him it is written, 'His name shall endure for ever; his name shall continue as long as the sun. All men shall be blessed in him; all nations shall call him blessed' (Ps. 72:17).

Solomon's name means 'peace', and his alternative name, Jedidiah, means 'beloved of God'. Yet to Christ belongs the title 'Prince of Peace' (Isa. 9:6), and of him the Father has declared (and more than once), 'This is my beloved Son, in whom I am well pleased' (Matt. 3:17).

The call, then, in 3:7 ('Behold') and in 3:11 ('Go forth'), each time directing attention away from everything else and everyone else and riveting every gaze upon Christ, leaves us in no doubt as to the matchless beauty and glory that belongs alone to him, and of which even all that could be said of Solomon fell far short. Without question, Solomon was a king who stood out and could not be missed. His reign was a remarkable time in history. His accomplishments were considerable. Yet only Christ, and never Solomon, can satisfy.

If Solomon is to be admired, how much more is Christ to be adored? If we are to approach Solomon with respect, how much more should we approach Christ with reverence? If to Solomon is due honour, how much more to Christ is due homage? If we may contemplate Solomon with wonder, how much more Christ with worship? Indeed ultimately Solomon fades out of the picture altogether, and the Lord Jesus Christ stands alone. Revelation 5 confirms that.

Chapter 4

THE GARDEN OF THE LORD

The speaker throughout the whole of this fourth chapter (apart from the closing verse, v.16) is the bridegroom. He has one extended theme and that is the praise of his bride, which he develops from the angles of his love for her, his delight in her, his desire for her, and her preciousness and sweetness to him. This is something which he is never ashamed or slow to engage in. Moreover, being the exemplary husband that he is, he knows how much his bride needs these encouragements and assurances frequently. Indeed, this is one of the most exquisite passages in the whole of the Bible for portraying what the Lord Jesus Christ thinks of his church, how he regards her, and what she means to him.

There are reminiscences here of some of the language which has already arisen in the Song, while fragrances of this chapter also recur later in the book. Of particular significance in the course of these verses is the description of the church as a garden.

4:1-5. She is beautiful

Behold, you are fair, my love! Behold you are fair! (4:1). We have had these very words before in 1:15. There is no wavering or inconsistency in Christ's view of his bride. What she means to him at one time she means to him at all times. Yet he does not content himself here with some general statement, then quickly passing on to something else. Having assured his bride again in a general manner of her fairness, her beauty, in his estimation, he now proceeds to apply it in several ways: to her eyes and hair (v.1), her teeth (v.2), her lips, mouth and temples (v.3), her neck (v.4), and her breasts (v.5) – eight different applications in all. This manner of pressing the details serves to underscore the

95

whole, namely the overwhelming, all-consuming and pleasurable nature of her beauty as he looks upon her. How appropriate this is, coming immediately after the account of the wedding day at the end of the previous chapter. Never is a bride more beautiful to her husband than at such a time!

You have dove's eyes behind your veil. We are familiar with the mention of dove's eyes, for this also appeared at 1:15 (see on that verse), with the addition this time of the mention of the veil (with NKJV and NIV, rather than AV's 'locks'). This is another suitable reference in connection with the wedding. The point has been made that it would be usual, in terms of the eastern background of the Song, for girls and women to wear head-dresses rather than veils, the veils being reserved for special occasions such as engagements and weddings. From behind her veil, the bride's eyes shine out, and they are, of course, lovingly directed to and fixed upon her bridegroom. She only has eyes for him.

It is important to understand that behind the various bodily parts that are being mentioned in these verses, it is of spiritual beauty that we are to learn, 'the inner man' (Eph. 3:16), 'the hidden person of the heart' (1 Pet. 3:4), the adorning 'the doctrine of God our Saviour in all things' (Tit. 2:10). 'For the LORD does not see as man sees; for man looks at the outward appearance, but the LORD looks at the heart' (1 Sam. 16:7). Grace in the believer is what is in view, that grace which the Lord Jesus Christ himself has implanted by his Holy Spirit, and which is a reflection of his own person. This is something which he takes close and careful notice of and which he loves to commend. Here it is the beauty of modesty, humility, tenderness and chastity that is intended – the very opposite of worldly pride, gaudiness, or any brash or coarse flaunting of self.

Your hair is like a flock of goats, going down from Mount Gilead. This will recur at 6:5. Gilead denotes a high plateau to the east of Galilee and Samaria, an area of high and rugged cliffs which, it has been stated, rise to some 3500 feet from the floor of the Jordan valley. The comparison of her hair to goats will refer to the long, black, glossy and wavy hair of the Palestinian goats, which has been described as having the fineness of silk and bearing a striking resemblance to the fine ringlets of a woman's hair. The picture is of a considerable flock of these goats moving around on the mountainside, or (so NKJV's 'coming down' and NIV's 'descending' may be translated) reclining, resting or sitting (sitting up) there, and so appearing to cover the hillside. It would be a beautiful sight.

This reposing and shining inclines us to think in terms of 'the incorruptible ornament of a gentle and quiet spirit, which is very precious in the sight of God' (1 Pet. 3:4), and the Lord Jesus' exhortation to his disciples, 'Let your light so shine before men, that they may see your good works and glorify your Father in heaven' (Matt. 5:16). Grace and holiness in a believer's life, and in the life of the church, will show; it will shine.

The pictures continue. **Your teeth are like a flock of shorn sheep which have come up from the washing, every one of which bears twins, and none is barren among them** (4:2). This time, as the bridegroom looks upon his bride, he thinks of the whiteness of sheep that have just been shorn and have come out of the sheep wash. 'Sheep' actually has to be provided; the Hebrew is literally 'a flock of shorn (ones)'. The word is supplied, however, when this verse is repeated at 6:6. The mention of 'twins' indicates symmetry: each ewe with her lambs, and the teeth of the upper and lower jaws all corresponding to one another, with none missing.

In interpreting these verses it is the overall impression which gives us the clue. So it is here. Purity, unity and fruitfulness are the things that are to the fore: purity illustrated in the shearing and the washing, unity in the mention of each sheep with its twin, and fruitfulness in the absence of barrenness. Each of these comprise definitive characteristics of the church of the Lord Jesus Christ. They are the things he desires and delights in, and the things he would be sought for, for all things come from him.

The bridegroom is the supplier of all that his bride needs, and of all that he requires for her and loves to see in her. 'And my God shall supply all your needs according to his riches in glory by Christ Jesus' (Phil. 4:19). In and from him is all our purity, unity and fruitfulness, in every sense of each of these, for they are all supernatural, and not of human wisdom, invention or cultivation.

The fourth and fifth items follow next: the lips and mouth. **Your lips are like a strand of scarlet, and your mouth is lovely** (4:3). The bride's lips are likened to a strand (thread, ribbon, cord) of scarlet (or crimson). Red is often used to describe lips, and would indicate healthiness, rather than the opposite which might be signified by pale lips. There is some question, regarding the second part of the sentence, whether the translation should be 'mouth' or 'speech'. Or a suggestion has been made (incorporating the two) that the mouth as the instrument of speech is intended. The word 'lovely' is also 'comely', 'delightful' or 'becoming'.

The meaning of the whole speaks for itself. Here is the edifying conversation of the Christian, the words of our mouths that are made acceptable to God (compare Ps. 19:14 and Mal. 3:16 on this same theme), speech which 'may impart grace to the hearers' (Eph. 4:29). Here too is 'the sacrifice of praise to God, that is, the fruit of our lips, giving thanks to his name' (Heb. 13:15). Such is choice and pleasing to Christ.

Your temples behind your veil are like a piece of pomegranate. This is reported as being a frequent simile in the east. The word for temples is only used in the Song (here and similarly at 6:7) and three times in the book of Judges (including the celebrated occasion in Judges 4–5 when Jael, the wife of Heber the Kenite, killed Sisera, the Canaanite general, by striking a tent-peg through his temple). The temples are that part of the face between the eyes and the ears, but here may be meant the upper part of the cheeks near them as well. Since the slices of pomegranate would be red/ruby/ruddy in colour, a freshness and rosiness of the cheeks is most likely what is in view.

Attention has been drawn in interpreting these words to what have been called the blushes of Christ's bride. The thought is a proper one, and contributes in no small way to her attraction in Christ's eyes. Again, it is the opposite of pride and self-esteem. Here once more the bride is an absolute picture of humility and modesty, as was stated above (note the mention of the veil, as in verse one), along with shamefacedness and consciousness of sin. This also is exceedingly attractive to Christ, who delights to beautify his bride still more by giving her more grace.

Next comes the neck. **Your neck is like the tower of David, built for an armoury, on which hang a thousand bucklers, all shields of mighty men** (4:4). The reference to the tower of David may be to that mentioned in Nehemiah 3:25, though precise identification cannot be made. It was no doubt a familiar landmark at the time of writing the Song. 'Armoury' may also be 'fortress' or 'arsenal', though it is difficult to know where NIV's 'built with elegance' comes from, even though elegance can be an appropriate word when describing a neck. This is the only occurrence of the word in the Old Testament, hence the NIV footnote about its meaning being uncertain. Another translation suggested is 'built in terraces', in the sense of building towers like terraces, with one above the other. Bucklers and shields are parts of a soldier's equipment, the former evidently being a smaller round shield. There is a mention in 1 Kings 10:16-17 of Solomon's shields. 'Mighty men' is the same word as in 3:7.

Very likely this tower of David was decorated in some way with bucklers and shields of various heroes, maybe of the king's bodyguard (observe Ezekiel 27:11 further for such a picture); as a result the height and strength of the tower was a natural picture for a neck, and the ornamentations upon it fitted well for the jewels, necklaces and such like which would grace a woman's neck (compare 1:10-11). The mention of 'a thousand bucklers' indicates the abundance of the supply of grace available for us in Christ (John 1:16). Among the spiritual graces and beauties of the Christian represented here are courage, strength, boldness, fortitude and perseverance in the life, walk and triumph of faith. There is more than a hint of 'but the people that do know their God shall be strong, and do exploits' (Dan. 11:32, AV).

The grace of faith (itself the gift of God) greatly honours and exalts our glorious head and bridegroom, who is the author and finisher of it (Heb. 12:2). With the shield of faith we are enabled 'to quench all the fiery darts of the wicked one' (Eph. 6:16). The whole of Hebrews 11 is very much an exposition of this verse of the Song.

Your two breasts are like two fawns, twins of a gazelle, which feed among the lilies (4:5). This is the final one of the eight bodily illustrations given in these verses of his bride's beauty in the eyes of the bridegroom, Solomon viewing the Shulamite (though if one takes the lips and the mouth in verse 3 as being one item rather than two, the total number would be seven, the classic scriptural number for fulness and perfection). Nothing immodest is intended by this reference to her breasts, which were often drawn attention to in a more public manner in eastern culture and poetry than would be the case in the western. The bride's breasts are compared here to the twin fawns of a gazelle, and the picture is simply, and delightfully, of youthfulness, tenderness, desirableness, the warmth of spiritual affections and the beauty of conjugal love. Breasts are mentioned again in this connection in 7:3, 7-8 (compare also 8:8-10). There is a savour also (not for the first time in the Song) of Proverbs 5:19: 'As a loving deer and a graceful doe, let her breasts satisfy you at all times; and always be enraptured with her love.'

A further word is necessary before moving on. In the comments upon verses 1-5 great care has been taken once again to steer a careful course between saying too little and saying too much. It is vitally important to be clear that the chief thing in view is the bride's spiritual beauty in the eyes of her bridegroom (and so the Christian's and the church's spiritual beauty in the eyes of the Lord Jesus Christ, who is the sure and competent judge of these things). Set forth here, in the loveliest language, is the proportion, the symmetry, the completeness of true Christian character. Here is the beauty of holiness in the heart, life and testimony of the believer and the church.

There is danger in going beyond this, and into such a minute detail of interpretation that becomes (at best) speculative and (at worst) far-fetched. On that basis, to take just one example, the two breasts just considered in verse 5 become for some the Old and New Testaments, or the twin sacraments of baptism and the Lord's Supper, or the ministers of the gospel as spiritual nurses to the people of God. But such interpretations are unwise, and miss the main, substantial and glorious point. The several parts in these verses must always be held together, for the total picture is one, not many, and takes us straight to the apostle's great statement: '... just as Christ also loved the church and gave himself for it, that he might sanctify and cleanse it ... that he might present it to himself a glorious church, not having spot or wrinkle or any such thing, but that it should be holy and without blemish' (Eph. 5:25-27).

4:6-7. The meeting place

The bridegroom continues, using, to begin with, words which are already familiar from 2:17, although then they were upon the lips of the bride. **Until the day breaks and the shadows flee away** (4:6). See the comments on the earlier verse. The words that follow now, however, break new ground: **I will go my way to the mountain of myrrh and to the hill of frankincense**, although myrrh and frankincense have already been explained at 1:13 and 3:6. There is a sense in which Christ's words here form an answer to the request of the bride back in 2:17, in her reference to 'the mountains of Bether'.

What is in view here? What is meant by the mountain of myrrh and the hill of frankincense? No specific geographical location is intended. It is rather a spiritual location; that is to say, a reference (true to the language and expression of the Song as a whole) to a meeting place, or a trysting place, where bridegroom and bride may be together and enjoy one another's company in an unhindered and uninterrupted manner. It is very appropriate that these words should follow hard upon the previous verses which have been filled with the speaking of the bride's praises. The words must not be understood as the language of Christ withdrawing from his people. Indeed, they are the very opposite. He must see her and be with her, since she is all his own. There is an emphaticness about what he says: it is literally 'I myself will go', thus assuring us of his presence waiting for us. 'Listen, O daughter, consider and incline your ear; forget your own people also, and your father's house; so the King will greatly desire your beauty; because he is your Lord, worship him' (Ps. 45:10-11).

A garden of heavily perfumed spices is in view for this place of union, which itself prepares the way for the more extended mention of spices and perfumes later in the chapter. There is a significance in the words chosen here which must not be missed. We have already noted that myrrh and frankincense (along with other spices) were used as part of the holy anointing oil and the incense in the tabernacle, and then later in the temple. This makes 'the mountain of myrrh and the hill of frankincense' a highly suitable designation of fellowship with God and communion with Christ, and so the verse becomes one of the Lord Jesus Christ's gracious promises and undertakings to meet with his people in the house of the Lord, and in the appointed ordinances (means of grace) thereof. Here he quiets us with his love and rejoices over us even with singing (Zeph. 3:17). This accords with the risen, ascended, glorified Christ walking 'in the midst of the seven golden lampstands' (Rev. 2:1). It would be a pleasant experience to walk upon a literal hill fragranced with myrrh and frankincense, and to breathe the attractive odours. How much more pleasing to the soul to dwell with Christ where he promises always to be found.

It has been observed that myrrh is bitter while frankincense is sweet, and that while communing with Christ here upon earth there is a 'bitter-sweet' aspect to Christian experience, sometimes mourning and repenting, sometimes rejoicing and delighting. It will be different in heaven, where neither mourning nor repenting will have any place. Then (after the day has broken and the shadows have fled away) 'we shall be like him, for we shall see him as he is' (1 John 3:2). The Lord Jesus Christ himself longs, too, for that day. This verse 6 is the assurance of that.

This section of the chapter closes as it began, with Christ eulogising over his bride, who he finds so beautiful and whom he loves so much. **You are all fair, my love,** he says (4:7), and continues, **and there is no spot in you**. Evidently the word here translated 'spot' usually appears in the Old Testament to describe the perfect sacrificial animals which were required for the sacrifices. What a magnificent summary of his love to us, his bride, this verse is, and what a welcome encouragement to seek him and meet him continually upon 'the mountain of myrrh and the hill of frankincense'. Since he will not stay away, how can we?

Every true believer is all too aware of having many 'spots' (recall 1:5), and the more we are enabled to behold Jesus' glory, the more wretched we feel and know ourselves to be. But the Lord Jesus Christ looks upon his church with different eyes. He who has become for us 'righteousness and sanctification and redemption' (1 Cor. 1:30) has the end in sight, for which his bride was chosen in the first place, 'that we should be holy and without blame before him in love' (Eph. 1:4). He regards us as such already, in our justified state. Though nothing of our present sin ever escapes his all-seeing eye, and though sin is always sin and can never be excused, yet he is absolutely taken up with us in that beauty which he himself has put upon us – his own.

4:8-11. Declaring the bride's praises
This most luxurious statement from the Lord Jesus Christ concerning his bride continues, setting forth in the most

wonderful language all that she means to him, and how lovely she is in his sight. The word 'spouse' (NIV, bride) occurs here in five consecutive verses (vs.8-12), and then again in 5:1.

The section begins with an invitation. **Come with me from Lebanon, my spouse, with me from Lebanon** (4:8). For the first time in the Song, the oft-repeated 'my love' now becomes the even more intimate 'my spouse' (or, literally, just 'spouse'). **Look from the top of Amana, from the top of Senir and Hermon, from the lions' dens, from the mountains of the leopards.** A number of places are mentioned here. Lebanon will refer to the Lebanese mountain range. Amana denotes a mountain in what is known as the Anti-Lebanon (or Anti-Libanus) range, from which issue the springs of the river Amana (this may be that river mentioned in 2 Kings 5:12 in connection with Elisha and Naaman, the Syrian commander, although that cannot be certain and the spelling there is different – Abanah, though compare the footnote). Senir (the Amorite name for the Hebrew named Hermon) is evidently the highest peak in that mountain range, being over 9200 feet in height. In Solomon's time lions and panthers roamed these mountain areas. The Lebanon and the Anti-Lebanon range are separated from one another by a valley of some fifteen miles.

There is some question as to whether 'look from' should be translated 'descend from' (NKJV has the former, NIV has the latter). The problem arises because of separate roots having identical forms, one meaning 'to descend' or 'to journey', the other meaning 'to look at' or 'to gaze'. It is striking to observe that in Scripture Lebanon is mentioned alongside the phrase 'those pleasant mountains' (Deut. 3:25), while Isaiah 35:2 speaks of 'the glory of Lebanon' and Hosea 14:6 of its 'fragrance'. As well as this, there is a reference to 'the dew of Hermon' in Psalm 133:3, and to Hermon rejoicing at the Lord's name (Ps. 89:12).

Why does the bridegroom speak of these places, with the invitation 'come with me'? It is the old story: he must have her company, she must be near him. He cannot suffer there to be any distance between them. He will not leave her alone, or to look after or fend for herself in the midst of all sorts of enemies and snares. She must be with him and cleave to him, out of danger, under his protection, separated from the world, delivered from its grips, supported by his comforts, in his embrace. Those who are united to Christ fellowship with him.

The company of Christ should have far more weight and reason to keep a believer close to him, than the seductions of the world should ever have to keep a believer away from him. It all fits beautifully with what he said in verse 6 concerning 'the mountain of myrrh and ... the hill of frankincense'. From all the dangers of the world, the flesh and the devil, the company of Christ at the throne of grace is a sure refuge. There, in the language of Psalm 91:1, we may 'dwell in the secret place of the Most High' and 'abide under the shadow of the Almighty'. 'No lion shall be there, nor shall any ravenous beast go up on it; it shall not be found there. But the redeemed shall walk there' (Isa. 35:9). Moreover, it has been noted that from the tops of these mountains of verse 8, Canaan could be seen, which is suggestive of the believer continually looking forward to a better country, and being with Christ there (Phil. 1:23).

The emphasis upon her being his spouse/bride is a solemn yet joyous reminder of there being a marriage covenant between Christ and his church, issuing in a relationship which has well been described as the best match. Compare the language of Hosea 2:19, where the Lord says to his people, 'I will betroth you to me for ever', and Isaiah 62:5, where he says, 'and as the bridegroom rejoices over the bride, so shall your God rejoice over you.'

You have ravished my heart, my sister, my spouse; you have ravished my heart with one look of your eyes, with one link of your necklace (4:9). The bridegroom in no way lets up in his esteemed appreciation of his bride's beauty, saying that she has 'ravished' (NIV, stolen) his heart, and, indeed, saying it twice. This is the only verse in Scripture where this verb is found

105

in the piel. It is as if a word actually has to be coined specially to express such an exalted truth as is set forth here, namely the sheer strength of Christ's love for and pleasure in his church. She is his great love and desire. His heart is upon her. Added to 'my spouse' here is 'my sister', but this should not be thought strange. The sibling figure occurs again at 8:1, and appears in the literature of the ancient near east as a term of endearment between those who are lovers. It serves to heighten even further the togetherness, closeness, purity and vitality of the union. Matthew 12:46-50 is relevant. No one relationship can set forth adequately how things are between Christ and his church. While that of husband and wife is fundamental, so that of brother and sister lends its own emphasis as well, including that of Christ's taking of our nature upon him, though without sin (Phil. 2:7), and making us 'partakers of the divine nature' (2 Pet. 1:4). Compare also Hebrews 2:11-12:

> For both he who sanctifies and those who are being sanctified are all of one, for which reason he is not ashamed to call them brethren, saying, 'I will declare your name to my brethren; in the midst of the congregation I will sing praise to you.'

There is a great tenderness to the language here: just one look of her eyes (those dove's eyes of 4:1, beautiful and holy), just one link of her necklace (those chains of gold of 1:10, gifted to her), and what an effect these have. Is it not the most amazing thing to realise that the Lord Jesus Christ finds his church absolutely irresistible? And if his heart was ravished by one look and one link (a partial view of his bride's loveliness), what will be the effect upon him of the full disclosure of her beauty?

The next two verses explore in more detail what it was (and what it is) about his bride that so ravishes Christ's heart. **How fair is your love, my sister, my spouse!** (4:10). This is the first thing: he praises her love. As in 1:2 and 1:4 (when the bride was speaking) this is the plural, 'loves'. There is something here which takes some grasping. He is saying that his church's love for him is a fair (or delightful) thing to him. It gives him pleasure and it rejoices his heart. That Christ's love is a delightful thing to his church prompts no surprise, because it is his love; yet here he is enthusing over his church's love to him, even though it is hindered and spoiled by so much sin and infirmity on our part.

How much better than wine is your love, and the scent of your perfumes than all spices! This is the second thing: he praises her graces. Again the word is 'loves'. The word here for 'spices' has a special reference to the balsam tree, as well as being used of scents and perfumes more generally. Both parts of this statement are familiar, for similar language was used of the bridegroom by the bride right at the very beginning in 1:2-3, the wine and the perfumes (ointments). All is mutual between Christ and his church. On a number of occasions in the Song the one takes up the other's words, just as lovers do.

By perfumes and their fragrance Christ refers to his people's spiritual graces and virtues, the fruit of the Holy Spirit coming to blossom in our lives. And what are these graces? They are features of likeness to Christ himself, Christ being formed in us (Gal. 4:19), the adornments of the gospel (Tit. 2:10), which bring him glory and show that our profession of Christ is not an empty, vain or hypocritical thing but that we are truly united to him, belong to him and are abiding in him. Love to Christ and a holy obedience to him are what he looks for and looks upon with much pleasure. What condescension he shows towards us.

Your lips, O my spouse, drip as the honeycomb (4:11). This is the third thing: he praises her words. This recalls 2:14, where Christ said, 'let me hear your voice; for your voice is sweet', and again he testifies for our encouragement. A honeycomb, when it drips (or drops) honey, does so thickly, richly, sweetly and gradually. It does not come pouring out like water from a tap, gushing forth at great speed and with strong force; one drop appears, hangs there for a moment, and drops, and then another, and so on. Such are the lips that the Lord Jesus loves to listen to, the speech that he is pleased to hear, from his church, and that he praises her for: lips like the honeycomb, words (speech) like the honey from the honeycomb. In other words: rich words, rich prayers, rich praises, rich worship, rich preaching, rich conversation. Not that which is hasty, superficial, thoughtless, careless or false. 'Pleasant words are like a honeycomb, sweetness to the soul and health to the bones' (Prov. 16:24).

There is an in-built reminder here of Malachi 3:16: 'Then those who feared the LORD spoke to one another, and the LORD listened and heard them; so a book of remembrance was written before him for those who fear the LORD and who meditate on his name.' The language, tongue, and speech of the Christian are to be altogether different from that of the world.

The same verse continues: **honey and milk are under your tongue.** This is the fourth thing: he praises her thoughts. Words under the tongue speak, surely, of thoughts: those things that are ready to be spoken (or may never be spoken) but which are there in the form of thoughts, meditations, contemplations and the like. Milk and honey were the two things with which God promised the Israelites that the promised land was flowing: good, refreshing, wholesome, nourishing and pure. There is the sense here, and in the previous phrase, of Psalm 19:14: 'Let the words of my mouth and the meditation of my heart be acceptable in your sight, O LORD, my strength and my redeemer.' Christ takes notice in his bride not only of what is spoken but of what is unspoken. Compare Psalm 139:1-6.

And the fragrance of your garments is like the fragrance of Lebanon. This is the fifth thing: he praises her works. Sometimes Scripture speaks of righteousness as a garment (as in Isa. 61:10), but here it is sanctification which is in view, and the works (or deeds) in which sanctification issues. A cross-reference would be 'the righteous acts (or, literally, righteousnesses) of the saints' (Rev. 19:8). The thought is of the believer/the church doing all for Christ and to Christ in everyday living and serving. Lebanon is mentioned again. It abounded in different varieties of trees that gave off the most ravishing scents and fragrances. Maybe we may find an echo here of Genesis 27:27, and observe that as Jacob's clothing held for his aged father Isaac 'the smell of a field which the LORD has blessed', so for Christ the garments of his beloved bride give forth a delightful odour. Evidently the word used here for 'garments' is not the one frequently employed in the Old Testament, but signifies the outer garment which doubled as a daytime cloak and a night-time covering.

In connection with what is said here, it is important to affirm that while our works can never be the ground of our acceptance with God, our justification, our relationship with the Lord Jesus Christ, yet the works and holiness of a believer, done in faith and gratitude and the enabling of the Holy Spirit, are required by God, are acceptable to God, and are pleasing to God. Having been saved by grace through faith (and that itself the gift of God), 'we are his workmanship, created in Christ Jesus for good works, which God prepared beforehand that we should walk in them' (Eph. 2:8-10).

Here then is the bridegroom declaring his bride's praises, not ashamed to do so, indeed delighted to do so. It should not surprise us, in one sense, that a bride so very dearly bought should be a bride so very dearly loved. What encouragements abound here for us to seek him and enjoy him. The effect it should have upon the church or the believer, however, is not to blow us up with fancy ideas of ourselves, or to imagine we are receiving some well-deserved credit. Far from it. Surely we should be humbled and laid in the dust, to think that he should ever speak so of us, and be brought to recognise afresh the great and searching truth of 1 Corinthians 4:7: 'And what do you have that you did not receive? Now if you did indeed receive it, why do you glory as if you had not received it?'

4:12-15. Christ's garden

In this section we are introduced to a fresh picture of the church in Christ's esteem: that of a garden, in relation to which is also mentioned a spring and a fountain. The language of fruits, spices and perfumes continues to be to the fore.

A garden enclosed is my sister, my spouse (4:12). In Ecclesiastes 2:5-6 Solomon records: 'I made myself gardens and orchards, and I planted all kinds of fruit trees in them. I made myself waterpools from which to water the growing trees of the grove.' It would be customary for royal palaces to have extensive and magnificent gardens and grounds for the king's pleasure and delight. These gardens would often be enclosed in one way or another (usually by a hedge or a wall), and would only be accessible to the owner. Further, since here in the imagery of the Song the garden is also the bride, it is appropriate to note that eastern wives would also be secluded from the public gaze and kept for their husbands' eyes alone. This would be regarded as a token both of protection and affection.

A garden is a fitting description of the church of Christ, particularly with the thought behind it of what was once a barren, unattractive and fruitless wilderness having been reclaimed, cultivated and made into a thing of great beauty and pleasure. Keeping in mind the eastern background of the Song, some of the loveliest and most luxuriant and magnificent gardens in the east were (and indeed are) often actually in the midst of a wilderness, surrounded by miles of sandy desert or acres of uncultivated land, but themselves alive, beautiful, fragrant and fruitful. The apostle John captures something of this when he writes, 'We know we are of God, and the whole world lies under the sway of the wicked one' (1 John 5:19).

The description of this garden as 'enclosed' (NIV, locked up) is also appropriate, for the church has only one owner and head, namely the Lord Jesus Christ. She can never belong to any other, for the church is the covenant gift of the Father to the Son (John 6:37), which he 'purchased with his own blood' (Acts

20:28). Jesus himself says of her, 'you are not of the world, but I chose you out of the world' (John 15:19). He has set his church apart for himself (compare Ps. 4:3). Her 'life is hidden with Christ in God' (Col. 3:3). She is his own pleasure garden. For her own part, the believer/church is to ensure complete and unequivocal devotion, affection and obedience to Christ. Christ's watchfulness over his garden is to be mirrored by her watchfulness over herself (compare Proverbs 4:23: 'Keep your heart with all diligence, for out of it spring the issues of life').

This is underscored in the two related pictures that follow in the same verse: **a spring shut up, a fountain sealed**. Springs and fountains would be familiar features in the oriental gardens envisaged here. It is even recorded of the garden of Eden, in the beginning, that it was well watered (Gen. 2:10; compare 13:10). These figures (enclosed, shut up, sealed) point eloquently to the peculiar nature of the church (peculiar in the sense not of odd but of being special), her safety and protection, her separation and distinctiveness from the world, her purity (a sealed fountain would be one shut against all impurity), and her character as a place where Christ delights to dwell and to hold secret converse and communion which, of necessity, he can never have with the world. Gardens, with springs and fountains (and, as this section continues, with fruits and perfumes), can be the most delightful places where people very much enjoy going; but there is no garden like Christ's garden, and no one who enjoys his garden as Christ does.

Important companion Scriptures are Isaiah 58:11 ('You shall be like a watered garden, and like a spring of water, whose waters do not fail') and Jeremiah 31:12 ('Their souls shall be like a well-watered garden'), along with verses like Ephesians 1:13 which speaks of believers having been 'sealed with the Holy Spirit of promise', and Ephesians 4:30 which records that they have been sealed by the Holy Spirit 'for the day of redemption'.

Your plants are an orchard of pomegranates with pleasant fruits (4:13). Not surprisingly, fruitfulness and fragrance (by now familiar Song themes) now come into view. The church is not merely a garden, but a fragrant garden and a fruitful one. Verse 13 continues: **fragrant henna with spikenard,** and there then follows, **spikenard and saffron, calamus and cinnamon, with all trees of frankincense, myrrh and aloes, with all the chief spices** (4:14).

Noting the various words first of all in verses 13-14, pomegranates have already been mentioned in 4:3, henna in 1:14, spikenard in 1:12, frankincense in 3:6 and 4:6, and myrrh in 1:13 and in connection with frankincense. The mention of 'all the chief spices' is the same word as in 4:10. Making their first appearances are saffron, calamus, cinnamon and aloes. Saffron comes from a small crocus, crushed and dried (it has been stated that to get a single ounce of this spice would require over 4000 individual blooms). Calamus (the Hebrew is just a 'stalk' or a 'reed') has been identified either as the giant reed or as sweet cane, the latter being the more likely. Cinnamon, another of the ingredients in the holy anointing oil of Exodus 30, is got from the bark or oil of the cinnamonum zelancum tree. Aloes has been identified as various things, including eaglewood or sandalwood. It is very costly and was used mixed with myrrh in connection with the body of Jesus after it had been taken down from the cross and given into the care of Joseph of Arimathea and Nicodemus (John 19:38-42).

Unmistakably, the emphasis continues to be on the delight of Christ in his garden and the exquisite effects upon the eyes (sight) and the nose (smell) of all that is to be found there. These are described as 'your plants' and as comprising 'an orchard ... with pleasant (or, excellent, choice) fruits'. The word for orchard is of a garden or park which would contain all manner of foreign, ornamental and fragrant plants. Hence the feature that all of these perfumes mentioned here have in common is the rich and pleasing fragrance they exude. It has been observed that none of them would be found growing naturally in any Palestinian gardens, thus making the point (which will be enforced in verse

16) that the things in his garden that give Christ pleasure are not those that grow there naturally (the product of human sin) but those that grow there supernaturally (the product of divine grace). They are 'the planting of the LORD, that he may be glorified' (Is. 61:3).

This major section (which began with verse 1) in which the bridegroom declares his unrestrained praises of his bride now concludes. She is **a fountain of gardens, a well of living waters, and streams from Lebanon** (4:15). Verses 13 and 14 developed the picture of the garden from verse 12a; verse 15 now develops the picture of the spring and the fountain from verse 12b. This is very much a picture of liveliness, fertility and refreshment, all of which (while it flows out of the life of the believer and the church) is derived from Christ himself, by his Spirit. It explains the source of the fruitfulness and fragrance which has just been described.

The phrase 'a fountain of gardens' is an interesting one. It has been translated 'a garden-fountain', though that is rather narrowing. Retaining the NKJV rendering, a fountain of gardens would signify a very full or copious fountain, which would be sufficient for the watering of many gardens. This garden of the Lord is watered and fructified by 'a well of living (or, flowing) waters' pictured as combining with 'streams from Lebanon' (cool and refreshing streams from Lebanon's snowy tops, pure and crystal clear). A traveller has recorded that on the side of Lebanon are fountains falling down in pleasant cascades; at the bottom, the streams all unite and become a full and rapid torrent. The streams themselves are visible, but their source is out of human view. The spiritual application of that stands out. It is very striking that in 5:15 it is written of Christ that 'his countenance is like Lebanon', while here in 4:15 it is the streams of his grace to and in his church which are likened as proceeding from Lebanon.

There is no contradiction between the church being both 'a spring shut up, a fountain sealed' and 'a well of living waters'.

The church is shut up and sealed by Christ for himself, yet at the same time from his church (through each believer) spiritual life flows, the glory of Christ is displayed and the purposes of Christ and his everlasting kingdom are accomplished (on this, compare Eph. 3:8-13). The very church which is such a delight to Christ, is intended to be a blessing to all mankind. The abundance of grace that is given to believers is not for proud or selfish hoarding, but for the benefit of the church and the world. Where grace dwells, it will be evidenced in fruit and fragrance.

How precious, then, to Christ is this garden (his own church, the soul of each believer). The fountain is the life of the garden, and dovetails exactly with the words of the Lord Jesus in John 4:14: 'whoever drinks of the water that I shall give him will never thirst. But the water that I shall give him will become in him a fountain of water springing up into everlasting life.' Compare also John 7:38, where Jesus says, 'He who believes in me, as the Scripture has said, out of his heart will flow rivers of living water.' Christ himself is the fountain of living waters, and he it is who, by his Spirit, makes believers, and makes the church, a well of living water. Indeed, without the vital influences of the Holy Spirit, his copious flowings given to us by the Lord Jesus Christ, there can be no fruitful or fragrant spiritual life. But when his influences are known and felt, everything is changed. Spiritual life flourishes, holiness thrives, fruitfulness abounds, and (this is the point in the context here) Christ is both delighted and glorified. All of which prepares the way precisely for the closing verse of this fourth chapter.

4:16. The north and south wind

For the first time in this chapter the bride speaks, and does so by way of a most appropriate response to all that the bridegroom has been saying. Warmed and encouraged by all the praise, delight and affection that has been heaped upon her, her response is to desire more and more of the felt presence and joyful experience of the bridegroom. In spiritual terms, this is the believer/church desiring more of Christ in his garden (v.16b). In order that this can be so, however, what is needed is a greater measure of the powerful and felt ministry of the Holy Spirit, who ministers Christ to his church and fits the church to receive him (hence v.16a). It is always timely to remember that the Holy Spirit (although he is the third person of the Godhead) is never concerned to draw attention to himself, but is always determined to glorify Christ. The Lord Jesus Christ has himself said of him, 'He will glorify me, for he will take of what is mine and declare it to you' (John 16:14).

Awake, O north wind, and come, O south! (4:16). The word 'wind' does not appear in the Hebrew, but is clearly understood. The Holy Spirit is often likened in Scripture to the wind, so this verse is in no way unusual. In this connection, compare Ezekiel 37:9 (revival), John 3:8 (regeneration) and Acts 2:2 (Pentecost). The picture is very suitable. Both the wind and the Spirit are powerful, and both are unseen in themselves, though you can point in each case to their effects. Both are refreshing and reviving, cooling and fructifying. Both are very necessary, for if everything remains motionless, dead calm and lifeless, disease can flourish and the air becomes unwholesome; while equally the lively motions of the Holy Spirit are absolutely necessary for the Christian's well-being and the church's spiritual life.

What is the point, however, of likening the Holy Spirit to the north wind and the south wind? The answer is not hard to find. In the world God has made, there is a clear distinction between these two winds (the north wind coming from the north, the south wind from the south). They are often mentioned separately on weather forecasts. The north wind is sharp, piercing, biting and shivering. The south wind is more balmy, melting, gentle, and ripening. Both are needed at different times. Both come from God's treasuries and fulfil his will and word.

So it is with the Holy Spirit of God. The teaching of 4:16 is that there is a clear distinction in the ministry of the Spirit (whether upon the believer or the church) which corresponds to the distinction in the natural world between the north and south winds. The north wind of God's Spirit may be seen in Christ's words in John 16:8, where it is said: 'And when he has come, he will convict the world of sin, and of righteousness and of judgment.' This wind is a convicting, convincing, disturbing, exposing, awakening wind of the Spirit. In contrast, the south wind of God's Spirit may be seen in Paul's prayer in Ephesians 3:16ff, that God would grant to the Ephesian Christians, 'according to the riches of his glory, to be strengthened with might through his Spirit in the inner man, that Christ may dwell in your hearts through faith ... to know the love of Christ which passes knowledge; that you may be filled with all the fullness of God.' This wind of the Spirit is a warming, kindling, healing, refreshing, soothing, comforting, ripening of spiritual fruits wind.

It may be that this distinction is reflected even in the two verbs that are used in 4:16. 'Awake' is the summons to the powerful, strong north wind. 'Come' is the call to the south wind that breathes more softly. How much this wind of heaven is needed. And while in nature you cannot have the north and south wind both blowing upon you at the same time, in grace you can.

To what purpose is this request for the Spirit made to Christ? **Blow upon my garden, that its spices may flow out.** The wind of heaven is called for that the fragrance of heaven may waft forth. Verses 13-15 have just pictured a delightful garden, full of fruitfulness and fragrance, precious in value, beautiful to all the senses, and pleasurable to walk in. In eastern lands the sweet fragrance and perfume that met someone when they entered such a garden would be indescribably pleasant and memorable. The same can sometimes still be experienced in English cottage gardens. This garden is a royal garden (King Solomon's garden), and just as Solomon is a type of Christ, so the garden, as has been seen, is a type of the believer/church.

So what the words here amount to is a request therefore to Christ for more of the sanctifying and spiritually fructifying work of his Holy Spirit. There is an implicit acknowledgment (as there needs to be) that we cannot produce Christ-likeness, holiness or spiritual fragrances on our own, notwithstanding the serious commands and vigorous exhortations with which Scripture abounds, to flee this, to pursue that, and so on. Yet nothing can be accomplished without dependence upon the Holy Spirit, for he it is, ultimately, who quickens grace where it is found and who produces it where it is not. God has promised to give more of his Spirit to his people, but he would still be enquired of for this.

Let my beloved come to his garden and eat its pleasant fruits. Here is the climax to the petition, and is completely in line with what was observed above about the Holy Spirit directing to Christ and not to himself. The believer's and the church's end in view in desiring holiness and spiritual fragrance is that the Lord Jesus Christ would desire all the more to come into his garden and eat his pleasant (excellent) fruits. More of Christ is the intent and desire (his visits, his presence, his love, his openings of his heart), and that with the motive not only of enjoying more of him, but he himself being all the more satisfied with and glorified in his church. The things Christ finds attractive and inviting in his garden are not the weeds that grow there naturally, but the Christ-like graces that can only flourish there supernaturally. The graces (or fruit) of the Spirit are many and various, rare and excellent, much desired in his people by Christ. He has already made this plain himself in the earlier verses of this chapter. What care needs to be taken, therefore, that we would not turn him away or grieve his Holy Spirit. The spiritual soul will always long to be in a more fit condition to entertain Christ in his garden. This leads directly into the first verse of the next chapter.

Chapter 5

THE ALTOGETHER LOVELY ONE

Before any fresh scenarios develop in this new chapter, the first verse carries on precisely from the end of the previous chapter. Chapter 4 is full of Christ's praises of his bride, in the course of which he employs the picture of a garden to describe his church – a garden that is his own possession, that is enclosed by his gracious choice and protection, that is the object of his intense admiration and delight, and from which flow out the odours and aromas of spiritual life, fruitfulness and grace. The closing verse (4:16) records the earnest desire of the believer/church for the north and south wind of the Holy Spirit to blow upon her (Christ's garden), in order to make her all the more attractive to him, and that he would be pleased to 'come to his garden and eat its pleasant fruits'. The bride does not have to wait long. Indeed, she does not have to wait any time at all.

5:1. Christ in his garden
What follows immediately is very much another case of 'before they call, I will answer' (Isa. 65:24). **I have come to my garden, my sister, my spouse** (5:1). In accord with his promise of John 14:21 ('And he who loves me will be loved by my Father, and I will love him and manifest myself to him'), Christ comes to his garden – indeed, he says 'I have come', the sense being, 'I am here already', 'I am come'. He was present in his garden anyway, even though his presence was not felt. He loves to answer such a request without delay, for it is not irksome to the Lord Jesus Christ to come to his own. The church is his church. Her graces are his graces. Her life is his life. In an expression of deep affection, he combines once again the terms 'sister' and 'spouse' of the one he loves. He owns his people in the nearest and dearest

relationships. See the comment on 4:10.

I have gathered my myrrh with my spice; I have eaten my honeycomb with my honey; I have drunk my wine with my milk. This speaks for itself, and incorporates words (myrrh, spice, honeycomb, honey, wine and milk) which are already familiar Song words. It was not altogether unusual for wine and milk to be mixed and drunk together (and it cannot be forgotten that the two are mentioned side by side in the glorious gospel invitation of Isaiah 55:1 to 'come, buy wine and milk without money and without price'). The gathering, eating and drinking indicate that the picture is of a celebration, a feast, a banquet. Evidently such gatherings were (and are) often held in gardens in the east, so the figure is a very natural one given the Song's background. There is also a strong savour of the words of Christ to the church at Laodicea: 'If anyone hears my voice and opens the door, I will come in to him and dine with him, and he with me' (Rev. 3:20), even though it is not the garden imagery that is used there.

The point of the verse so far is clear. The Lord Jesus more than delights to answer prayer of the nature that has been expressed, and takes pleasure (wonder of wonders) in coming to hearts that desire him and have been made ready to receive him. That pleasure (see how he accommodates himself to his people in explaining his delights in being with his own) he likens to the delights of a man dwelling in a beautiful garden, walking amid its delicious perfumes and fragrances, and tasting its sweet and healthful fruits. What is such a pleasure to him should also provoke great delight and enjoyment to his own.

Christ continues speaking in the second part of the verse. **Eat, O friends! Drink, yes, drink deeply, O beloved ones!** To whom is he speaking, and what does he mean? He is obviously expressing the wish that his own pleasure in his garden should be shared by others also, rather than be exclusively his own enjoyment. But who? It has been interpreted as referring to angels, those 'ministering spirits sent forth to minister for those

119

who will inherit salvation' (Heb. 1:14), who 'desire to look into' the Lord's gospel dealings with men (1 Pet. 1:12), and in whose presence there is joy 'over one sinner who repents' (Luke 15:10).

It would seem simpler, however, as well as far more natural and straightforward, to direct these words also to the church (believers), and to do so in a dual sense. Firstly, what is such a pleasure to Christ should also provoke great delight and enjoyment to his own, thus maintaining the emphasis present throughout the Song on the mutual nature of the delights of Christ and his church's communion together. He desires all whom he has called his friends to share his joy (compare John 15:9-16, especially verses 11 and 15). He is never fully satisfied at his own feast until all his friends are feasted also. Then secondly, referring once more to Revelation 3:20 quoted above, the importance of the individual aspect of 'if anyone', thus serving as a reminder of the necessity of each individual believer being careful to maintain unbroken and unsullied communion with Christ, and not being able to hide behind 'the church' or blame others if all is not well with their souls in this respect.

While the Lord Jesus Christ has been anointed by God 'with the oil of gladness more than (his) companions' (Ps. 45:7), he would have his companions (those whom, in another Scripture figure, 'he is not ashamed to call (his) brethren', Heb. 2:11) rejoice with him. There is no over-extravagance in the language in 5:1b, for there is never any danger of overdoing the communion between Christ and his church. God's provision of salvation in the gospel is itself described in terms of a feast, as some of Christ's parables, with their gracious offers and invitations, show. He has prepared and provided for his people 'a feast of choice pieces, a feast of wines on the lees ...' (Isa. 25:6). 'They are abundantly satisfied with the fullness of your house, and you give them drink from the river of your pleasures' (Ps. 36:8).

* * * * *

It would not be out of place here to repeat something which was said earlier, namely that it is not necessary always to feel under pressure to impose a chronological sequence upon the different sections of the Song. That applies again here, as the scene now changes completely. Yet the fact of this section following upon the previous one is a further reminder of the changeful nature of our communion with Christ, and that it does not just proceed along a level path from day to day. As we get to know our own hearts, it is alarming to discover how quickly fervour can give way to coolness, prosperity to decay.

5:2-8. Another bad night
The first experience of a bad night for the believer was in 3:1-5, which recorded the nightmare shock of fearing that the Lord Jesus Christ had departed, never to return. A deep and disturbing area of Christian experience (the sense of desertion) was there unfolded. Here, now, is another one, also set during the night, but dealing with a different matter. In these verses it is the bride who is speaking, recounting her experience in her own words to the daughters of Jerusalem. This will then lead, in the next section of the chapter, to a further conversation between them concerning the bridegroom.

These are sad verses, recounting the bride's folly and her improper conduct towards Christ, the consequences of which were heavy to bear. The problem that is exposed here (in a picture taken directly from married life) is one which is all too familiar in the Christian life: indifference towards Christ, carelessness regarding him, taking him for granted, provoking him to withdraw for a season from our soul's company and enjoyment, and leaving us without any felt sense of his comforting and loving presence. No information is given as to how the bride got into this state, but no doubt pride, self-satisfaction, worldly cares, the wiles of the devil, and the frequent snare of resting on spiritual laurels (achievements, works, even spiritual progress in the growth in grace and knowledge department) were present in differing degrees somewhere along the line. They usually are.

I sleep, but my heart is awake (5:2). The state described here is that of being half-asleep and half-awake. Unlike chapter 3, this is probably not a dream, but rather that state of near-sleep, just going off to sleep, when the mind still has some conscious alertness to it, though everything is beginning to drift. It is a picture of listlessness and self-indulgence, ever-present dangers. There are actually two participles here – sleeping, waking – which shows that what is recorded here will not be a one-off occurrence in the Christian life. Indeed, the whole of that life is a history of revivings and withdrawings, revivings and withdrawings, and so on, one after the other. The 'heart' refers not to the blood-pumping physical organ, but to the whole gamut of racing emotions and feelings and thoughts. The combination expressed here of sleeping but the heart being awake is suggestive of that state described in Matthew 26:41: 'The spirit indeed is willing, but the flesh is weak.' Very instructively, that comment of Christ with respect to the three disciples who were with him in Gethsemane arose in the context of him saying to them, 'Watch and pray, lest you enter into temptation'.

In this state a voice is heard: **it is the voice of my beloved!** The voice is heard and recognised. **He knocks, saying, 'Open for me, my sister, my love, my dove, my perfect one; for my head is covered with dew, my locks with the drops of the night.'** The beloved knocks and speaks, and does so once more in terms of sweet affection which exhibit his desire for renewed fellowship with his bride. Once again, Revelation 3:20 is to the fore. Christ does not stand by in a disinterested fashion when his church shows this half-hearted, lackadaisical frame of mind, heart and soul. He comes, he knocks, he awakens her, and chooses the most endearing words with which to do so. Sister (family bonds), love (deep affection) and dove (purity) have already been commented upon. Here also is 'my perfect one' (or flawless, NIV; undefiled, AV), which is all of a piece with the language of 4:7. The chief idea here is of blamelessness.

The word occurs in Job 1:8, in God's assessment of his servant there, and in Psalm 37:37 as part of the description of the righteous man, as opposed to the wicked. Those who are his, and so who are clothed with his righteousness, the Lord Jesus looks upon as perfect. By such means as his words of love here, he would seek to engage afresh his bride's love to him.

'Open to me' (AV, NIV) would be better than 'open for me'. It is a call which expects and requires a welcoming response. As if to say, how could entrance ever be denied to such a loving and glorious Christ? The Lord Jesus Christ is not finished with a soul once he has brought to it the forgiveness of sins. He would pay regular visits, both in the secret place and in the congregations of his people. When he knocks, it is our duty to open to him. You would hope that once he had made his entrance into a sinner's heart, he would be welcomed at all times. Yet, regrettably, it is not so.

The description he gives of himself (head covered with dew, and so on) is very much in keeping with Solomon's world in which the Song was written. The nights were cool and the heavy dew which fell during the long dry summer period was vital in providing refreshing moisture for the vineyards. 'Covered' can be translated 'filled' (AV) or 'drenched' (NIV). The two statements ('for my head ... dew' and 'my locks ... night') are in parallel. All of this brings home potently the utter grievousness of a bride shutting and locking her husband out of their home on a rainy night, and so, in spiritual terms, the absolute disgrace attaching to the believer who would treat Christ in a similar fashion. Yet how often it happens, and how unkindly is he used who has done and suffered and accomplished all for his people at such appalling cost.

The very poorest of excuses are offered by the bride, which show just how far carelessness towards Christ can go. **I have taken off my robe; how can I put it on again? I have washed my feet; how can I defile them?** (5:3). In other words, she has settled down for the night, and has no wish to be disturbed or troubled by anyone, not even her husband. By 'robe' is meant the garment worn next to the body. The washing of the feet was necessary having walked barefoot or in open sandals along dusty roads. It is not that she cannot get up out of bed, but that she will not. Impossibility is not the problem; unwillingness is. The bed is too warm, she is too comfortable, and getting up again would be too inconvenient. She thinks only of herself.

The personal pronoun 'I' is very prominent in this whole section. She is overtaken with sloth. She has lost her first love. Far from fulfilling Christ's wishes expressed back in 4:8, and rapidly forgetful of her own desires expressed so passionately in 4:16, she would rather just stay put. Any effort to do anything else is too great. When that is the case, any old excuse is presented on the grounds that any old excuse will do. Instead of rising up and running to meet Christ in the means of grace and places of duty (compare 2:17 and 4:6), any pathetic, trivial and selfish excuse is offered. In one season of the Christian life, nothing is too much to do or to suffer or to deny oneself for Christ, and omission of duty would cause great unease and a guilty conscience. Yet the very next moment a condition arises such as is recorded here, where Christ himself can be turned away with no sense of concern at all.

What a wretched state of affairs this represents. A very significant portion of Christ's teaching which addresses this is Luke 12:35ff. 'Let your waist be girded (Be dressed ready for service, NIV) and your lamps burning,' is how it begins, and then proceeds to expound the need for continual wakefulness and watchfulness in the whole of Christian life and service. The poverty of miserable excuses that slight Christ comes out in his parable of the great supper (Luke 14:15-24). The call to awake from sleep occurs several times in the New Testament (for example, Rom. 13:11, Eph. 5:14, 1 Thess. 5:6f).

Thus far, Christ's entreaty meets with no response. Yet he does not leave matters there. He will not so easily be turned down, nor will he take no for an answer from his own. The strength and ardour of his love to his bride is such that he comes to her and comes to her again, even in her coldness and her laziness, even after she has replied to him (more or less), 'Go away'. The patience of the Lord Jesus with unconverted souls is a wonderful thing; however, his patience with his own people is even more remarkable. This time his approach is represented as being in more than words; he takes action. **My beloved put his hand by the latch of the door** (5:4). The sort of door in mind would either have had a keyhole which was large enough to admit a human hand, or (possibly) a small window through which a person inside and a person outside could communicate with each other. The word can be 'latch-opening' (NIV), 'opening', 'hole'; 'door' itself is not in the Hebrew. It is recorded that some houses would have a hole in the door, above the lock. Those whose house it was would open the lock by putting their hand through the hole and moving the bolt and/or turning the key on the inside.

The bridegroom is seeking to let himself in, stretching his hand through this opening as if to unlock it on the inside, and the sight of this has an immediate and arousing effect upon the bride: **and my heart yearned for him**. A yearning, longing, sighing, pounding and stirring of her whole being is intended (which AV translates 'and my bowels were moved for him': often in Old Testament terms such inner organs were viewed as the seat of tender emotions). She can no longer be content with the thought of him remaining outside in the damp and dewy night air. This is the very opposite of the carelessness she had just been showing when she could not even be bothered to get up out of bed. Now, however, she is up in a flash and cannot get to the door fast enough. She demonstrates here something of that 'godly sorrow' of which the apostle Paul speaks in 2 Corinthians 7:10. By a fresh conquest of divine grace, Christ working by his Spirit, an unwilling bride is made a more than willing one again. Yet she is in for a surprise.

I arose to open for my beloved, and my hands dripped

with myrrh, my fingers with liquid myrrh, on the handles of the lock (5:5). The bride speaks of Christ here as her beloved – though it is worth observing that even in her indifferent state (half-asleep and half-awake) she spoke of him then also as her beloved, upon recognising his voice (v.2). Even in the midst of what was a backslidden state, the assurance of her relationship to Christ and her vital interest in him had not been altogether removed. Faith stirs into exercise again, desiring (as faith does, working through love) to embrace Christ and all that is in him, and having done so to hold fast to him and not let him go.

It took her some little time to manage to get the door open. Myrrh makes another appearance in the Song at this point, described here as 'liquid myrrh' (or flowing myrrh). It is not clear whether the perfume was on the bride's hands already (as part of her preparations for the night), whether she took time after getting out of bed to anoint herself with it, or whether it was left on the handles of the lock from the bridegroom's hands. However it was, she fumbled somewhat in dealing with the lock. Eventually, though, the door was open, and she expected to see straightaway her beloved who had just been speaking to her, and seeking to gain entrance to her. That is when she had her surprise.

I opened for my beloved, but my beloved had turned away and was gone (5:6). Before she was ready to receive him and to welcome him, he had gone again. There was nobody there. The verb translated here 'turned away' has the sense of 'to turn aside', or 'to take a different direction'. The use of two verbs, one straight after the other, heightens the effect, as if to say 'he has gone, he has gone'. As a result (as in the experience recorded in chapter 3) she had to set off searching for him once more, though this time things were going to be more uncomfortable than on the previous occasion. How necessary it is in the life of faith to observe the vigour of that call, 'Whatever your hand finds to do, do it with your might' (Eccl. 9:10), and to follow the example of the psalmist who 'made haste, and did not delay' (Ps. 119:60). This the bride here had failed to do. She had taken her time. She had not rushed into Christ's arms. She delayed and suffered for the delay. How many precious times with the Lord Jesus Christ that we might have enjoyed have been lost because we did not redeem the time without delay.

We are faced here again with the mysterious reality of the withdrawings of Christ. The effect upon the bride was quite devastating. **My heart went out to him when he spoke.** There is no 'to him' in the Hebrew. The full force is 'my soul went out' or 'my soul failed'. The discovery of his absence was a soul-stopping moment. Sometimes people use the phrase, 'I nearly died', or, 'I could have died'. There is something of that here. The same verb occurs in Genesis 42:28 of Jacob's sons, when they found their money in their sacks: 'Then their hearts failed them and they were afraid.' The 'when he spoke' does not mean 'while he was speaking' (for he had been silent for some moments and she had not rejoiced to hear his voice anyway), but signifies 'in consequence of/after his speaking' (as she now 'heard again' his words and meditated upon them).

This might appear to be an extraordinary moment for the Lord Jesus Christ to withdraw, having just a moment ago been so earnestly desirous of his bride opening the door to him. Yet he always knows what he is doing, as well as when and why he is doing it. As for her, the trial is not over yet. There is still more to endure before the presence of Christ will be enjoyed afresh. How she must have wished (though in vain) that she had arisen and opened the door to him at his first knock. Where there is true grace residing in a soul, few things grieve a believer more, in missing Christ's presence, than to know that their own sin, idleness and slighting of him is the cause. This must have been impressed sorely upon the bride here. Under a strong sense, then, of wrongs done to him, the bride cannot rest satisfied or content until she has him to herself again. Far from returning to bed, immediately she set about looking for him, but it proved no easy task. While she had paid all too little attention to his voice, his withdrawings have now stirred her up.

I sought him, but I could not find him; I called him, but he gave me no answer. Appropriate means must be employed diligently in order to recover a missing Christ (especially self-examination, repentance, the word and prayer). On this, compare the reference back in 3:2 to her going about the city streets and squares, and see the comments on that verse. Yet there was no quick discovery, and no rapid response. The bridegroom treated the bride as she had treated him, though not in a manner of revenge or wrath, but of loving rebuke and correction.

The watchmen who went about the city found me (5:7). These watchmen we identified in 3:3 as spiritual overseers, pastor-teachers, those who have the care of souls; in other words, ministers of the gospel. That identification holds here, though the words that follow appear strange, at least at first sight. **They struck me, they wounded me; the keepers of the walls took my veil away from me.** It appears that these men set about the bride in the manner of an assault. What is being conveyed here?

It has the look of what is often referred to these days as 'heavy shepherding', but need not necessarily be taken for such. The point is that those to whom the bride turned for help were at pains to impress upon her the serious nature of her spiritual declension. This was not intended (nor should it ever be intended) as cold comfort to believers, or the language of 'I told you so'. Rather, as those who 'watch out for' or 'keep watch over' souls (Heb. 13:17), a word which carries the sense of spending sleepless nights over the church, like shepherds with their sheep, Christ's ministers are not to flatter, entertain or speak smooth words to needy souls but are to rebuke, correct and instruct (2 Tim. 3:16).

However, this passage does require an important caution to be entered, lest those who are taken for true and faithful gospel ministers are in reality false and uncalled. For even though 'the word of God is living and powerful, and sharper than any two-edged sword, piercing even to the division of soul and spirit, and of joints and marrow, and is a discerner of the thoughts and intents of the heart' (Heb. 4:12), it must never be applied roughly or harshly, but always out of heartfelt love and concern for the believer and with a desire above everything else to see Christ glorified afresh. May all of Christ's ministers be enabled with all needful grace, experience and skill to be shepherds and pastors after his own heart and example, in order to do Christ's people good and not harm. 'A bruised reed he will not break, and smoking flax he will not quench' (Isa. 42:3).

The keepers of the walls are the same people as the watchmen; there is no need to look for any distinction between them. As for the removing of the bride's veil, this speaks poignantly of the humiliation and shame arising from her mistreatment of Christ. The literal taking away of her veil would be the greatest indignity that could be done to an oriental woman. Having said that, the word actually used here (which NIV translates 'cloak') is probably best understood as a lightweight summer overgarment. Its only other Old Testament occurrence is Isaiah 3:23, where it appears in a list of items of clothing and various ornaments which the women of Israel would have taken away from them when the days of the exile came, and is translated (plural) 'robes' (NKJV). It is a different word from that rendered 'veil' in 4:1 of the Song.

There is an important difference to be observed between this episode and that in chapter 3. On the earlier occasion, while Christ was absent it was not on account of neglect on the believer's part. Consequently, the search for him was rewarded comparatively swiftly. The present case, however, is very much a case of neglect of Christ, and so it is not surprising that the search to recover his presence and fellowship again takes longer and is accompanied with greater difficulties and trials. It is much more difficult to recover the enjoyment of Christ again than it is to lose it through our folly. It may be that it was in order to learn that lesson for the future that the bride was permitted here to receive this rather untender treatment from the watchmen.

It seems that the ministry of the watchmen did not profit the bride (because of its oversharp and unfeeling nature?), so she now turns once again to the daughters of Jerusalem and gives them a solemn charge (compare 2:7, 3:5, 8:4). **I charge you, O daughters of Jerusalem, if you find my beloved, that you tell him I am lovesick!** (5:8). It is literally, 'if you find my beloved, what do you/will you tell him? That I am lovesick'. She recounts to them her experience and acquaints them with her sorrows and exercises, and (to all intents and purposes) asks them to pray for her. The 'if you find my beloved' is indicative of the fact that in seasons of spiritual darkness or desertion it will often be assumed by the troubled soul that other believers who are in a better condition will know exactly where to find Christ and will have access to him on their behalf to seek his help and presence for them. This the bride hopes is the case here. Even though pride will sometimes hold Christians back from asking, it is part of the privilege and duty of Christian fellowship and belonging to engage earnestly for one another before God. Believers holding up one another's cases before him is pleasing to Christ, and nothing, surely, pleases him more than for our desire for him to be expressed, that we are lovesick for him. It is striking to learn (since we identified these daughters of Jerusalem as those younger in the faith, see comments on page 32) that such ones may on occasions have an access to Christ and felt communion with him which others may not.

Indifferent she may have been, but no longer; now lovesick is the word she chooses to describe herself. This lovesickness over an absent Christ may be contrasted with the earlier lovesickness arising from a surfeit of Christ (2:5-7). He is to be rejoiced in when present and sought when absent. 'Hope deferred makes the heart sick' (Prov. 13:12), especially when the sweetness of Christ's love and fellowship, having once been known, and then despised, is longed for again. His presence is the soul's health, while his absence is its sickness.

This charge leads directly into the second half of the chapter, as the daughters of Jerusalem take things up with the bride.

5:9. A leading question

Why do Christians enjoy so little of Christ, compared with all
that there is of him for us to enjoy? The root answer from this
chapter thus far is that so much of the time we are so greatly
taken up with ourselves, and so little taken up with him. The
bride paid the price for her indifference towards her husband.
Yet she has come to her senses, and realises again that she cannot
live without him, and that there is no one else like him in all the
world. She has engaged the help of the daughters of Jerusalem
in finding him again, and has given them a message to convey
to him on her behalf.

This brings us to the next section of chapter 5, though there
is no break of which to speak. Everything flows on. The bride's
charge to them (v.8) draws from the daughters of Jerusalem a
very important question (v.9), which has the effect on the bride
of her uttering a most exquisite description of her beloved, and
so giving a most glorious poetic portrait of the Lord Jesus Christ
(vs.10-16). This has long been one of the favourite portions of
the whole of the Song to those who love the Saviour, and builds
up to the never-to-be-forgotten climax of him being spoken of
as 'altogether lovely' (v.16).

> **What is your beloved more than another beloved, O fairest among
> women? What is your beloved more than another beloved, that
> you so charge us?** (5:9).

The tightness of the language is apparent when it is realised that
neither the 'is' nor the 'another' (both of which appear twice in
the English translation) are actually there in the original. The
meaning of the question is clear: as if to say, 'this beloved of
yours – what's so special about him? how does he stand out so
much from anyone else's beloved?' Putting it in rather more
colloquial terms, 'what is there to write home about him? why
do you go on about him so much?' On 'O fairest among women',
see comment on 1:8, where the same words are spoken by the
beloved himself. Compare also the use of 'fair' in 1:15 and 4:1,

131

and 'all fair' in 4:7. It is Christ's own grace and likeness in her which makes his bride fair (beautiful, lovely).

That the daughters of Jerusalem (younger believers) should ask such a question of the Shulamite (the bride) should not appear strange, nor need it tie us up in interpretative knots. The whole purpose of verse 8 is to lead on into the verses that follow it. The daughters themselves are not strictly ignorant of the answer, for Christ is precious to them too, but it will do their own faith in and communion with the Lord Jesus Christ good to hear the answer, that he would come to mean more and more to them. Babes in Christ should always be able to benefit from those older in the faith, and should learn to esteem them. It may be also that they intended to comfort and encourage the Shulamite by their question, that they too might do her good.

Mutual conversation between believers upon the glory of Christ is highly desirable (compare Mal. 3:16). If only there was more of it! One believer's passion for Christ may prove to be a means of stirring up the passions of other believers for him, as well as of causing unbelievers (to whom, left to themselves, Christ means nothing at all) to enquire concerning his glory and beauty. How important it is that everyone would learn from every true Christian that there is a preciousness, a desirableness and a satisfaction to be found in Christ which is absolutely missing everywhere else. Yet how little, very often, that impression is given.

5:10-16. The glory of Christ

Stirred by the alarming experience of verses 2-8 and the inviting question of verse 9, the bride launches into a most beautiful description of all that the Lord Jesus Christ is to her and means to her. There is a staggering richness of language here, thoroughly suitable in the light of who it is whom the words are extolling. The bride's heart is full of him, and what now follows is very much in the spirit of Psalm 45, with its beginning, 'My heart is overflowing with a good theme; I recite my composition concerning the King; my tongue is the pen of a ready writer. You are fairer than the sons of men; grace is poured upon your lips; therefore God has blessed you for ever' (Ps. 45:1-2).

The verses through to the end of chapter 5 leave the matter in no doubt. The Lord Jesus Christ is infinitely superior to any and every other 'beloved' anyone might have, being wiser, richer, changeless, and able to be loved with the whole heart, without there ever being any possible danger of loving him to excess. The other beloveds of verse 8 stand for whatever people would put in the place of Christ, and so are what are called regularly in Scripture, idols. Compare 1 John 2:15-17, with its telling reference to 'all that is in the world – the lust of the flesh, the lust of the eyes, and the pride of life'.

A word needs to be said in general terms, first of all, about the interpretation of verses 10-16. This is in line with the comment made in connection with 3:10. The point is that great care is needed in striking a right balance between overall impression and particular detail. There is much to be gleaned from the details (as will be shown as the commentary proceeds), for Christ's excellence is made up of a whole (indeed, an endless) variety of particulars. Each part is suggestive of something to be found in him. However, the general picture, setting out both strikingly and memorably the magnificence and incomparableness of Christ, must not be missed.

My beloved is white and ruddy, chief among ten thousand (5:10). It has been remarked that love songs describing the physical beauty of loved ones were common in the ancient near east, though tended to describe the female rather than the male. Here, however, after the extensive eulogy upon the bride's beauty in chapter 4 (with more to come in chapters 6 and 7), it is the beauty of the bridegroom that is in focus. After this opening statement of verse 10, the physical order in the description proceeds downwards from head to foot. It is indeed a full-length portrait. We cannot help being reminded of Revelation 1:12-16.

'White' may be translated 'bright', 'dazzling', or (with NIV) 'radiant'; 'shimmering' has also been suggested. The word occurs only four times in the Old Testament. Purity is what is especially in view. 'Ruddy' conveys the picture of a fresh and healthy complexion, plenty of colour, anything but pale of face. The thought of manliness is being conveyed. It will be seen that there is no contradiction here between white and ruddy, should it ever be enquired how someone can be both at the same time, rather than one or the other. The force of 'chief' is 'outstanding' (standing out), completely distinguished from any competition (standing alone, beyond compare, in a class of his own), while 'among ten thousand' adds to the sense of superlativeness, even uniqueness. It could be that there is a military analogy implicit here: the one who stands out from the whole company of ten thousand men, as a banner lifted up among an innumerable army. In this connection, notice Isaiah 11:10: 'And in that day there shall be a Root of Jesse, who shall stand as a banner to the people; for the Gentiles shall seek him, and his resting place shall be glorious.' Again, the truth is being emphasised that there is in Christ what cannot be found in or said about anyone else. There is a sense in these words of what is said of Christ in Philippians 2:9, having been given by the Father 'the name which is above every name'. In him resides everything that makes him lovely to our souls, and captures our admiration and affection.

In 1 Samuel 16:12 David is described as 'ruddy, with bright eyes, and good-looking', indicating a roundedness and wholeness of health and appearance. How much more is this true of great David's greater Son. All eyes would rest on him. All attention would be taken by him, to whom shall 'the obedience (or, gathering) of the people' be (Gen. 49:10). The beauties of Christ's divine and human natures have been seen here (white in his glory as God, ruddy in his taking upon himself the nature of man). He who is 'the brightness of (God's) glory and the express image of his person' (Heb. 1:3), is the one 'who is holy, harmless, undefiled, separate from sinners' (Heb. 7:26).

His head is like the finest gold; his locks are wavy, and

black as a raven (5:11). The finest/purest/choicest/most refined gold is next to be employed in setting forth the glory of Christ. The thought is likely that of gazing upon an exquisitely sculptured head. 'Wavy' (AV, bushy), describing the locks (the area around the temples), only appears this once in the Old Testament. The word may have something to do with palm leaves or vine branches. The picture being conveyed is of a profusion of hair in flowing clusters, with the added detail of them being 'black as a raven'.

The kingliness, dignity and nobility of Christ may be seen here: the one who is 'Wonderful Counsellor, Mighty God, Everlasting Father, Prince of Peace' (Isa. 9:6), 'head over all things to the church' (Eph. 1:22), 'the head of all principality and power' (Col. 2:10), and who 'in all things (has) the pre-eminence' (Col. 1:18). Evidently both by the Jews and the Romans black hair was regarded as being especially beautiful, such that those whose hair was not naturally black would seek sometimes to make it so by various means available to them. Christ's magnificence, stateliness and beauty, however, is his own, and is neither borrowed nor derived.

The same root that gives the adjective 'black' in this verse gives also the word translated in Ecclesiastes 11:10 'youth' (or, it could be 'prime of life'). In application here to Christ this speaks of the youthful vigour and freshness of him who is 'the same yesterday, today, and for ever' (Heb. 13:8), and who at all times is fit and qualified for all his undertakings for his people. He never changes or decays. He is always the same. He continually retains his beauty and glory. In this again, he stands alone.

His eyes are like doves by the rivers of waters, washed with milk, and fitly set (5:12). The focus moves now to the eyes. Again the language is exquisite and well-chosen. The picture is of doves washing themselves by darting in and out of rivers of waters; though then the poetic detail is added that the washing is actually in milk. Special focus falls upon the bridegroom's eyes being likened to these doves (note that it is not 'his eyes are like doves' eyes', but 'his eyes are like doves': on the former comparison, see 1:15 and 4:1, both re the bride). Doves by the rivers, in the manner described, represent the pupil of the eye surrounded by the clear and healthy-looking white of the eye. To complete the imagery, his eyes are 'fitly set' (not sunken in their sockets or, as the saying goes, sticking out like organ stops). This conveys the idea of jewels set in a ring; the translation 'stones beautifully set' has been offered. A literal translation would be 'sitting on a setting'.

The emphasis this time is surely upon the gentleness and compassion of Christ, his tenderness and grace, his sympathy and consolations. He says of himself, 'for I am gentle and lowly in heart, and you will find rest for your souls' (Matt. 11:29). The apostle Paul appeals movingly to the Corinthians 'by the meekness and gentleness of Christ' (2 Cor. 10:1). His eyes are pure eyes (unable to approve of any sin), knowing eyes (thoroughly acquainted with his people), discerning eyes (in loving wisdom ordering all things for our good), loving eyes (forever looking upon us with complacent delight), and on more than one occasion in the four Gospels they are weeping eyes (feeling for us and bearing us upon his heart). 'The Lord knows those who are his' (2 Tim. 2:19).

'For the eyes of the LORD run to and fro throughout the whole earth, to show himself strong on behalf of those whose heart is loyal to him' (2 Chron. 16:9). While this may cause great consternation to unbelievers, the firm bonds of the eternal covenant make it exceedingly comfortable to believers. Peter rejoices in the comforts of such a verse as this in the Song in confessing to Christ, after the resurrection, 'Lord, you know all things; you know that I love you' (John 21:17).

His cheeks are like a bed of spices, like banks of scented herbs (5:13). Next it is the cheeks which are singled out for mention. The second phrase of the sentence may be rendered 'a raised bed (or, towers) of aromatic herbs'. Maybe trellises covered with deliciously perfumed flowers is what is in view. The dominant theme, clearly, is fragrance and beauty arising from the sweet perfumes. This applies very well to the Lord Jesus Christ. His cheeks are mentioned in Isaiah 50:6: 'I gave my back to those who struck me, and my cheeks to those who plucked out the beard; I did not hide my face from shame and spitting.' Linking the Isaiah and Song verses together, the fragrance of Christ in his passion, humiliations, sufferings, agonies and death is inexpressibly sweet and precious. Compare, on this, Ephesians 5:25 (for the church as a whole) and Galatians 2:20 (for each believer individually), as well as Ephesians 5:2.

The cheeks are only part of the complete face, which prompts again the reflection that if just a measure or part-view of Christ is so pleasing to his people, what effect will his fulness have. Even what have been called the half discoveries that he makes of himself to our souls are reviving and ravishing, so what will the complete discovery be. Scripture regularly uses the language of the spiritual senses (taste, sight, smell and so on) when exploring the relationship between God and his people, Christ and his church.

This same verse continues: **His lips are lilies, dripping liquid myrrh.** Christ's lips have already been mentioned implicitly in 1:2 ('the kisses of his mouth'), while he spoke of his bride's lips in 4:3, 11. Myrrh has already been commented upon, having appeared a number of times in the Song so far (see comment on). Lips, as well as for kissing, are for speaking, and so the words of Christ come into view here. His words themselves are kisses of his mouth. They are not merely intended to fill our heads with knowledge but should also minister deeply to our very souls and affect our affections. The word the bride uses to describe her husband's lips is 'lilies'. A lily of a deep red colour is very likely intended, rather than the white one we are often most familiar with. Here is Psalm 45:2 once more: 'grace is poured upon your lips.' Compare Isaiah 50:4: 'The Lord GOD has given me the tongue of the learned, that I should know how to speak a word in season to him who is weary. He awakens me morning by morning, he awakens my ear to hear as the learned.'

The words of Christ are pure, precious, true, desirable, comforting and powerful. Where necessary they are chastening as well: 'As many as I love, I rebuke and chasten,' he says in Revelation 3:19. They are as precious as (or more precious than) the choicest liquid myrrh. 'More to be desired are they than gold, yea, than much fine gold; sweeter also than honey and the honeycomb. Moreover by them is your servant warned, and in keeping them there is great reward' (Ps. 19:10-11). The word 'dripping' (or, flowing) in association with myrrh signifies abundance and fulness – again, very appropriate considering whose lips they are. The whole of the Song itself, of course, is testimony to the beauty and matchlessness of Christ's words. Well is it said of him, 'No man ever spoke like this man!' (John 7:46). Where Christ's words are despised, he will himself be despised, which was exactly what was happening in the first half of the chapter. 'Let the word of Christ dwell in you richly' (Col. 3:16), is the divine command and counsel.

His hands are rods of gold set with beryl (5:14). Several matters arise with the translation. For NKJV's 'hands', NIV has 'arms'; evidently the word can be used for any part of the arm. NKJV/NIV's 'rods of gold' can be 'rings of gold', or even 'golden cylinders' has been suggested. The phrase 'set with beryl' is difficult to be precise with, in terms of the precious stone intended. Possibilities include 'jewels' itself, as a general term, or else beryl, chrysolite, topaz, lapis lazuli or even 'stones/ jewels of Tarshish'. Beryl or topaz, being themselves goldish/ yellowish in colour, might fit best with the mention of gold itself. It may be that the thought is of the hands being the gold rings, having fingernails which were as the jewels set in those rings.

Men wear gold rings on their hands (fingers), but Christ's hands themselves are described as rings of gold. He is in every way superior to all. This ties in with the original question to the bride from the daughters of Jerusalem. They asked how her beloved was better than other beloveds, and in the course of these verses she is responding by seeking to show that he is better not just in some ways but in every way. Observe Psalm 115 for the contrast between the true God and false gods, and so between the true beloved (Christ) and 'other beloveds' who cannot compare with him.

The mention of hands invites reference to 'the works of his hands', whether in creation, providence or grace, for just as in the previous verse the lips are the instruments of speech, so here the hands are the instruments of action. Christ's words and Christ's works go together, and are both alike matters of adoring contemplation to the believer. In connection with the central theme of Christ and his people, compare the very significant mentions of his hand in Psalm 95:7 ('For he is our God, and we are the people of his pasture and the sheep of his hand') and in John 10:27-28 ('My sheep hear my voice, and I know them, and they follow me. And I give them eternal life, and they shall never perish; neither shall anyone snatch them out of my hand').

His body is carved ivory inlaid with sapphires, completes the verse. 'Carved' can also be bright or polished, while 'inlaid' may be rendered overlaid, decorated, covered or encrusted. The sense of these words has been put forward in the phrase 'a work of art'. The polished whiteness of ivory is combined here with the azure blue of the choicest sapphires. Beauty, perfection, symmetry, form are suggested, even that of the one who says of himself to mankind, 'You are from beneath; I am from above. You are of this world; I am not of this world' (John 8:23). Still the Shulamite does not digress from her theme: how utterly incomparable her beloved is.

His legs are pillars of marble set on bases of fine gold (5:15). The word for 'leg' may also be rendered 'thighs', and can be descriptive of the entire leg from the thigh right down to the ankle. This is the sole appearance of the word in the Song. It does appear, however, as many as eighteen times elsewhere, twelve of these being used in the Pentateuch of the heave offering (comprising the right leg/thigh of the sacrificial animal which formed the portion belonging to the priest). Compare Leviticus 7:32, 34.

Strength (well depicted by pillars of marble) is the chief thing here, linked very much with Christ's ability to support and uphold his people, and his unswerving trustworthiness and stability in doing so. The whiteness of the marble, taken with the gold of the bases upon which the pillars are set, conveys the sense of kingliness; in other words, this is no ordinary strength but is royal strength, kingly strength, with all the magnificence and dignity that accompanies it. To the Lord Jesus Christ belong 'the nations for (his) inheritance and the ends of the earth for (his) possession'. The Father says to him: 'You shall break them with a rod of iron; you shall dash them to pieces like a potter's vessel' (Ps. 2:8-9). He is 'King of kings and Lord of lords' (Rev. 19:16). The government is upon his shoulder (Isa. 9:6) – the government of the whole universe, but in particular the government of his church. The perfection of his ways and the settled and skilful nature of his purposes are also gathered up here.

A sight of all of this is full of unspeakable consolation and assurance for Christ's people, and contributes greatly to their appreciation of his beauty. He who has borne their sin, bears up his own in all their fears, trials and temptations, fulfils all his purposes for them and keeps them from falling.

His countenance is like Lebanon, excellent as the cedars. Lebanon is famed for its beauty. Just as the bridegroom had rejoiced over his bride with the words 'the fragrance of your garments is like the fragrance of Lebanon' (see on 4:11, and compare also the comments on 4:8), so now Lebanon is employed by the bride of her beloved. For 'countenance', NIV has 'appearance'. The word conveys not merely 'face' (which is often spoken of as 'countenance') but the whole sense of deportment and (that old word) mien – in a sense, everything about him, every aspect of him, how he looks, how he is viewed, the effect of his presence, the impression he makes, every part of a person in the whole of his proportions, and such like. This is no slight or passing view of Christ but rather carries the sense of his fulness, grandeur and prominence. This being so, the reference to the excellent (choice, stately) cedars of Lebanon is well chosen and absolutely appropriate. For height, strength, beauty, whole appearance, these trees excelled all others.

Piece by piece this unfolding of the glory of Christ by his bride is reaching its climax. **His mouth is most sweet** (5:16). The word for 'mouth' can be translated 'palate', and was used in 2:3 with respect to taste. The sentence here recalls the first thing the Shulamite said, right back in 1:2, when she referred to 'the kisses of his mouth'. See on that verse and on 5:13b; and also on 4:3 where Christ refers to his bride's lips and mouth. The word 'sweet' is a plural, so literally 'sweets', or even 'sweetnesses'; 'sweetness itself' might catch the sense well. Whether in terms chiefly of the mouth as the instrument of affection (kisses), or of wisdom (speech), or of looks (beauty), the Lord Jesus Christ, once again, stands alone.

Then follows this: **Yes, he is altogether lovely.** The total picture has been expressed and the height has been reached. All the exquisite particulars dwelt upon so lavishly in verses 10-16a come together here at their highest and most all-inclusive point – not merely the loveliness but the altogether loveliness of Christ. The 'yes' does not appear in the Hebrew. Literally the phrase reads, 'and all of him is lovely/desirable'. Again, the word is a plural: as well as his sweetnesses there are his lovelinesses. There is no perfection or excellence lacking in him, and no comparable perfection or excellence to be found in anyone else. There is this thoroughness to Christ's loveliness and desirableness: all of him, and all of all of him, is lovely and full of delights.

Against the background of the whole of Scripture, this works out in various ways, especially in the light of Jesus' own remark, 'You search the Scriptures ... and these are they which testify of me' (John 5:39). He is altogether lovely in his person (all the eternal and radiant glories of his Godhead and all the perfect and gracious features of his Manhood, the whole great mystery of the union of the two complete natures in the one person). He is altogether lovely in his offices (Prophet, revealing, by his word and Spirit, the things of God, not least for our salvation; Priest, offering up himself as a sacrifice to satisfy divine justice, to reconcile us to God, and to make continual intercession for his people; and King, subduing us to himself, ruling and defending us, restraining and conquering all his own and our enemies). He is altogether lovely in the many relations he bears to his own (such as, our great Redeemer, our only Saviour, our glorious Bridegroom, our complete Surety, our loving Shepherd, our great High Priest, our gracious Master, our mighty King, our matchless Lord, our royal Head, our powerful Advocate, our sure Foundation, our victorious Captain, our immovable Rock, our unfailing Comforter, our best Beloved and our faithful Friend, these last two about to be focussed upon in this very verse 16). In a word: he is altogether lovely as our All-in-all. To all 'who believe, he is precious' (1 Pet. 2:7). There is no blemish, defect or shortfall in him whatsoever. He is absolutely faultless.

This is my beloved, and this is my friend, O daughters of Jerusalem! Neither time in the Hebrew does the 'is' appear, thus once more tightening the language, the 'this' being emphatic each time, as if underlined. 'This my beloved, and this my friend': this one, and him alone. The title 'beloved' for Christ is already familiar in the Song (compare 1:14, 16; 2:3, 8-10, 16, 17; 4:16; 5:2, 4-6, 8, 10, along with 3:1-4). There is now added the title 'friend'. The two titles, of course, belong together, and are both expressive of Christ's overarching character as husband/bridegroom of his bride.

The portrait of Christ as the believer's friend is drawn very richly in Scripture. Proverbs presents him in this way: 'A friend loves at all times, and a brother is born for adversity' (17:17); 'there is a friend who sticks closer than a brother' (18:24). When

Christ's opponents accused him, despisingly, of being 'a friend of tax-collectors and sinners' (Matt. 11:19), little did they realise the glorious truth they spoke. There is also that statement, 'having loved his own who were in the world, he loved them to the end' (John 13:1). As the sinner's friend and the believer's friend, the Lord Jesus Christ pays all our debts, carries all our sins, supplies all our wants, bears all our burdens, comforts us in all our troubles, sweetens all our afflictions, warns us of all dangers, rebukes lovingly and corrects all our faults, tells us his secrets, subdues all our enemies, defends us in all dangers, manages all our concerns, entrusts us with his interests, counsels us in all our perplexities, takes our part against our adversaries, secures for us eternal life and glory, and gives us himself. He is faithful, he is dependable, he is constant, he is true. Well may it be said of him that he is both a friend in need and a friend indeed.

The bride is determined that the daughters of Jerusalem will get the message. They had asked their question in verse 9, and she has answered them in no uncertain terms in verses 10-16, as if to say, 'Do you really desire to know what my beloved is more than another beloved? Then I shall tell you'. And having done just that, it is a case of 'Now do you see? How can there possibly ever be anyone to compare with him?' Which is exactly how every true believer regards the Lord Jesus Christ, and longs that everyone else should be of the same conviction and affection. 'My soul shall make its boast in the LORD; the humble shall hear of it and be glad' (Ps. 34:2).

Chapter 6

THE BEAUTY OF CHRIST'S CHURCH

In the previous chapter, the daughters of Jerusalem enquired of the Shulamite concerning her beloved. She replied in rapturous terms, and this has the effect not only of stirring up again her own affection for him, but increasing also the desire of these daughters of Jerusalem for him as well. In the spiritual terms of the Song, the believer's own passion for Christ is revived, and her glowing and adoring testimony concerning him causes the younger believers to crave for more of Christ for themselves. This is apparent straightaway in the opening verses.

6:1-3. Christ gathering lilies
Where has your beloved gone, O fairest among women? Where has your beloved turned aside, that we may seek him with you? (6:1). With these words the daughters of Jerusalem pursue matters with the Shulamite. Earlier she had asked them to help her find her beloved (5:8). Now they are as keen as she is to discover where he is, showing their serious intent by repeating their question as soon as it is asked. Their desire for Christ is united and mutual, rather than causing jealousy or rivalry. The seeking and finding of Christ is the true and high end of all spiritual duties, in which the whole of his church should be engaged; without him they remain empty.

It is striking that their mode of address for the bride ('O fairest among women', compare 5:9) accords once again with his own (1:8, compare 4:1). The verb 'turned aside' indicates 'which way has he taken? in which direction has he gone?' It underscores that Christ's absences from his people are only temporary turnings aside, not permanent withdrawings. Compare Isaiah 54:7-8.

It is a blessed thing when one Christian's delight in the Lord

Jesus Christ makes such an impression upon a fellow believer that their spiritual desires are kindled afresh also (or, for that matter, when a believer's enthusiastic and devoted setting forth of the excellences of Christ is used by God in drawing sinners to Christ). Let Christians not be reticent or backward either in speaking with one another about Christ or proclaiming his fulness of grace to sinners. The fire of love to Christ needs to burn ever more brightly and warmly. If we would be of any use in commending Christ to others (whether they are believers or unbelievers), we must be in earnest about him ourselves. Indeed, one regular end of Christ's dealings with his people (as here) is not only for their own good but that they may be the means as well of leading others to know and possess him themselves. Recall, in this connection, the psalmist's phrase 'the generation of those who seek him, who seek your face' (Ps. 24:6), and the description of Christians as those 'called to be saints ... who in every place call on the name of Jesus Christ our Lord, both theirs and ours' (1 Cor. 1:2).

The bride is ready with her answer. **My beloved has gone to his garden** (6:2). The garden (4:12; 5:1) is a description of Christ's church as a company gathered out of the world, so the bride's answer to the question as to where Christ has gone is to say, 'He is in his church, he is to be found among his people.' She recalls his own words of 5:1. Note the emphatic personal pronoun of possession: he is in 'his' garden, which he has planted and of which he takes care (compare 'the planting of the LORD, that he may be glorified', Isa. 61:3, as well as 27:3). The church belongs to the Lord Jesus Christ, who is both its bridegroom and its head. If it be asked why the bride did not know this all along, thus making the whole business of chapter 5 unnecessary, any Christian who knows his or her own heart with any degree of accuracy knows how prone that heart is to be forgetful, unbelieving, distracted, sinful and confused. We can forget the most elementary things and get into the most foolish scrapes.

The reference to Christ being in his garden (where he was all along, though unregarded and unenjoyed by his bride) is amplified: he has gone **to the beds of spices, to feed his flock in the gardens, and to gather lilies**. These words bring together related themes already expressed in the Song. The mention of beds of spices recalls the whole of 4:12–5:1. For Christ feeding see 1:7; as there, 'his flock' is an addition, not in the Hebrew text, while 'feed' can also be translated 'browse' (with NIV). The plural 'gardens' appeared in 4:15, while lilies are descriptive of believers (2:2). Although he may withdraw his felt presence from the believer for a season, Christ is always to be found somewhere in the spiritual garden of his church.

Christ is pictured here, then, in the place he most delights to be, enjoying the fellowship of his people on earth and the presence of his people in heaven. Mindful of the Solomonic background to the Song, just as a king would enjoy going from his royal palace into his gardens (often a fair distance), there to browse, to walk, to rest and to converse, so the Lord Jesus Christ (the King of kings, who has travelled the far greater distance) takes great pleasure in being present among his people, fellowshipping with his own and manifesting himself in ever increasing degrees of glory to their souls. Pursuing the analogy a step further, just as the earthly king might pick some of the flowers (or have them picked for him) that they might be taken back to adorn the palace, so the heavenly king, in his regular visits to his garden, gathers some of his lilies and takes them to be with him in heaven itself, to adorn that holy and happy place. Heaven is very much a place of gathered lilies.

What a tender and inviting picture Christ's gathering of his lilies is. The entire plan and work of divine grace in salvation may be seen precisely in those terms: election in Christ before the foundation of the world, the coming of Christ into the world to save his people from their sins (the active obedience of his life and the passive obedience of his death), the pouring out of the Holy Spirit at Pentecost (along with the wonders of the new birth and effectual call), the Christian life as a life of deepening communion with Christ and growing likeness to him, and, finally, the taking of his saints to glory and all that follows at his coming return that has been prepared for the endless ages of eternity 'with Christ, which is far better' (Phil. 1:23; compare Ps. 16:11). All of this is a gathering of Christ's lilies which are precious, fragrant and beautiful in his sight. As was observed at 2:1-2, Christ is the lily and his people are lilies (having no natural holiness of their own but clothed now with the white and pure garment of Christ's own spotless righteousness). They are the pure in heart who shall see God (Matt. 5:8). All the church's beauty and garments are taken out of her bridegroom's wardrobe. It is her own, but by gift; yet being once given it is her own for ever. Here, the church is 'like a lily among thorns' (2:2); in heaven, there will be no thorns, only lilies. Believers are to be patient with respect to Christ's timings, and are never to begrudge him the lilies that he gathers.

I am my beloved's, and my beloved is mine. He feeds his flock among the lilies (6:3). The shared enjoyment takes hold again, with the return of a deep assurance on the bride's part of her firm and settled relationship with her beloved, and the sublime wonders of covenant grace. Here the language of faith and hope revives.

When testifying in this way in 2:16, the bride's words were 'My beloved is mine, and I am his.' This time she says, 'I am my beloved's and my beloved is mine.' While both statements come to the same thing (being an intimate expression of the mutual belonging, mutual affection, mutual familiarity, mutual delight, mutual contentment and mutual likeness one to the other of Christ and his church), there is a significance in the change of order in the wording this time round. In 2:16 the Shulamite's first thought was of her claim upon Christ (he is mine), after which she mentioned his own claim upon her (I am his). In 6:3 she is now thinking first of his claim upon her (I am his), and then proceeds to her own claim upon him (he is mine). In other words, there is a maturing, a growing in grace, to be observed, with the Lord Jesus more and more taking the pre-eminent place in her thoughts, her heart and her life. So it should be, for the relationship between Christ and a believer should not remain static. Indeed it cannot. The next time something similar is said by the Shulamite (7:10), Christ fills the whole picture.

For 'he feeds among the lilies', see on 2:16 and 6:3, with this added comment: for all the intensely individual nature of the believer's relationship with Christ, his presencing of himself in his church ('among the lilies') must never be overlooked or undervalued. Christians are to 'consider one another in order to stir up love and good works, not forsaking the assembling of ourselves together, as is the manner of some, but exhorting one another, and so much the more as you see the Day approaching' (Heb. 10:24-25). Christ is to be enjoyed not only in secret but among the lilies.

6:4-7. In praise of the bride

There has been much grieving of her beloved on the bride's part, but all is now well again and things are restored. Now, without any hesitation or delay, the bridegroom opens his heart again and speaks in praise of his bride, enlarging upon her beauty and all that she means to him. He does not take her to task or set about her, but adopts the tenderest language towards her, speaking very much to her and not merely of her. His love does not change, nor do his assurances of it cease. Remember how the Lord Jesus appeared to Peter, after his resurrection, and restored so graciously the one who had denied him three times (John 21:15-19). Christ always delights to return in love to his people who return to him in penitence.

The word for 'my love' is the feminine form of the word used by the Shulamite in 5:16, 'my friend', and could be translated so here. The companionship of love is one of the emphases of the relationship upon which the Song focuses. Some of what Christ says in these verses we have had before in the Song; some of it is new.

O my love, you are as beautiful as Tirzah (6:4). There are three separate (though dovetailing) expressions of affection and pleasure in this verse, being worded in three comparisons. Calling her by the now familiar appellation 'my love', even after all her coolness and wretched behaviour, the first phrase compares her beauty to that of Tirzah ('beautiful' is the first word of the sentence, in the place of emphasis: 'Beautiful you (are), O my love').

Why Tirzah? Tirzah was a city in Samaria whose name means pleasantness, sweetness, delight, agreeable. For some time it was the residence of one of the ancient kings of Canaan (see Josh. 12:24) and then some of the kings of Israel. It continued a chief royal city until in Omri's reign the city of Samaria itself became the capital of the northern kingdom, after the division into north and south (see 1 Kgs. 16). A location suggested for Tirzah is Tell El-Farah, some seven miles north-east of Shechem on the main road towards Beth-Shean. This was evidently a most beautiful site, with gardens, groves and an abundant water supply.

We may take the poetic reference here as indicative of the spiritual beauty of the church of Christ, and (more particularly) her beauty to Christ, in his eyes: her holiness, her graces, her ornaments of Christ-likeness, her continual delightfulness to him. In other words, those very things which he has touched upon already in the Song.

He continues: **lovely as Jerusalem**, the second of these three expressions of affection. Lovely is also comely, and the description carries the sense of lovely to look upon, lovely to be with, lovely to speak with. Why Jerusalem? If Tirzah was striking, Jerusalem was even more so. At first it was a stronghold of the Jebusites, then became the metropolis of all Israel and centre of the Davidic-Solomonic empire, and then the residence of the kings of Judah after the division of the kingdom. Its name means city or foundation of peace.

In a special sense Jerusalem was seen as the place where God dwelt (his earthly dwelling-place), where he was worshipped and glorified; 'the city of our God, ... his holy mountain, beautiful in elevation, the joy of the whole earth', 'the city of the great King', 'God is in her palaces', 'the city of the LORD of hosts, the city of our God' (Ps. 48); the place to which the tribes went up 'to give thanks to the name of the LORD', where 'thrones are set ... for judgment', 'the house of the LORD our God' (Ps. 122); 'the perfection of beauty' (Lam. 2:15). 'Glorious things are spoken of you, O city of God!' (Ps. 87:3).

We may take this poetic reference as speaking of the spiritual worship of the church of Christ, and the glory which that brings to him. 'The LORD loves the gates of Zion' (Ps. 87:2), and the Lord Jesus Christ takes great pleasure in the sacrifices of praise and worship that are rendered to him by his people. In and by his church the Lord is reverenced and adored, his name is exalted, his word is proclaimed, his sacraments are administered and his discipline is exercised.

The third expression of affection follows: **awesome as an army with banners!** The word 'army' (NIV, troops) is understood, rather than actually being in the original, which reads 'as bannered'. With NKJV's 'awesome', compare 'terrible' (AV) and 'majestic' (NIV). 'Imposing' and 'commanding' have also been offered as translations. The picture intended is that of an army marching forth with banners unfurled, confident of victory, afraid of no man. The church of Christ is not only beautiful and lovely, but awesome as well. This is very significant, and not how the church is usually thought of, even by those who by grace belong to her.

Here are believers in their true colours as 'kings and priests' to God (Rev. 1:6); radically separate from the world and wholly consecrated to Christ and filled with his Spirit (2 Cor. 6:16–7:1; Eph. 5:18); walking in good order and paying careful attention to discipline throughout the ranks (1 Thess. 5:12-15; Heb. 13:7,17); 'endeavouring to keep the unity of the Spirit in the bond of peace' (Eph. 4:3); standing 'fast in one spirit, with one mind striving together for the faith of the gospel, and not in any way terrified by (her) adversaries' (Phil. 1:27-28); 'strong in the Lord and in the power of his might', having 'put on the whole armour of God' and so 'able to stand against the wiles of the devil' (Eph. 6:10-11); the owners and exercisers of faith, 'the victory that has overcome the world' (1 John 5:4); adorning 'the doctrine of our God and Saviour in all things' (Tit. 2:10); and doing 'all to the glory of God' (1 Cor. 10:31).

The poetic reference this time is to the spiritual potency of the church of Christ. An army with banners, or a bannered army, is a distinctive company of people (in this case, chosen by God in his Son before the foundation of the world, purchased by grace, born of the Spirit) who wage a continual warfare in the world under their great king and head, the Lord Jesus Christ, the 'Commander of the army of the LORD' (Josh. 5:14). Her glorious bridegroom is her mighty ruler, to whom she is captive and obedient as a people made willing in the day of his power (compare Ps. 110:3, AV). However much the true church of Christ is mocked, disregarded or despised, she ought (at her best) to provoke awe, amazement, terror, respect and fear – in the devil and in the heart of all her king's enemies.

This recalls such Scriptures as Joshua 2:11 and Deuteronomy 2:25 (and compare also Deut. 11:25). In the former, the testimony of the Lord's enemies was 'the terror of you has fallen on us (i.e. the enemies), and ... all the inhabitants of the land are fainthearted because of you (i.e. God's people)'; their hearts melted and all their courage departed in the face of reports of God's mighty works for and presence among his people. In the latter, the Lord encourages his people with these words: 'This day I will begin to put the dread and fear of you upon the nations under the whole heaven, who shall hear the report of you, and shall tremble and be in anguish because of you.' Consider also 2 Corinthians 10:3-6.

There is no contradiction, of course, in these several characteristics being put together as they are here. Beauty, loveliness, majesty, dignity, awesomeness and grace are all very fitting terms to be applied to the bride of Christ, for they belong so very appropriately first of all to her bridegroom, and she bears his likeness. Moreover, the fairer and more beautiful his church is in Christ's eyes, the more awesome and terrible will she be in the eyes of her adversaries.

Completely in keeping with his view of his bride and the effect she has upon him, Christ proceeds: **Turn your eyes away from me, for they have overcome me** (6:5). One look from his bride has completely overwhelmed the bridegroom! The verb 'overcome' can be 'disturbed', signifying a state of holy agitation. He is deeply affected and moved. (In a different setting, namely one of great grief and sorrow, note the strong verbs used to describe Christ's emotions at the grave of his friend Lazarus, John 11:33-38). Her eyes (her love, her faith, everything about her as his) ravished him. What a graciously condescending way of speaking. Compare 4:9. He does not mean to imply that the church should cease to look to him. Rather, in the context here (chapter 6, following on from the varied experiences of chapter 5), the Lord Jesus is testifying to the Shulamite that he has overlooked (pardoned, forgiven) all her sins and neglects, and loves her as earnestly, passionately and desiringly as ever. She need have no fear on that count. Here is Psalm 45 yet again: 'So the King will greatly desire your beauty; because he is your Lord, worship him' (45:11).

Immediately he underscores this in verses 5b-7 with a rich expression of love and delight towards his bride which is virtually identical with what he said in parts of 4:1-3. **Your hair is like a flock of goats, going down from Gilead:** compare 4:1b. **Your teeth are like a flock of sheep which have come up from the washing; every one bears twins, and none is barren among them** (6:6): compare 4:2. **Like a piece of pomegranate are your temples behind your veil** (6:7): compare 4:3b. See the comments in those places. The only slight differences are 'Gilead' for 'Mount Gilead' and (strictly) 'ewes' for 'sheep' (which was understood in 4:2).

Not for one moment is this needless repetition. The language of mutual love often repeats itself. This is a great part of its attractiveness and reflects the constancy and changelessness of true love. There is no truer love than that of the Lord Jesus Christ for his church, and for each believer who comprises his church. So there is every reason to be thankful that he says the same things again and again. He would 'stir us up by way of reminder' (2 Pet. 3:1) of his love in all its depth and height, its breadth and length, its purity and intensity. For him it 'is not tedious' to do so, and for us 'it is safe' (Phil. 3:1). His kindness and affection to his bride after his withdrawings remains just as before. For even his withdrawings are in love, not from lack or diminishing of love.

How important it is for believers to grasp this, for after we have sinned and grieved the Lord we would easily begin to imagine that he will not have the same love to us as formerly, that our interest in him may not be so secure as before, and that his attitude towards us will have changed completely, or may at least be in doubt. These are the very things that the devil, the enemy of our souls, would have us think. Christ, however, is the free forgiver and the full forgetter of his people's failures, as the royal welcome accorded here to his returning and repenting bride assures us. At such times he would confirm and strengthen our faith and assure us that to him we are as beautiful as ever; he would recall to us our true character and calling as his holy bride, that we should be all the more careful to walk consistently in the light of it; and he would remind us that he is 'Jesus Christ ... the same yesterday, today, and for ever' (Heb. 13:8), and that the divine covenant made with us is 'an everlasting covenant, ordered in all things and secure' (2 Sam. 23:5).

6:8-10. The only one

In that choice expression she used in 5:10, the bride declared the absolute uniqueness of her beloved: 'chief among ten thousand'. He stands out both from and above all others. He is beyond compare. Now it is the bridegroom's turn to return the compliment and to express a similar conviction regarding his bride. **There are sixty queens and eighty concubines, and virgins without number** (6:8).

The word picture here is of a vast collection of women. They are described variously as queens (wives of kings – though evidently the word is used only here and of Esther, Vashti and the Queen of Sheba, not of the wives of either the Israelite or Judean kings), concubines (a sort of second rank of wives in polygamous society, who possessed such privileges and protections as distinguished them from those women who were neither wives nor concubines), and virgins (a straightforward denoting of unmarried women). Put them all together, line them all up in a row, speak of all their individual or collective attractions, and they come nowhere near the Shulamite. She stands out and she stands alone. She is beyond compare.

It remains something of an open question as to whether there is any particular significance in the increasing numbers of the women (going up in the order 60, 80, without number) and the decreasing rank (starting at the top with queens, and then proceeding downwards, so to speak, through concubines to virgins). Any significance there is, is likely to be just this: there are many of 'them' but only one of 'her'. So to that extent the uniqueness of the bride is emphasised all the more. Historically it is the case, regrettably, that in due time when Solomon's heart turned away from the Lord, 'he had seven hundred wives, princesses, and three hundred concubines' (1 Kgs. 11:3). There is no need, however, to build such a reference in to the present passage.

The next verse sees a development of this theme of the bride's uniqueness. **My dove, my perfect one, is the only one** (6:9), is how the bridegroom continues. This, it must be remembered, is Christ speaking of his church. Nor is it the first time in the Song that he has spoken in this way. On 'dove', see 1:15, 2:14, 4:1. On the bride's perfection (AV has 'undefiled' here), compare

4:7. The beauty of holiness is the beauty of all beauties. The phrase 'the only one' (NIV, unique) is interesting. It captures the sense of 'the one and only', and underscores the fact that she cannot be compared with any other women, however grand or beautiful any other women might be. All others just pale into significance, blend into the background, disappear completely from view when compared with this one. This, of course, is how every true husband ought to view his wife, having no eyes at all for any other women, and being very much a 'one-woman-man'. In such a way Christ looks upon his church, his bride. The word 'one' is actually the first word of the verse. So a literal rendering would be: 'One, she, my dove, my perfect'. Look also at the repeated 'my'. The matter could not be made any plainer. Christ has no other love. Kings have their queens, their concubines, and their virgins. Christ has his one bride, and she is all his desire, she is everything to him, she has the assurance of his complete and undivided love.

This sentence in verse 9 is not yet complete, however. It continues: **the only one of her mother, the favourite of the one who bore her.** Still there is the emphasis upon uniqueness: 'the only one', 'the favourite/choice one'. The meaning of Christ's words here is this: his bride is as dear and precious to him as is an only child to her mother, the choicest offspring of the womb, the darling of the heart. Compare a similar figure of speech in Proverbs 4:3: 'When I was my father's son, tender and the only one in the sight of my mother.' Although the Lord Jesus Christ possesses all the kingdoms of the world, and the glory of them, they are all as nothing to him compared with his church, his beloved one. His 'little flock' (Luke 12:32) is more beautiful and precious in his eyes than all the rest of mankind put together, whatever may be their striking features, for he has put his own beauty and comeliness upon his own. She has more in herself alone, than others have in themselves all put together. This puts us in mind of Jehovah's words to Israel, 'You only have I known of all the families of the earth' (Amos 3:2).

Then others are brought in as well, who also delight in the bride. **The daughters saw her and called her blessed, the queens and the concubines, and they praised her.** The thought is a familiar one of a bride being the centre of attention, the focus of admiration, as wedding guests (for example) admire her beauty and speak well of her. Here it is the bride of Christ of whom they speak, as her pre-eminence among women is acknowledged without jealousy or rivalry on all sides. The beauty of holiness, the excellence of godliness, the sublime exquisiteness of likeness to Christ cannot be overlooked or disregarded, however much men would sometimes wish it could be. It always stands out. It does so right now, 'in the midst of a crooked and perverse generation' (Phil. 2:15), and it will do so all the more 'when he (Christ, the heavenly bridegroom) comes, in that day, to be glorified in his saints and to be admired among all those who believe' (2 Thess. 1:10).

The Lord Jesus takes particular note and makes careful record of all that men think or speak of his church, and he is delighted when his people are honoured. Yet again we are taken into the realm of Psalm 45, especially here the second part of that psalm, verses 9-17. Compare also Isaiah 60:15, 61:9 and 62:7. In calling her 'blessed', the thought is of counting her happy and most highly favoured – as indeed the church is, being 'blessed ... with every spiritual blessing in the heavenly places in Christ', and having been chosen 'in him before the foundation of the world, that we should be holy and without blame before him in love' (Eph. 1:3-4). Whenever his bride is well spoken of and commended, the Lord Jesus receives much pleasure; equally, whatever is spoken against her, he takes as spoken against himself, and will hold men responsible for their words (Matt. 12:36-37).

Before passing on, it is worth noting two alternative lights that have been shed upon verses 8-9. The first is to regard queens, concubines, virgins, mother and daughters as the same as the dove herself. That is to say, none of these parties are distinct from the bride herself, the church, but all are expressive of the bride, though in diverse ways. It is argued that they represent between them the visible church (beautiful in her external profession and order) and the invisible church (real and true believers, whose graces are particularly commended). Upon this interpretation we are reminded that the church herself is the 'mother' who bears the 'daughters', the mother of all who believe (compare Gal. 4:26: 'but the Jerusalem above is free, which is the mother of us all'). The oneness of the church is also to the fore here, the unity of the true church of Christ (Eph. 4:4-6); just as the church is one garden, with many beds of spices (6:2), so the church is one company, with many different and smaller congregations.

The second takes us into the heavenly court of the King of kings. Surrounding the Lord Jesus Christ there are 'an innumerable company of angels' (Heb. 12:22), as well as archangels, cherubim, seraphim and all the heavenly host, of every rank and grade. Among all these, however, the one to whom belongs all the affection of Christ, the one who is the object of his very special endearment, is his bride, the redeemed of the Lord. In herself, as the bride of Christ, she excels all these created beings, even as the Lord Jesus Christ himself is superior to them all (Heb. 1:4). When actually made like Christ as he is in glory (compare John 17:5 and 1 John 3:2), what surpassing glory will be hers. Yet there will be no jealousy whatsoever among the heavenly beings towards the bride of Christ; rather, she will be praised, honoured and delighted in on every side.

There are a number of vital questions posed in the Song, such as 3:6, 5:9 and 8:5. Here is one now, as the Lord Jesus Christ continues to speak in the most exalted terms of his bride. **Who is she who looks forth as the morning, fair as the moon, clear as the sun, awesome as an army with banners?** (6:10). This is a beautifully poetic portrait of the church. Notice the way in which there is an increase in brightness in the words that are used: first morning (or dawn), then moonlight (which is still visible in the morning sky before the sun has risen), then the full sunlight itself. The word for moon is literally 'the white or milky one', while that for 'sun' is 'the hot one'. The appearance of the Shulamite is like the morning red of the dawn beginning to break through the darkness; the soft whiteness of the moon as it continues to shine in the heavens in the early morning; and the pure brightness of the sun, high in the sky, shining in full splendour at midday.

A possible connection between verses 8-9 and verse 10 should not be overlooked, in this sense: the former verses having ended on the note of the praise of the bride from all sides, it may be that the encomium of verse 10 is illustrative of that praise, and that the bridegroom takes it and makes it his very own. Coming ultimately from him gives it both an authority and a sweetness which it would otherwise lack, for the praises of men are fickle while the praises of Jesus are true and lasting. Moreover, the interrogative form gives added force to his words.

What is the overall intention and application of verse 10? The Lord Jesus Christ continues to speak in praise of his bride, and to express her superiority over all-comers. This he does in detail by way of a four part description. First, his bride 'looks forth as the morning'. There is a natural contrast here with the night which precedes the morning. The night is dark, with the morning comes light. Christ's bride is like the morning: light, fair, welcoming, delightful, joyous. Indeed these are the very things she is to him. Compare Isaiah 58:8: 'Then your light shall break forth like the morning....'; and the reference in Psalm 30:5 to joy coming in the morning after a night of weeping. She is not dark, she does not droop. There is an animation about her, she is full of life, 'the joy of the LORD is (her) strength' (Neh. 8:10).

Secondly, she is 'fair as the moon'. When, at the creation, 'God made two great lights', the moon was described as 'the lesser light to rule the night' and 'to give light on the earth' (Gen. 1:16-17). His bride is like the moon in that she is the light of the world on account of her union with him who is himself the light of the world (John 8:12; Matt. 5:14). She reflects his glory, she shines in a world of darkness. Her light, borrowed from him, is a thing of great beauty both to earth and to heaven.

Thirdly, she is 'clear as the sun'. As the sun is compared with the moon there is an increase in splendour, for the sun is 'the greater light to rule the day' (Gen. 1:16). So there is an ever increasing splendour and beauty attaching to the church of Christ, whose husband is 'the Sun of Righteousness' (Mal. 4:2). This is what is adverted to by the apostle when he writes of believers, 'But we all, with unveiled face, beholding as in a mirror the glory of the Lord, are being transformed into the same image from glory to glory (NIV, with ever-increasing glory), just as by the Spirit of the Lord' (2 Cor. 3:18). Compare Judges 5:31: 'Thus let all your enemies perish, O LORD! But let those who love him be like the sun when it comes out in its full strength'; Daniel 12:3: 'Those who are wise shall shine like the brightness of the firmament, and those who turn many to righteousness like the stars for ever and ever'; and also Matthew 13:43: 'Then the righteous will shine forth as the sun in the kingdom of their Father.'

What this all adds up to is the truth of the progressive sanctification of believers. They have their morning, their moonshine and their eternal sunshine. While justification is a state, a condition, not subject in any way whatsoever to degrees (a person is either justified or not justified), it is not so with sanctification. Having begun a good work in his people, the Lord will complete it, he will bring it to absolute fruition and perfection (Phil. 1:6; compare Prov. 4:18 and Gal. 4:19).

The four-fold portrait is climaxed with words which appeared as recently as verse 4: 'awesome as an army with banners.' (In passing, it is strange that although the wording in Hebrew is identical in 6:4 and 6:10, NIV, having translated it the first time as 'majestic as troops with banners', now changes track completely with the translation 'majestic as the stars in procession'). See the comment on 6:4. It has been observed that the distinction between the two verses is that verse 4 takes its comparison from terrestrial objects and verse 10 from celestial ones.

An army with banners should not provoke derision but terror, not laughter but fear, not disregard but amazement. The true church (as already described here in v.10), who is so fair and beautiful in the estimation of her beloved, should be awesome to the ungodly, and awesome to the devil. There is far too little of such awesomeness attaching to the contemporary church, which much of the time gives a most effeminate appearance. Hers should be a spiritual beauty joined with a fighting posture. It is when the church is preserved in her purity that she secures the victory. A church filled with the love of God, the life of God, the presence of God, the fear of God, the truth of God, the Christ of God, the Spirit of God and (not least) the holiness of God will not fail to have an effect. A church where the banner of the Lord Jesus Christ is held high, and where that blessed combination of truth and grace is found in abundance, will provoke all manner of opposition, yet will be owned of her bridegroom, who has given her the sure promises, 'I will build my church, and the gates of Hades shall not prevail against it', and 'I am with you always, even to the end of the age' (Matt. 16:18b; 28:20).

6:11-13. Nothing between

Verses 11 and 12 present a real difficulty in the matter of who is speaking: is it the bridegroom (Christ) or is it the bride (the believer/church)? NKJV opts for the latter, NIV for the former. Commentators are thoroughly divided among themselves. In one sense the 'problem' only arises because the union between Christ and his church is so complete, and because the communion between them (which had been spoiled temporarily by the bride's indifference and laziness) has now been sweetly restored. There is nothing between them. They are of one mind and heart and soul. So it can be argued that it scarcely matters who is speaking: either one of them could be, for they would very likely use much the same words, as lovers do.

All in all, however, if a judgment has to be made for the purposes of commentary and exposition, we shall come down on the side of it being the bridegroom, the Lord Jesus Christ himself, who says these words. This would follow on well from the previous section, as well as dovetailing smoothly with what follows, and means that the bridegroom is the speaker throughout the whole section 6:4–7:9 (though see the comment on 6:13). It also fits with his statement in 5:1 ('I have come to my garden, my sister, my spouse') and her statement in 6:2 ('My beloved has gone to his garden').

I went down to the garden of nuts (6:11). This is best understood as the beloved explaining what had happened while he had apparently disappeared from view, in withdrawing himself from his bride for a season. He had not done so in anger but in love, and although one believer may feel deserted on occasions in Christian life and experience, the Lord Jesus is still to be found elsewhere in his garden. He has not withdrawn altogether from his church as a whole. He is still here and there in his garden, ever ready to return to the one from whom he has withdrawn, keeping her upon his heart, desiring her company again upon her repenting of her sin and her seeking him and his grace afresh. This is a beautiful testimony to and assurance of the lofty and changeless character of Christ's love for his own, even though he is so often treated shamefully by them.

Why is the church described now as a 'garden of nuts' (NIV, grove of nut-trees)? The garden is already a familiar picture in the Song where the church is concerned (for example, 4:12). The nut in question is probably the walnut, having a hard shell with a sweet kernel. This would be suitable as a figurative expression of the church in its relations both to Christ and the world, going through many tribulations in entering the kingdom of God (Acts 14:22). The life of believers 'is hidden with Christ in God' (Col. 3:3). 'As the mountains surround Jerusalem, so the LORD surrounds his people from this time forth and for ever' (Ps. 125:2). Compare also the request of the Lord Jesus in his prayer to the Father: 'I do not pray that you should take them out of the world, but that you should keep them from the evil one' (John 17:15).

His reason for going to the garden of nuts is next stated: **to see the verdure** (new growth, fruits, blossoms) **of the valley, to see whether the vine had budded and the pomegranates had bloomed**. Christ is ever watchful over his garden, to nourish it, to take care of it, to see 'how it is doing'. Even when he seems to be out of sight, that care never ceases for one moment. Just as any gardener delights in a fruitful, fragrant and productive garden, so the Lord Jesus desires his valley to be covered in verdure, his vines to be in bud and his pomegranates to be in bloom – in other words, to have all spiritual liveliness and grace in evidence among his people. The language chosen in this verse is a reminder that grace is found in different stages (the bud, the blossom and the fruit). All are precious and pleasing to Christ. He loves his disciples to bear much fruit (John 15:8); equally, he delights in the very first buddings of grace, believers in their weak and tender beginnings, whose faith is as a mustard seed (Matt. 17:20).

He observes closely and carefully the spiritual condition and progress of his church, and of every believer in his church, going from one to the other, missing none. Though one soul may not be prospering so well at any given time, another will. Though in one place the condition of his church may leave much to be desired, in another the blessings of God abound. He knows precisely how it is, at all times, in all the many different parts and corners of his garden, in each of the individual 'beds of spices' (6:2), and with every single one of his 'lilies' (6:3). This is underscored even in the word for 'valley', which makes here its only appearance in the Song, though is often found elsewhere in the Old Testament. The picture in view, evidently, is of a deep and narrow valley, which during the rainy season would be like a torrent of water, but outside that time would be a dry channel. Such is very much a picture of the variety of Christian experience and the dryness and revivings of the soul.

Before I was even aware, my soul had made me as the chariots of my noble people (6:12). This is generally reckoned to be the most difficult verse in the whole of the Song to get a grip upon. That being the case, perhaps we should look deliberately for the most straightforward meaning possible. Such, in the context, would be as follows. The Lord Jesus had been spurned. He had gone down to the garden of nuts, and was attending to things there. All of a sudden the repenting, returning and longing bride caught his eye, ravished him (6:5), such that he could not but himself return to her, overcome as he was again with her stateliness and loveliness. This he did speedily, as if he was mounted on the swiftest chariots. The irresistible power of mutual love drew them together once more.

There is a translation matter to be sorted out here. NKJV's 'my noble people' (or 'princely' for 'noble') is fine. The people of Christ are indeed princes, heirs to a heavenly kingdom, with a crown of life, righteousness and glory laid up in store for them, a throne of glory prepared for them to inherit, princely garments to wear, princely fare to eat, and princely company to enjoy. However, the Hebrew can stand as it is, without translation, thus giving 'the chariots of Ammi-Nadib'. This could be the actual proper name of a place or a prince, intimating magnificent chariots belonging to some superior personage, famous for their unusual speed.

Another possibility arises from the fact that 'Ammi' means 'my people' (compare Hos. 2:1), and 'Nadib' is the same word which is rendered 'willing' in Psalm 110:3 (AV), in which case the present verse could be translated 'the chariots of my willing people'. This reading leads some to interpret the chariots as symbolic of the church's faith, love, hope, desires, prayers, longings and expectations – all of these, as it were, calling and drawing Christ back, as chariots sent to fetch him, and never returning empty without him. Even this is all of grace, all of the love which he bears in his heart towards her, and never of his people's merits; for he puts himself in the chariots of his people ('my soul had made/set me'), having first made them a willing people again.

The ultimate point is this: where his people long for him and must have him, there Christ delights to be, and takes no persuading to come. 'Before I was even aware' (NKJV; 'before I realised it', NIV; or, simply, 'I knew not/I did not know') is the gracious and kindly way in which Christ expresses himself. Strictly, nothing can take him by surprise, still less happen unexpectedly; yet he condescends to speak of himself in this most tender and moving way, that his people might be astonished all over again at the greatness of his love, even in the face of all the wrongs we have done to him. He never changes. Even when he has turned away from his own because of our neglect, his passion remains the same, and with him it is the work of a moment to return again, swiftly, as on the fastest chariots. There is a redolence here of Psalm 31:22.

All of this prompts a twofold response in the closing verse of the chapter (which is actually 7:1 in the Hebrew). **Return, return, O Shulamite; return, return, that we may look upon you!** (6:13), is the first part of that response. This is the only verse in the Song where the bride is actually called Shulamite. It has been thought by some to be a proper name (Shulamith), and by others to refer to the place from which she comes (Shunem, Shulem or Salem). It is much more likely to be the feminine form of the name Solomon, indicating 'Solomon's bride' or 'Solomon's lady'. Husband and wife share the same name. It has been urged throughout this commentary that, in the Song, Solomon is a type of Christ, and the Shulamite is a type of the church/believer. Christ's 'new name' is written upon his faithful people (Rev. 3:12). Since the name Solomon means 'peace', the bride's name is indicative of her character as the justified and reconciled one, for whom Christ is her peace (Eph. 2:14), 'having made peace through the blood of his cross' (Col. 1:20). Believers are complete in Christ (Col. 2:10). He being theirs, they possess all things in him (Rom. 8:17).

Who is speaking here? It is most natural to take the words as coming from the Lord Jesus Christ still, although the 'we' may indicate that here he invites the rest of the church (and even the angels in heaven, and perhaps even a reference to the triune Godhead, as in 1:11) to share in his delight in the return of his wandering one. An obvious parallel would be found in Jesus' parable of the lost (prodigal) son, where again the corporate dimension is very much to the fore when the son returned home: 'let us eat and be merry', 'it was right that we should make merry and be glad' (Luke 15:23, 32). Just as a repenting sinner is a sight to see, so is a returning backslider, a reclaimed wanderer, a revived believer. Gather round and look! The verb is a strong one, signifying not 'have a look at' out of mere curiosity but 'see with insight and understanding'; 'verify by examination' has been suggested as capturing its force. There is something remarkable to be seen in the beauty of restored fellowship between Christ and one of his own. Moreover, what gracious passion there is in the fourfold 'return', what holy earnestness, what kind offer of pardon, what wondrous assurance of welcome. Compare John 14:23: 'Jesus answered and said to him, "If anyone loves me, he will keep my word; and my Father will love him, and we will come to him and make our home with him." '

What would you see in the Shulamite – as it were, the dance of the double camp? This second part of the verse is taken by some to be the Shulamite's response, indicating her modesty and humility, even shyness, not wishing to have people staring at her or to be the focus of attention: what is there to see in me? how am I worth looking at? Compare 1:6, and the testimony of Job (Job 42:6), Peter (Luke 5:8) and Paul (who describes himself as 'less than the least of all the saints', Eph.

3:8). It can just as well, if not better, be taken as the words of the bridegroom, still rejoicing in his bride and the fully restored communion between them. He asks the question (what would you see?) and then answers it himself in the reference at the end of the verse, testifying to her grace and to her attractiveness in his sight. Indeed, he who asks it is best able to answer.

As with Ammi-Nadib, the question arises: do we translate the words or leave them as they stand? The Hebrew is Mahanaim, and means 'the double camp/the two camps'. It occurs in the history of Jacob when he was returning home to Esau, shortly before he wrestled with Christ at Peniel. 'So Jacob went on his way, and the angels of God met him. When Jacob saw them, he said, "This is God's camp." And he called the name of that place Mahanaim' (Gen. 32:1-2). Christ seems to be saying: I will tell you what you see in the Shulamite – a noble, majestic and exquisite sight; the one he has already described twice in this chapter as 'awesome as an army with banners'. Just as Jacob was overwhelmed with the sight of the angels of God, so here is an overwhelming sight: a trophy of grace, a redeemed soul, a bride of beauty, a wonder of the world indeed!

Where does the dance come in? Was there such a thing in Solomon's time as the Mahanaim dance or the dance of the two camps/army camps? Was there even something which became known as the angelic dance? Is this a reference to some circular dance, or a dance performed by two companies of dancers, weaving in and out, moving around one another or in opposite directions? All sorts of suggestions have been made and speculations advanced, but the fact is we do not know. It is striking that Mahanaim appears here with the article. Certainly it is the case in the Old Testament that joy and dancing are sometimes found together (such as in Exod. 15:20-21; 1 Sam. 18:6-7; 2 Sam. 6:14-15; and compare Ecc. 3:4).

All in all, it would seem that the memorable Genesis experience given to Jacob, and the mysterious mention of the dance are probably to be combined in this way: the Lord Jesus has as much pleasure in viewing his beloved bride, newly restored to him in love and devotion and faithfulness, as any number of people could have if permitted to gaze upon the hosts of heavenly angels in choreographed array celebrating the triumphs of grace and glory – a festive company of rejoicing hosts! Indeed his pleasure far exceeds all others' pleasures. A possible reference to Job 38:7 should not be overlooked: 'when the morning stars sang together, and all the sons of God shouted for joy.'

Chapter 7

THE PRINCE'S DAUGHTER

There is no stark change of mood or emphasis as the new chapter opens. Both bridegroom and bride speak in the course of it, and their mutual affection and mutual desire for one another continue to be very much in evidence. Our 7:1-13 is 7:2-14 in the Hebrew text, the Hebrew's 7:1 being our 6:13.

7:1-5. The bridegroom continues

Having begun his present contribution in 6:4, the bridegroom pursues his warm words to the Shulamite throughout this first section of chapter 7, not least by way of further encouragement to her, and assurance that notwithstanding her previous indifference towards him, his love to her has not changed at all. It is reminiscent of earlier portions of the Song in its delicate handling of the bride's beauty, spiritual truths being set forth in feminine physical pictures (compare 4:1-5, 6:5-7). The bride declared the bridegroom's beauty in a similar manner, using manly figures, in 5:10-16. In that latter passage the description began with the head and worked down; here things begin with the feet and work up. In each case ten features are mentioned. As the Shulamite's beauty (indeed, her perfection) is described in this way, the contrast cannot be missed with what she was by nature: 'from the sole of the foot even to the head, there is no soundness in it, but wounds and bruises and putrefying sores' (Isa. 1:6). How very wide apart are nature and grace!

It is important to remember again, as with similar passages earlier in the Song, that these portions descriptive of beauty are one whole, which is made up of various different parts. Consequently, a balance must continue to be maintained between understanding the significance of the parts while never losing

168

sight of the thrust of the whole. It is possible to end up with an interpretation which is too detailed or fanciful, as well as one which is not detailed enough and misses things which are intended for spiritual profit.

How beautiful are your feet in sandals, O prince's daughter! The curves of your thighs are like jewels, the work of the hands of a skilful workman (7:1). The bride's beauty has just been described in terms of a dance (6:13), and the swirl of the dance may be behind these words also: the gracious footwork of the dancer, and her shapely and attractive thighs in the dance, or the free movements of the thigh joints. The translation 'steps/footsteps' has been suggested for 'feet', which would add to this possibility. Certainly movement is implied in the words used. This is the only occurrence in the plural of 'jewels'. In the singular it refers to an ornament consisting of gold, silver or precious stones; here in the plural it is used because the lively movements of the thighs are being compared to the movings to and fro of a (pendulumed?) ornament. Sandalled feet were considered in the east to be an attractive and fashionable feature for both male and female wear, and would sometimes be very costly.

Of greater significance is the first reference in the Song to the bride (and so to the Christian) as a prince's daughter. The Lord Jesus Christ delights to discover new names and titles for his bride, reminding her thereby of the largeness and freshness of his love towards her. The word for 'prince' speaks of noble disposition as well as nobility of birth and rank, and so this ties in with a theme which is repeated at different points in Scripture, namely the royal birth, character and station of those who are in Christ. They are chosen from eternity (Eph. 1:4), born from above (John 3:3), redeemed with precious blood (1 Pet. 1:18-19), married to Christ (Rom. 7:4), 'heirs of God and joint heirs with Christ' (Rom. 8:17) and sons and daughters of the Lord Almighty (2 Cor. 6:18).

As well as Psalm 45 (to which attention has been drawn many

times already in this commentary), this is found, for example, in the record of God's grace to sinners in Psalm 113:7-8 ('He raises the poor out of the dust, and lifts the needy out of the rubbish heap, that he may seat him with princes – with the princes of his people'), and in the very similar language used in Hannah's prayer (see 1 Sam. 2:8, not least the phrase 'to set them among princes and make them inherit the throne of glory'). A classic statement of these matters is enshrined in such verses as 1 Peter 2:9-10 and Revelation 1:6.

It is also noteworthy that this beauty, gracefulness and sheer strikingness of the bride is ascribed to 'the work of the hands of a skilful workman'. Hers is not a painted-up, do-it-yourself sort of beauty. There has been a hand at work which is not her own. The beauty of holiness is the work of grace, the handiwork of the Spirit who glorifies Christ (John 16:14). This is always a highly practical matter, feet and sandals being suggestive of the believer's daily walk and life as God's workmanship (see Eph. 2:8-10 and Tit. 3:4-8). To walk barefooted is mentioned in Scripture as a mark of shame (Isa. 20:4). The Christian, in contrast, is well-shod, and is to lead a well-ordered and well-disciplined life, doing all to the glory of God (1 Cor. 10:31).

Your navel is a rounded goblet which lacks no blended beverage (7:2). Things move from the feet, via the thighs, to the navel. The picture is of a goblet (or rounded bowl or basin) filled with wine. The phrase NKJV translates 'blended beverage' only occurs here in the Old Testament. AV has liquor, NIV has blended wine. Other possibilities are mixed wine, mingled wine, or spiced wine. What is probably in view is wine either diluted with water or strengthened with spices and honey. The important thing, however, is not the precise identity of the drink involved, but rather the view of his bride which the Lord Jesus Christ is entertaining here.

It is worth connecting the second part of the verse with the first, before interpreting them. **Your waist** (AV, belly) **is a heap of wheat set about with lilies**. Some have seen here a reference to the Shulamite's dress, on the basis of the custom of placing heaps of wheat in rows when it was harvest time, and then decorating them with flowers from the fields. The two figures taken together (the navel and the waist) seem to convey the thought of spiritual health, graces in vigorous exercise, liveliness of soul, fruitfulness.

Letting Scripture be its own interpreter, a reference to the book of Proverbs is appropriate. Speaking of fearing the Lord, 'it will be health to your flesh, and strength to your bones' (Prov. 3:8). The word for flesh is literally navel, and that for strength is literally drink or refreshment. It may be wondered, in purely physical terms, what is so special about the navel. Significantly, it is very much at the centre of the body (both of newborn infants, and, in terms of length of body, of adults as well). When seen in the context of the fear of the Lord, however, things become clearer, for 'the fear of the LORD is the beginning of knowledge' and 'of wisdom' (Prov. 1:7; 9:10), and it is the true believer's earnest desire to continue 'in the fear of the LORD all day' (Prov. 23:17). This is the way of blessedness: 'Behold, thus shall the man be blessed who fears the LORD' (Ps. 128:4). This is a characteristic of great beauty and appeal, as the divine bridegroom contemplates his bride: not a sowing to the flesh, but a sowing to the Spirit (Gal. 6:8), not a making provision for the flesh but a putting on the Lord Jesus Christ (Rom. 13:14), not a drinking of the waters of the earth that fail but a drinking of the living water which Christ himself gives (John 4:13-14).

What of the waist? The same word is translated 'inmost body' in Proverbs 18:8, and 'womb' in Job 15:35. The picture is suggestive of fruitfulness as opposed to barrenness, the church giving birth to believers in the sense of the choice gospel promise, 'And of Zion it will be said, "This one and that one were born in her" ' (Ps. 87:5; compare also Ps. 87:6 and Isa. 44:1-5). In this respect, the church of the Lord Jesus Christ is not only a beautiful bride but a fruitful mother as well, and this is a great delight to her husband. The poetic way in which her waist is likened to 'a heap of wheat set about with lilies' combines the thoughts of beauty, fruitfulness, health and vigour all into one. There is also a sense of what Jesus speaks of in John 7:38: 'He who believes in me, out of his heart (AV, belly; NIV, from within him) will flow rivers of living water.'

These poetic pictures in the Song, let it be underscored, are never given so that we may go away and draw them; they are word pictures only, for spiritual purposes. Note how verse 1 (the believer's outward walk) and verse 2 (the believer's inward condition) are so well balanced, as they need to be for genuine spiritual health. Inward soundness of heart and outward holiness of life are both vitally important, and each has its own place in Christ's commendation of his people. He observes them both and takes pleasure in them both. Moreover, he desires with a positive desire to see these things; the words 'which lacks no blended beverage' may evidently be rendered along the lines of 'let it not be wanting/may there be no lack'.

Nor are these images left behind in the next verse. **Your two breasts are like two fawns, twins of a gazelle** (7:3). This verse is a repeat of 4:5, with the omission this time of 'which feeds among the lilies', the figure of the lilies having just been used. See the comment on that verse. This is no vain or pointless repetition, however. The fawn-like breasts follow on very suitably from the goblet of wine and the wheat/lilies as figures of beauty, fruitfulness and nourishment. In connection with the nourishment: just as it was observed earlier that the church is likened to a fruitful mother (the born in Zion theme), so it is in the church, by means of the public means of grace, that the head and bridegroom of the church has made rich provision for his people's spiritual growth and development along the pilgrim path to glory and to himself. A lack of breasts will be drawn attention to in 8:8, as a sorry condition. At several places in Scripture wives are commended for their bearing, nourishing and bringing up of their children, which is regarded as a blessing from the Lord and greatly engages and attracts their husbands to them. Compare (for the principle) Psalm 128:3, and (as examples) Genesis 29:34 and Luke 1:24-25.

Your neck is like an ivory tower (7:4). Next comes the neck, which will be followed in this same verse by the eyes and nose. The Shulamite's neck was first mentioned in 1:10 as decorated 'with chains of gold', and was then likened in 4:4 to 'the tower of David'. See on those verses. Now it is compared to a tower of ivory. Both here and in 4:4 ornamental towers are indicated. Just as ivory is white, costly and precious, so are believers who are joined to Christ their head (white, because washed clean from their sins, Isa. 1:18; costly, because redeemed 'with the precious blood of Christ', 1 Pet. 1:19; and precious, because that is the very manner in which the God of all grace regards his covenant people whom he has given to Christ, Isa. 43:3-4, and to whom he gives the grace gift of 'precious faith', 2 Pet. 1:1, 'more precious than gold', 1 Pet. 1:7).

The bridegroom continues: **your eyes like the pools in Heshbon by the gate of Bath Rabbim.** This place was the ancient Amorite capital of Heshbon (Num. 21:25-26) which had come to belong to Solomon. It enjoyed a richly watered situation, and on each side of its gate were deep pools (or fish-pools). Just as ancient cities would be built near a water supply, so the city gate would be convenient for going to draw the water from wells established for that purpose (compare 2 Sam. 23:15; also Gen. 24:11 and John 4:5-7). These pools in Heshbon put the Lord Jesus in mind of his bride's eyes: large, clear, deep, attractive, desirable. Her eyes have already featured in 1:15, 4:1, 9 and 6:5. The meeting of the eyes is very much the language of true love.

In the course of his prophecy, Jeremiah utters this poignant cry: 'Oh, that my head were waters, and my eyes a fountain of tears, that I might weep day and night for the slain of the daughter of my people!' (Jer. 9:1). It may be that this feature of his bride was also in the bridegroom's mind here – her eyes weeping for sin, mourning before the Lord over her own sins and those of his people. Those who mourn in Zion, the Lord Jesus delights to console, for he is the mourners' comforter and brings 'the oil of joy for mourning, the garment of praise for the spirit of heaviness' (Isa. 61:2-3).

It is also striking that the particular pools chosen by the Lord Jesus Christ are those 'by the gate of Bath Rabbim'. Bath Rabbim, not mentioned anywhere else in the Old Testament, means 'daughter of many/a multitude'. There would be a marked and visible contrast between the bustling thoroughfare in and out of the city gate, and the calm and serene pools on either side of it. This serves to enforce the contrast, insisted upon all through the Bible, between the church and the world, and that the believer/church must 'not be conformed to this world, but be transformed by the renewing of your mind, that you may prove what is that good and acceptable and perfect will of God' (Rom. 12:2). The world is blind and sits in darkness, whereas the believer has been given spiritual sight, understanding and discernment, and dwells in marvellous light (2 Cor. 4:6; Eph. 1:17-18; 1 Pet. 2:9).

Your nose is like the tower of Lebanon which looks towards (literally, peering toward the face of) **Damascus**, the desert city and capital of Syria (Isa. 7:8), on the eastern side of the Lebanon mountain range, captured by David but free again under Solomon (see 2 Sam. 8:6 and 1 Kgs. 11:23-25). This might give the impression of being some nose; yet in some cultures a prominent nose is regarded as an attractive feature, so this reference should not be considered strange. Presumably some famous watchtower is indicated. The features intended here would be courage, bravery, watchfulness and fortitude, all very important characteristics of the true believer and the true church, and a vital constituent part of true spiritual beauty. With this, compare the references in 6:4, 10, 'awesome as an army with banners.' Damascus can stand for the enemies of the church, the church being pictured here as being on guard, maintaining a careful vigilance, not going to sleep in the face of constant dangers and threats of danger to her doctrine, her testimony and even her very life.

This recalls the spirit of God's people in Nehemiah's day when the people were rebuilding the wall of Jerusalem after the return from exile in Babylon. Nehemiah records that 'we made our prayer to our God and because of them (the enemy) we set a watch against them day and night'; and he so arranged things that 'half of my servants worked at construction, while the other half held the spears, the shields, the bows and wore armour', and 'those who built on the wall, and those who carried burdens, loaded themselves so that with one hand they worked at construction, and with the other held a weapon' (Neh. 4:9, 16-17). The whole of the chapter is relevant here.

There is a natural progression from the nose/Lebanon (v.4) to the head/Carmel (v.5) which cannot be caught in any English translation. **Your head crowns you like Mount Carmel, and the hair of your head is like purple** (7:5). Literally the opening of the verse reads 'your head on you (as/like) Carmel'. The head stands for the crown, the crowning glory or feature. Of this, Carmel, a high mountain near the sea, appearing to rule the land and sea at its feet, is a suitable figure. Note important references to Carmel in 1 Kings 18 (Elijah's contest with the prophets of Baal) and Amos 9:3. The name itself means 'fruitful place'. Isaiah refers to 'the excellence of Carmel and Sharon' (Isa. 35:2). Just as in verse 4 the church was pictured keeping a careful, watchful and fearless eye upon her enemies, so now the mention of the head recalls Psalm 27:6, where David testifies to God's praise, 'And now my head shall be lifted up above my enemies all around me.' Holy boldness and holy protection are here together, and both come from the Lord himself.

The reference to the Shulamite's hair being 'like purple' is another implicit assurance of the royal status of believers. Purple is regarded very much as a royal colour, and was used for expressing what was considered most beautiful in colour. There is no contradiction here with the earlier mentions of her hair being black (the flocks of goats, 4:1 and 6:5: see on those verses). While purple and black are not the same, it has been suggested that what is intended is that the black hair shines and shimmers with a purple lustre. Again, however, it is the meaning of the purple that counts, and that, as just stated, is the bride's royalty. Believers are married to the King of kings. The church is the bride of Christ. That is basic to the whole of the Song. For some reason NIV translates 'like royal tapestry' for 'like purple'; this brings out the emphasis on royalty, but there is nothing in the Hebrew for 'tapestry'.

The description in this verse closes with the words, **The king is held captive by its tresses.** Evidently the root meaning of 'tresses' is to run or to flow, giving a picture of her hair cascading down in flowing ringlets like rippling water. This appears exceedingly beautiful in her bridegroom's eyes; he is captivated by it. The thought of a loved one held fast in the long hair of the woman he loves is a familiar theme in Eastern poetry. One translation of the present phrase that has been offered is 'a king fettered by locks'. AV's 'in the galleries' appears to proceed from a different word from the same root, but does not give appropriate sense (compare 'rafters', 1:17). The analogy of Scripture gives the reminder that a woman's long hair 'is a glory to her; for her hair is given to her for a covering' (1 Cor. 11:15). The spiritual glory of the bride of Christ is her likeness to him; not 'that outward adorning of arranging the hair, of wearing gold, or of putting on fine apparel; but ... the hidden person of the heart, with the incorruptible ornament of a gentle and quiet spirit, which is very precious in the sight of God' (1 Pet. 3:3-4).

His church exerts a most attractive power in the Lord Jesus Christ's estimation. He delights in the loveliness and preciousness of grace to be seen in her. He does not look and immediately look away; his gaze is fixed upon her, he is overcome by her (recall 6:5). Psalm 45 comes to the fore yet again (especially the emphasis in 45:11 upon the king greatly desiring her beauty). His bride's holiness has a potent influence both on attaining and enjoying the richest visits and manifestations of her heavenly bridegroom. A cross-reference to Zephaniah 3:17 would not be out of place either, with its expression of the tender complacency of the divine love: 'He will rejoice over you with gladness, he will quiet you in his love, he will rejoice over you with singing.' It is a matter of continual amazement to believers that the Lord Jesus feels this way; that what captivates his attention and his affection is not the glory of the angels, the cherubim and seraphim, or the rest of the heavenly host, but his own people. Well has it been observed that Christ's bride is, to him, the fairest sight in heaven or on earth, next to his Father.

7:6-9a. Precious moments
Having taken great pleasure in detailing some of the features of beauty belonging to his bride, and having owned himself to be utterly captivated, the Lord Jesus Christ now utters what is really a summary of the way he feels about her, before then launching off again into a fresh expression of holy delight and desire. This is the bridegroom's final major contribution in the Song, only 8:13 remaining.

How fair and how pleasant you are, O love, with your delights! (7:6). This is by now very familiar Song language. The words 'fair' and 'pleasant' have both occurred already, on both sides. They combine both outward physical attractiveness and inward spiritual loveliness. Their use here is to declare once more how highly Christ regards his bride's beauty, and never wearies of telling her. It is, of course, his own beauty that he has put upon her, for the believer/church is clothed with Christ and has put on Christ (compare Isa. 61:10 and Rom. 13:14). To him, she is all beautiful (4:7). So is he to her (1:16). This love that binds the two as one is the most wonderful working of divine grace.

The phrase 'with (or, in) your delights' (or we may render the verse 'how fair/beautiful and how pleasant are you in delights, O love!') is striking. It recalls how the Lord names his people Hephzibah, 'for the LORD delights in you', followed swiftly by

177

'and as the bridegroom rejoices over the bride, so shall your God rejoice over you' (Isa. 62:4-5).

If it be enquired why the Lord Jesus takes such delight in his bride, or what her 'delights' are to him, the answer may be given: that she has been given to him by the Father in the eternal covenant of grace; that she has become his bride bought by his own blood (and what bride ought not to be the delight of her husband's heart and eyes, especially such a costly one as she is?); that the Holy Spirit has made his abode in her (not least in order to form Christ's own image there); that she glorifies him in the world and adorns 'the doctrine of God our Saviour in all things' (Tit. 2:10); and that she is being prepared for that blessed day when she will behold and share his glory in heavenly places for ever. For the bride's part, how careful should every Christian and every congregation be to ensure that they really are being a true delight to Christ and are not (as was discovered earlier in the Song) grieving him and causing him to withdraw. How remarkable it is that he calls her 'love', attesting thereby that not only is she lovely, but love itself.

There is a particular force accompanying the repeated 'how': 'how fair' and 'how pleasant'. As if to say, exactly how fair and how pleasant you are cannot be told, cannot be expressed. The sense being conveyed is of the Lord Jesus Christ's bride being incomparably beautiful, beyond all ordinary thought or expression.

This stature of yours is like a palm tree (7:7). The next picture used of the Shulamite is a palm tree. This is new to the Song. The tree intended here will be the date palm, a tall and slender tree, noteworthy for both its height and its branches, and ideally symbolising stateliness, gracefulness and elegance. In the former verses of this chapter, the Lord Jesus has taken a piece-by-piece view of his bride. Now, as he takes what might be called a full-length look at her, this is how she appears to him. This Hebrew word for palm tree is also used as a woman's name in the Old Testament (Tamar: Gen. 38:6, 2 Sam. 13:1 and

14:27 are examples). Branches of palm were used in the joyful feast of Tabernacles (Lev. 23:40) and by the multitudes celebrating the entry of the Lord Jesus Christ into Jerusalem (John 12:12-13). They are also spoken of as being in the hands of the praising company of the elect in glory, 'standing before the throne and before the Lamb, clothed with white robes, with palm branches in their hands' (Rev. 7:9).

The picture of the palm tree is spiritually very suggestive when applied to the believer/church. Here is the Christian's uprightness, balance, proportion, steady growth and ultimate glorious victory (the palm being an emblem of victory). Here is what the apostle Paul testifies to: 'but one thing I do, forgetting those things which are behind and reaching forward to those things which are ahead, I press towards the goal for the prize of the upward call of God in Christ Jesus' (Phil. 3:13-14). Here is the challenge set out to the whole church, 'till we all come to the unity of the faith and the knowledge of the Son of God, to a perfect man, to the measure of the stature of the fullness of Christ' (Eph. 4:13).

It is used to great effect in Psalm 92:12-14: 'The righteous shall flourish like a palm tree.... Those who are planted in the house of the LORD shall flourish in the courts of our God. They shall still bear fruit in old age; they shall be fresh and flourishing.' Speaking of bearing fruit, that also is in the bridegroom's mind, as he continues: **and your breasts like its clusters.** In 4:5 and 7:3 the bride's breasts were likened to 'two fawns, twins of a gazelle'. Now the figure employed is the clusters of dates upon the palm tree, which have been described as dark-brown or golden-yellow clusters, crowning the summit of the stem and adding greatly to the overall beauty of the palm; a sweet fruit into which, at the appropriate season, the blossoms are ripened. By breasts is no doubt to be understood the love and affection which the bride entertains towards her beloved and with which he is himself entertained. 1:13 of the Song (as well as Proverbs 5:19) are relevant.

The mention of the clusters is highly significant. The more a palm tree is loaded with clusters of dates, the better it is observed to flourish. Similarly, if in the believer's life (and in the corporate life of believers together in the church) there is to be a vigorous spiritual flourishing, then there must be a ripening not only of this or that distinct grace, but of all spiritual graces and virtues together. That is to say, not merely a particular individual fruit, but the whole cluster. When Paul writes of these things, he refers not to the fruits of the Spirit but to 'the fruit of the Spirit' (Gal. 5:22). The individual segments of that fruit are mentioned one by one, for each is important; yet so is the whole. There must be no picking and choosing in the area of spiritual grace.

If it be asked why the church is made fruitful and caused to flourish, Psalm 92:15 has the answer: 'to declare that the LORD is upright; he is my rock, and there is no unrighteousness in him.' In other words, it is for his own praise: 'that they may be called trees of righteousness, the planting of the LORD, that he may be glorified' (Isa. 61:3).

The bridegroom warms even further to his present theme in the next verse. **I said, 'I will go up to the palm tree, I will take hold of its branches'** (7:8). The verb 'go up to' can be 'climb' (with NIV), while 'take hold of' may be 'grasp/seize'. The boughs and branches of palm trees do not grow out of the side or on various levels of the trunk, as is the case with many trees. Rather, they are only at the top. So in order to harvest dates it is necessary first to climb the tree, so the point then of taking hold of the branches is to pick the fruit from under the leaves. To facilitate the climbing process the trunk of the tree has rings in its bark which fulfil the function somewhat of steps. Skilled climbers accomplish this with great speed.

What does the Lord Jesus Christ intend by speaking in this way? It is the language of embrace, of the enjoyment of love, of the bridegroom being welcomed by the bride and finding rich delight and refreshment in her company and affection. His 'I said' is his promise and assurance. He does everything deliberately. What Christ has said he will do, first marrying his bride and then relishing her. She is his choice. This, like everything to do with the divine everlasting love, goes back before the foundation of the world, when, with the Father, the Son's 'delight was with the sons of men' (Prov. 8:31), and when Christ engaged to be the redeemer of his people. Compare John 17:24 for what might be termed 'the other end' of this eternal love for and treasuring of his own. Then, once and for all, the Lord Jesus Christ 'shall see the travail of his soul, and be satisfied' (Isa. 53:11). In the meantime, Christ manifests himself to his bride in ways and degrees that he appoints, and never removes his love from her or leaves her without some sense of that love, 'for he who promised is faithful' (Heb. 10:23).

Let now your breasts be like clusters of the vine, is how the bridegroom continues. From clusters of dates from the palm tree the picture now transfers without fuss to clusters of grapes from the vine. As well as resembling the palm tree, the believer/church also resembles the vine. Indeed the vine and the vineyard is a richly worked piece of biblical imagery. Two leading examples are: 'You have brought a vine out of Egypt ... Look down from heaven and see, and visit this vine' (Ps. 80:8, 14); and, 'For the vineyard of the LORD of hosts is the house of Israel, and the men of Judah are his pleasant plant' (Isa. 5:7).

The Lord Jesus' own claim in John 15:5 needs mentioning as well, for it is a key statement of his people's union with himself, leading to communion. 'I am the vine, you are the branches. He who abides in me, and I in him, bears much fruit; for without me you can do nothing.' The 'let now your breasts be like' intimates 'let them be so to me'. It is only as the bride abides in Christ that she is fruitful and brings forth any clusters at all. It is his presence with her and his love for her which causes the bride of Christ to be productive in any way, otherwise she would be as a barren tree or a dry stick. Moreover, these fruits are his own property by right. Coming from him, they belong to him. The John 15 context, just mentioned, suggests that another reason Christ may have for going up to the palm tree and taking hold of its branches is for pruning purposes, so that his people may bear even more fruit (John 15:2). In such pruning, his wise trying and afflicting of his people will always play a vital role (Acts 14:22).

Verse 8 concludes, **the fragrance of your breath like apples**, and runs straight into **and the roof of your mouth like the best wine** (7:9). This is a continuation of the sentence which began 'let now', whereby is expressed a strong wish: let it be so. One after the other, the clusters of the vine, the fragrance of apples and the richest of wines are employed in order to supply a memorable picture of the deep pleasure the fellowship of his dearly loved bride gives to Christ. There is a mutual comfort of love here. It is very striking, in the whole connection of these present verses, that the delight which the heavenly bridegroom finds in his bride is vitally related to his finding in them spiritual graces. This is brought out in verses like Psalm 149:4 and Jeremiah 9:24, which provide a very appetising encouragement to the believer/church in the direction of true holiness and godliness, and to be done completely with all hypocrisy or false love.

A number of familiar Song themes re-emerge here. Fragrance (the features of scent and smell) occurred in 1:3, 13 of Christ and in 1:12 and 4:10ff of the believer/church. Breath links in with the bride's initial longing, right at the beginning, for Christ to kiss her 'with the kisses of his mouth' (1:2), and Christ's words concerning his bride in 4:3 (her lips and mouth). The phrase 'the roof of your mouth' is literally 'palate', in the sense both of the instrument of taste ('sweet to my taste', 2:3) and the mouth itself (as in 5:16). Apples recall the Shulamite's description in 2:3 of her beloved, and her desire concerning him in 2:5. Those apples upon which she had fed had the effect of perfuming her breath, which is yet another way which the Song has of setting forth the truth that all the Christian's graces come alone from Christ. Here is an application of the principle 'what do you have that you did not receive?' (1 Cor. 4:7). Wine also made an early appearance: Christ's love was described as 'better than wine' (1:2), while he returned the identical compliment in 4:10.

The word translated 'breath' may be 'nose' (with AV). The thought is of breathing in and breathing out, and usually in breathing the nostrils are used with the mouth closed. It was a custom evidently to anoint the nostrils with fragrant perfumes. This was reckoned to be healthful and refreshing for the person whose nostrils they were, as well as giving a pleasant smell when the breath was exhaled. Some of these perfumes or ointments gave a smell like apples. In addition, the Lord Jesus makes a particular point of likening the roof of his bride's mouth not just to wine but to 'the best wine'. There is wine and wine, and this is the very best. The wording is a superlative.

There is a reference here, in the joint mention of the breath and the mouth, both to kisses and words, and in each case they are kisses and words of intense love from the bride to her husband. Here are the Christian's desires and longings, confessings and repentings, sighings and groanings, thanks-givings and praises. These are the expressions of the new life, the breathings of the new creature, which are highly pleasurable to Christ (as well as being hugely profitable, quickening and warming in their effect upon fellow believers). All of this makes the figure of the best wine very appropriate. Once more, in tune with the repeated emphasis of the Song, this fragrance breathed by the believer will be in proportion to how he/she walks with Christ and is filled with his Spirit. No 'corrupt communication' is to proceed out of the mouth of a Christian, 'but what is good for necessary edification' (Eph. 4:29); herein is the believer distinguished from the unbeliever, the soul who is united to Christ from the soul who is not. What exquisite refreshment the ardent love, the holy speech and the spiritual mindedness of a true believer is to the heavenly bridegroom.

7:9b-13. Devoted to Christ

There is a phrase in regular use in the English language whereby someone says 'you have taken the words right out of my mouth'. That is exactly what seems to happen now, part way through verse 9. As just observed, Christ has been speaking, and has described the roof of his bride's mouth as being 'like the best wine'. Immediately the bride breaks in, snatches the words from Christ's mouth, and continues herself, finishing his sentence.

The wine goes down smoothly for my beloved, moving gently the lips of sleepers. The unexpected change of speaker may appear to be very abrupt, yet clearly takes place. The word 'beloved' is only used in the Song for the bridegroom, and never for the bride. The word 'smoothly' may be translated 'uprightly' or 'straight' (compare discussion of this word at the end of 1:4), though 'smoothly' gives a better sense here in terms of the swallowing of wine. It is not bitter, it does not catch in the throat, it does not cause any choking, but slips down smoothly and sweetly, and gives refreshment and pleasure.

This interjection from the Shulamite must not be considered impertinent. She is keen to seize the opportunity (for Christ's own glory) to express the reason for the roof of her mouth being like the best wine. It is that all her loving, all her desiring, all her praising, all her serving, all her very being is for her beloved. No one else can come before him, and no one else can take his place. He alone is worthy of her love and has claims to it, and he alone shall possess it. There are strong shades here of Philippians 1:21.

The second part of the sentence is difficult. Literally it is 'moving/flowing/gliding gently/softly (over?) the lips of sleepers/sleeping ones'. The main verb is only known in the Hebrew here. What is meant? One interpretation offered is to imagine the bridegroom falling asleep in the bride's arms, while she remains awake and muses with delight upon the fact that even while he is asleep her love continues to flow out to him, just as wine glides smoothly down. The picture of a sleeping

Christ is very strange, however; and, anyway, he has up to this point been very much awake.

A clue is perhaps to be found back in 2:14, where Christ spoke most tenderly to his bride: 'Let me see your countenance, let me hear your voice; for your voice is sweet, and your countenance is lovely.' As was remarked at the time, the Lord Jesus loves to see and to hear from his bride. The sight and the sound of her are indescribably precious and lovely to him. That being so, the reference in 7:9b may be this: as the bride gives delight to her bridegroom in the manner of which he has been speaking, so this has an effect also upon others. These others are the ones described as 'sleepers', which may refer to dead sinners still asleep in sin, or sleepy Christians who have lost their first love and gone right off the boil where Christ and the things of Christ are concerned.

The love of Christ which the church enjoys, the gospel of Christ which she proclaims, the walk with Christ which she lives, the presence of Christ which she savours – these and many other such things cause sleepy ones to stir, to consider, to be revived, to seek the Lord and begin to receive a taste for spiritual things. Love to Christ leads to love for souls, and love for souls points needy ones to the love of Christ. Out of the abundance of the heart which is filled with the love of Christ, the mouth will speak his praises. Those who never knew Christ before, and had not a single good word to say of him and his grace, now have tongues that are loosed to declare his glory. Those who once rejoiced in him now do so again, speaking in the lowliest terms of themselves and in the highest terms of Christ. All such have either discovered or re-discovered themselves to be the chief of sinners, and Christ to be their glorious Saviour and bridegroom. Even when all of this has been said, however, it still has to be admitted that this remains a most elusive verse.

It is the most natural thing there could be for the bride now to testify in a beautifully simple and straightforward way, **I am my beloved's, and his desire is towards me** (7:10). No words could be more in place from her at this juncture, the more so since she has been silent for some time. They are immediately reminiscent of 2:16 and 6:3. See on those verses. Once again the 'am' and 'is' are supplied in English, thus making the original far tighter and more expressive: 'I my beloved's, and towards me his desire.'

This, however, is no vain repetition. The only other Old Testament occurrences of this word for 'desire' are both in Genesis (3:16, speaking of Eve's desire being for her husband, Adam; 4:7, referring to sin's desire to have Cain). It is a strong word, as these other references imply, and here in the Song it expresses the believer's blessed and assured response to all that the Lord Jesus Christ has been saying throughout the extended section 6:4–7:9. Here is something for every Christian to revel in. Here is 'the full assurance of hope' (Heb. 6:11), and equally 'of faith' (Heb. 10:22) and 'of understanding' (Col. 2:2). This is the language of one who, like John, the beloved disciple, leans upon Christ's bosom (John 13:23). It is a case (as it should be) of none of self and all of Christ, in whom is to be the Christian's and the church's boasting and rejoicing all the day long, now and for all eternity. Ezekiel's wife was 'the desire of (his) eyes' (Ezek. 24:16); how much more so is the church to her husband, Christ. The clearer a believer's grasp of this, the richer the comforts that will abound and the readier the willingness to confess Christ before others.

Underscored here is the vital teaching of Scripture that he who is the Saviour of his people is also their Lord, and no wedge or division must ever be driven between the two. The one who has saved us and made us his bride is (by virtue of that very act) the one who owns us and rules over us. 'You call me Teacher and Lord, and you say well, for so I am,' he has declared (John 13:13). He who is prophet (to teach us) and priest (to die for us and intercede for us) is also king (to govern us).

This verse speaks the language of possession, and very personally so ('his desire is towards me'). This very desire towards his own covenant seed, which existed from eternity and brought the Lord Jesus from heaven to earth the first time, will bring him again a second time, though not then to bear our sins but to bring in the fullness of salvation to all those who are waiting for him (Heb. 9:28). His desire is continually towards his bride, and is never removed from her. He who has set his love upon her, bears with her, sympathises with her, upholds her, undertakes for her, protects her, and in every way imaginable is all in all to her. Her blessedness now and her eternal happiness hereafter are in his gracious and firm hands. The greater the discoveries we are enabled to make of the love of Christ (as here throughout the Song), the greater will be our readiness to serve him and to suffer for him, to seek him and to submit to him. That which brings such spiritual comfort also brings serious spiritual duty, which, in all seasons, is to be rendered willingly, cheerfully, wholeheartedly, exclusively and entirely.

That this is so becomes apparent straightaway, for the verses that follow, to the end of the chapter, recount how the Shulamite is herself impelled to action on the basis of her fresh assurance of Christ's desire towards her. **Come, my beloved, let us go forth to the field; let us lodge in the villages** (7:11). The inviting verb 'come' is a shared word in the Song between the bridegroom and the bride (compare, on his part, 2:10, 13; 4:8). She must be alone with the one who loves her so much, and whom she loves, walking with him, talking with him, confiding in him, listening to him. Four times this 'let us' appears, in two verses. There are times for sharing Christ with others and relishing the fellowship of kindred minds with regard to him. Equally there are times when privacy is required so that the beloved one can be enjoyed alone. His words back in 2:10-14 are a further encouragement in this direction.

Recall the precious experience of the two disciples travelling from Jerusalem to Emmaus towards the evening of the day of the Lord Jesus Christ's resurrection (Luke 24:13-35). Theirs was a most blessed spiritual heartburn. The apostle Paul's constant desire (as much when he was a mature believer as in the earlier days following his conversion) was 'that I may know him (Christ)' (Phil. 3:10). This is something which the true Christian never outgrows, and which is continually in need of perfecting.

For NKJV's 'villages', NIV footnote has 'henna bushes'. Evidently the verbal root has to do with covering or sealing, though a series of different, similarly-spelled nouns exist, related to the root, including both villages and the copper coloured dye which comes from henna plants. The Shulamite's use of 'lodge' as well as 'go forth' intimates the desire for extended time spent with Christ, leisurely fellowship, unmarked by rush or hurry (remember 1:13).

Let us get up early to the vineyards; let us see if the vine has budded, whether the grape blossoms are open, and the pomegranates are in bloom (7:12). This recalls the similar language used by the Lord Jesus Christ in 6:11. An early start is envisaged, for that would be a good time to observe the facets of nature that are here described. Moreover, continuing to give full value to the Solomonic background of the Song, early rising was an established feature of eastern life, whether of the king in his palace or the meanest of his subjects. Being up and dressed before dawn was customary, and much important business was dealt with at an early hour. The women, by and large, would rise earlier than the men. The Lord Jesus' own practice in this regard is well documented in the Gospels. One example, very appropriate in the present context, is Mark 1:35: 'Now in the morning, having risen a long while before daylight, he went out and departed to a solitary place; and there he prayed.' He would have his bride do the same, in order to be with him, cultivating the enjoyment of his company and giving careful attention to the oversight and examination of her spiritual graces.

Believers may be absolutely clear as to their interest in Christ, but it is necessary also to take stock regularly of their present state and condition in practical terms. In the verse just referred to (6:11) it was Christ who was observing his bride's state; here

(7:11-12) she is examining herself in his presence, and is doing so in the way that this work needs to be done, namely both in earnest and in detail. He who takes loving and wise care of his own people would not have them careless of themselves. There is also here a concern to know how things are in the various congregations of Christ's people, if it is well with them, if the cause of Christ and the gospel is flourishing among them (compare the words of Paul to Barnabas in Acts 15:36).

With the mention of the field, the villages and the vineyards, there is a strong sense of getting away from it all. This supplies a necessary reminder to the Christian and the church of not belonging to the world (John 17:16), of going outside the camp (Heb. 13:13), of avoiding anything and everything which would detract or distract from communion with Christ (Eph. 4:22-23), and of deliberately seeking spiritual affections and setting them upon heavenly things (Col. 3:1-3). Isaac was so engaged in Genesis 24:63. The Lord Jesus Christ counsels this very thing to his disciples in Matthew 6:6. To be alone with Christ is not to be alone, for he would have us find his company to be the choicest of all. Let us be all the more careful, therefore, not to wander where he would not wish us to go or would not be willing to go with us.

And to what purpose is this trip into the country? The bride continues, **there I will give you my love**. Not for the first time, 'love' is in the plural, 'loves'. At the beginning of the Song the Shulamite rejoiced at the thought of Christ's loves, and now she desires to give all her loves to Christ, in response to his own. The sense is of 'all my loving', with no rivals admitted and nothing held back. This is one of the tests of true love to Christ: it not only desires to be with him, but it desires to serve him and to 'do' for him, in a way of self-denial and self-sacrifice, nothing being too much to render to such a husband and master. There is, without contradiction, this desire of the believer to be completely alone with Christ and a balancing desire to work for him, which labour is a true labour of love. A heart and a life loving Christ is a mark of true spirituality. The worship and fellowship of retirement with Christ, along with the vigour and diligence of service for Christ, constitute together the giving him of our 'loves'.

Attention has also been drawn from these verses to the missionary calling of the church. In an earlier chapter Christ described her as 'a garden enclosed ..., a spring shut up, a fountain sealed' (4:12), though only a few verses later he went on to speak of her as 'a fountain of gardens, a well of living waters, and streams from Lebanon' (4:15). The bride comes in to be with Christ and goes out to proclaim Christ. She comes in to know him and she goes out to make him known. The one with whom she dwells in secret is the one whose name she testifies to all. The church is at one and the same time, therefore, 'a spring shut up' and 'a well of living waters'. So whether in the field, in the villages, at home or away, near at hand or to the ends of the earth (Matt. 28:19-20; Mark 16:15; Luke 14:21-23; Acts 1:8), the church is to declare the good news to a world in desperate need of the gospel. In the light of the repeated 'let us' here in the Song, the principle is clearly established that the Lord's own presence with his church is always necessary if the work of evangelism and missions is ever to be attended with success. He it is who prospers his own work and word. Without him we can do nothing (John 15:5).

Following the pictures of fruitfulness and blessing conveyed by the vines budding, the grape blossoms opening and the pomegranates being in bloom (with their triple application to communion with Christ, growth in spiritual likeness to Christ, and owned and blessed service for Christ), the chapter concludes on a similar note, with great joy and anticipation.

The mandrakes give off a fragrance, and at our gates are pleasant fruits, all manner, new and old, which I have laid up for you, my beloved (7:13). Mandrakes (they may also be called love-apples) are potent-smelling plants of the potato family, described as having whitish green flowers and yellow apples the size of nutmegs. This is the only occurrence of the word apart from Genesis 30:14-16, where it is mentioned four times. It will be seen from the context there that mandrakes were considered to be something of an aphrodisiac, which is to say the eating of them was understood to stir up sexual desire and passion and overcome problems of barrenness of the womb. The mention of them here in the Song indicates afresh the bride's longing to bring real joy and pleasure to her bridegroom, and so is illustrative of the believer's/church's priority to be a delight and a glory to Christ at all times, not a grief or cause of dissatisfaction. The believer enjoys Christ, but would have Christ enjoy her. This mutuality of love has been present throughout the Song, as has been noted.

The phrase 'at our gates' (NIV, 'at our door'; or it could be 'over our doors'), is used elsewhere in the Old Testament mostly in a literal sense (such as the door of the tabernacle, Lev. 15:29, or the entry gates of cities, 1 Kgs. 17:10). It does have metaphorical uses as well, however ('the valley of Achor as a door of hope', Hos. 2:15; 'guard the doors of your mouth', Mic. 7:5). Here the picture is of choice fruits that have been preserved on a shelf above the inner doors of a family dwelling. This was a familiar eastern custom with both fruit and flowers, including the doors of the homes of newly married couples. The phrase 'pleasant fruits, all manner' is literally just 'all pleasant' (or excellent; NIV has 'every delicacy'); fruits, however, is rightly understood. The 'all' refers to the many different kinds of pleasant fruits which, after they have all been gathered, are divided into new and old.

This verse is full of mature Christian experience. The fruits pertaining to the believer/church that are pleasant to the Lord Jesus are (consistent with the Song throughout) spiritual virtues and graces. There are not just one or two of these; they are manifold. They are marked both by plenty and variety. Reference has already been made in the commentary, in this connection, to passages like the Beatitudes and the fruit of the Spirit. To these may be added such as Romans 5:3-5, Colossians 3:5-4:6 and 2 Peter 1:5-11, along with several others. Our souls should be well stocked with these pleasant fruits, rather than the shelves being empty or the goods being in short supply. This all makes the mandrakes a very suitable illustration, given their associations just mentioned. Christians are married to Christ, 'to him who was raised from the dead, that we should bear fruit to God' (Rom. 7:4). The church of Christ is not to be a barren woman but 'a joyful mother of children' (Ps. 113:9). True ministers of the gospel, like the apostle Paul, 'labour in birth again until Christ is formed' in his people (Gal. 4:19).

Not only will such fruits be fragrant and pleasant, but 'new and old'. This is reminiscent of Jesus' words in Matthew 13:52, the preserving of the old and the bringing forth of the new. There will be past grace, present grace and future grace; grace already received, grace being received and grace yet to be received; graces matured, graces maturing and graces yet to mature. All these dimensions continually apply. While the past is highly important (there can be no present and future without it), yet the past is not all, in the Christian life – for the very reason that it is the Christian *life*, and life is something that lives, breathes, grows and develops. That which is lifeless and static quickly becomes stale. Holiness is not won in a day. The old needs constant reviving and renewing, while the new should be regularly in evidence. In the church as a whole, in an important sense, there needs to be this vital combination of the new and old: the deep and tried experience of those believers who are ripening for heaven and whose walk with God and devotion to Christ goes back a long way, and the fresh and younger experience of those who have only set out upon the pilgrim path more recently.

A useful comparison is also John 1:16, which reminds us that just as all grace comes to us in and through the Lord Jesus Christ (he is the conduit, the channel, of all the riches of divine grace, as is made plain in Ephesians 1:7), so it is all for him as well as from him. Hence, 'which I have laid up for you, my beloved' (literally the word order is 'my beloved, have I laid up for you'). There is no place for self-boasting here or anywhere else. Christ is to be the first and the best. Everything about his bride (her affections, her desires, her service – everything) is laid up for Christ, set apart for Christ, devoted to Christ and directed for Christ, just as Mary's 'pound of costly oil of pure spikenard' was best employed in anointing the feet of the Lord Jesus. It is recorded specifically that the whole of the house was filled with its fragrance (John 12:3).

Chapter 8

COME, LORD JESUS!

The previous chapter ended upon a high note of loving desire, with the Shulamite speaking of those fragrant and pleasant things, new and old, which she has laid up for her beloved. She wished to give him her love. Now, in the final chapter of the Song, she continues to speak, and in the same vein. In addition, there are one or two interjections from other quarters, and then the whole finishes with a final word each from the bridegroom and the bride. There is no dousing of the flames of passion or the ardour of mutual affections. Things continue as before.

8:1-4. Bridegroom and brother
The bride speaks in these verses, addressing herself first to her husband (verses 1-2) and then to the daughters of Jerusalem (verses 3-4).

Oh, that you were like my brother, who nursed at my mother's breasts! (8:1). This 'Oh, that' has the force of an 'If only' (with NIV). The phrase 'like my brother' is 'like/as a brother to me'. The sibling figure appeared earlier in 4:9, 10, 12, on those occasions upon the lips of the bridegroom. The Lord Jesus Christ spoke of his church as his sister, as well as his bride. This time the speech is reversed: the bride speaks of Christ as her brother. This is the only occurrence of the word in the Song.

The bride's wish is not so much a literal one that she and her husband were really brother and sister. Rather (as was observed in the comments on chapter 4), the expression emphasises kinship, closeness and purity. There is no place here for 'the lust of the flesh, the lust of the eyes, and the pride of life' (1

194

John 2:16). This picture fills out further the uniqueness of the relationship which exists between Christ and every believer, which bursts the bounds of any one way of describing it. It is very appropriate that the strongest bonds of affection and mutual concern for one another should exist between those born of the same mother, who were nursed (or, who sucked) at her breasts.

For her own part here, the bride is still desiring a greater intimacy with her beloved. Without this, she cannot be truly satisfied. She longs to show her care for him, to tend to all that will give him pleasure, to make some fresh return to him for all that he has lavished upon her, and to do so in a public rather than in a hidden or secretive way. Such, surely, is the attitude of the true Christian, who does not begrudge Christ anything that he requires, or look to personal profit in Christian service and devotion, but is anxious to render a heartfelt response to him, after the manner of Psalm 116:12 ('What shall I render to the LORD for all his benefits towards me?'). In this connection, note the apostle's urging in Romans 12:1-2.

The thought of Christ as his people's brother is a most comforting and suggestive one. It recalls the truth stated in the letter to the Hebrews: 'Inasmuch then as the children have partaken of flesh and blood, he himself likewise shared in the same' (Heb. 2:14). He is described in Proverbs as 'a friend who sticks closer than a brother' (Prov. 18:24). It asserts Christ's great condescension, his feeling sympathy and his readiness to take his bride's part, upholding her in her trials and confirming her testimony to him before men.

This same theme continues: **If I should find you outside, I would kiss you; I would not be despised.** The eastern background of the Song comes into its own again here, shedding further light on the choice of the brother/sister language. Brothers and sisters from the same mother would be permitted to kiss one another in public, without drawing attention to themselves or causing offence, whereas a husband and wife would not do so. This completeness of display of love will be reserved for heaven, where (without any restraint, disturbance or reproach) Christ and his church will give themselves to one another for ever, in an exquisite holy delight and satisfaction. It is more of this very heaven right now upon earth that lies behind all that the believer utters here. Oh, to be able to love Christ and to know his love here and now, as shall be the case there and then, with nothing held back on either side, and no scorn from the ungodly who think nothing of him. Yet these things must wait their own time and place.

I would lead you and bring you into the house of my mother, she who used to instruct me (8:2). The believer proceeds to declare what she would do if Christ were her brother (in other words, if she could be as free with him as she would wish while still pursuing the pilgrim path). She would take him (the two verbs are used, lead and bring: literally, 'I would lead you; I would bring you') into her mother's house. This is not the first mention of the mother's house; it appeared in 3:4, where we interpreted it of the church and the believer's family. See the comment on that verse.

The phrase 'she who used to instruct me' may be translated in that way as a feminine, but may also be taken as a masculine. In that case the translation would run: 'you would teach me'. On the former rendering, the instruction to the believer comes from within the church; on the latter, it is Christ himself who will teach her. In one sense the two come together, since it is very specially in his church (among the gathered congregation of his people and through his appointed ministers) that Christ (by his Spirit, through his word) teaches believers all they need to know for their edification and sanctification (compare John 17:17). In this respect, the church may be regarded as the school while Christ himself is the teacher. Christ who is to be enjoyed in the secret place is to be enjoyed as well in the sanctuary.

What the believer is admitting here is her need of guidance, counsel, instruction, and that her beloved Christ is the one to give it to her. She would, like Mary, sit at his feet (Luke 10:39), and be devoted to him as her teacher. To him belongs the office of prophet (as well as priest and king) in his church. In him 'are hidden all the treasures of wisdom and knowledge' (Col. 2:3). He it is who says to his disciples, 'for all things that I heard from my Father I have made known to you' (John 15:15). A genuine love to Christ and desire for Christ will always be evidenced in a serious determination to learn from him. There is suitable Christian modesty here, for which individual believer or congregation of his people is yet the bride to Christ that they should be? The most mature believers should be the most earnest and humble students. A great deal still remains to be learned in the lifelong process of growing 'in the grace and knowledge of our Lord and Saviour Jesus Christ' (2 Pet. 3:18).

I would cause you to drink of spiced wine, of the juice of my pomegranate. Still the main thread remains: the desire of the Christian for greater and greater fellowship and intimacy with Christ. The juice of the pomegranate (for pomegranate, see on 4:3) was used both on its own in the manufacture of a flavoured wine and in mixed beverages along with other flavours. What is envisaged here is a drink of the richest and most refreshing sort the bride could offer. The language she uses is of welcome and enjoyment, the very language that the Song has exuded all the way through, with all her love and faith and hope flowing out upon Christ. Such welcome and readiness to receive him is a great refreshment to the Lord Jesus (Rev. 3:20). He promises and he delights to be with such a people. The next two verses are proof of this.

Verses 3 and 4, after the manner of 2:6-7, are to be taken as the words of the Shulamite addressed to the daughters of Jerusalem. **His left hand is under my head, and his right hand embraces me** (8:3). This is identical to 2:6. The earlier context of these words was lovesickness, arising from a surfeit (not an absence) of the felt love of Christ. The particular point this time is this: the bride has just expressed her desire to give a royal entertainment of love to Christ, but immediately affirms that all her rest and satisfaction is in him for himself, not in what she may do for him. She desires to give her very best to him (in terms of him being the worthy one), but acknowledges freely that the real nub of the matter is that he is everything to her. She has no other love. While she realises that there are ultimate heights and depths to the experience of the love of Christ that must wait for heaven (for the best is always yet to be, while still on earth), yet she recalls with relish those earlier seasons of his love and desires as much as may possibly be had of him right now.

There are sweet remembrances here of David's testimony, 'your right hand upholds me' (Ps. 63:8) and of Moses' words, 'underneath are the everlasting arms' (Deut. 33:27). Such is the believer's portion and assurance, in the Lord, and experienced on one occasion is greatly to be desired at all times. While the Lord Jesus Christ sometimes springs special surprises of his grace, it remains true that (by and large) the experience described here in verse 3 is enjoyed in proportion to the desire expressed after it.

The charge that follows is slightly different from the earlier wording of 2:7 and 3:5. As well as the omission of the reference to the gazelles and the does of the field, the bride's words now are cast as a question, although this does not come out in the English versions. **I charge you, O daughters of Jerusalem, do not stir up nor awaken love until it pleases** (8:4). It needs to be rendered: 'Why should you stir up or why should you awaken love until it (or, she) pleases?' The picture is of the two lovers, bridegroom and bride, in each other's tender embrace. What reason, then, could anyone have to disturb them? What could be more important than communion with Christ? The Shulamite speaks to the daughters of Jerusalem (which fits in with v.2: having spoken of bringing Christ into the church, she desires the church should keep quiet for him); yet she intends these words for herself as well. There is something solemn here. The utmost care needs to be taken in order to guard against any disturbing or spoiling influences while Christ's presence and love are being enjoyed. Let no Christian ever do anything to provoke the Lord Jesus Christ to withdraw the comforts of his love or the blessings of his presence. Let there be no insensitive words, no foolish deeds, no sinful weariness of him, nothing to cause him to leave when the church so much needs him to stay.

8:5-7. Christ unchanging

Who is this coming up from the wilderness, leaning upon her beloved? (8:5). The question about coming up from the wilderness appeared in 3:6, where the reference was to the bride. The same is the case here. It is not clear who is speaking. NKJV assigns the words to a relative, whoever that is meant to be. NIV attributes it to friends. The daughters of Jerusalem are the most likely candidates of all. They have just been addressed, and are very much taken with the happiness of the bride in the security of her husband's love.

For the thought of the church 'coming up from the wilderness', see on 3:6. It is an appropriate way of describing both what the state of the sinner is like before being saved by God's grace, and how the redeemed proceed safely to glory. Side by side with it may be placed Psalm 113:7-8, with its imagery of the sinner's poverty and need, in the dust and on the rubbish heap, and then being made to sit with the princes of God's people. From the wilderness of sin and misery and death the bride of Christ has been redeemed, and through the wilderness of this world she is being led and preserved.

The further description of her as 'leaning upon her beloved' emphasises all that she owes, and owes continually, to the Lord Jesus Christ, who himself never changes, since he is 'Jesus Christ ... the same yesterday, today, and for ever' (Heb. 13:8). He is the beloved upon whom she leans. The picture conveyed is of Christ as the sinner's hope and help, and as the believer's all in all. The pilgrim path to glory is surrounded by all manner of dangers, toils and snares. This world cannot satisfy the cravings of a spiritual soul. It is a vale of tears much of the time. It is the place where our enemy, the devil, prowls around like a roaring lion, seeking whom he may devour. So with her back towards the desert from which she came, and with her face firmly fixed towards heaven to which she is travelling, the church/believer presses on to God. The more the soul is taken up with Christ, the less of a wilderness everything appears, and the less laborious the upward journey to heaven becomes. It is he, and his presence, that makes the difference.

The verb for 'leaning' makes here its sole appearance in the whole of the Old Testament. The basic meaning is of support, taking someone's elbow, and so making progress in that way. Dependence and closeness are to the fore. The Lord Jesus Christ is the very one (and the only one) upon whom to lean. Not only is there salvation in no one else, 'for there is no other name under heaven given among men by which we must be saved' (Acts 4:12), but he 'became for us wisdom from God – and righteousness and sanctification and redemption' (1 Cor. 1:30).

In other words, the believer begins, continues and ends with Christ. A real, whole, known and firm Christ is the one to be leaned upon for everything (acceptance with God, growth in spiritual grace and knowledge, strength and wisdom for the performance of all duties, protection and perseverance, and glory at the last) and in all circumstances (whether bright or gloomy, in his felt presence or in his felt absence, in joy or sorrow, in assurance or perplexity, in believing or repenting, in life or death). All our weight is to be thrown upon him. All our confidence is to be in him. All our boast is to be of him. All our desires and affections are to be towards him. There is no risk or failure with him. Philippians 4:13 fits in here (weak in ourselves, but strong in Christ). This question of verse 5 presents a most expressive picture.

I awakened you under the apple tree. This introduces what is generally regarded as one of the most difficult and obscure passages in the Song. It seems natural and inviting to take these words (and those that follow to the end of the verse) as the words of the bridegroom, looking back to how he chose his bride before the foundation of the world, awoke her love and drew her to himself, making her his own, in all the wonders and glories of the covenant relationship. While that is a great biblical truth, it would require us here to change the pointing of the Hebrew text from masculine to feminine suffixes, which some commentators have done. However, the masculine endings in verses 5-7, as they stand, require the Shulamite to be the speaker throughout this section. She is addressing her beloved. Her words connect somewhat with what she was saying in the opening verses of the chapter.

Back in 2:3 she likened him to an apple tree. The reference here is again to him, and the focus seems to be this. The bride is recalling to Christ, or putting him in mind of, those earlier precious occasions of shared love and conversation when he spoke and acted on her behalf in answer to her earnest prayers and entreaties, came to her aid, undertook for her, and such like. These were themselves proven times when she discovered what it was to lean upon her beloved, and was never disappointed. To be 'under the apple tree' is to be near him, trusting in him, covered by him and refreshed by him. It was no wonder that she was desiring his company so much once more, for the thought of it in former times was a tremendous pull. The joys she had known before she desired to know again and to know continually.

Moreover, what was one Christian's experience in this regard was another's also: **There your mother brought you forth** (or, 'travailed with you'); **there she who bore you brought you forth** (or, 'there she travailed; she bore you'). The picture of the church as Christ's mother has already been explored (see on 3:4, 11; 8:1). What is in view here is the corporate experience of the church of Christ, her shared comforts, her parallel blessings. All the dealings of Christ with their souls are to be remembered and cherished by his people, from the first espousals of love right on throughout the Christian life in all its eventfulness. Those places (those apple trees) where, in particular, Christ has met with our souls will also be etched upon the believer's memory; the remembrance of them (so long as it is in a strictly non-superstitious way) will often stimulate and revive love to him who first loved us. The same is true of his special visitations in his word, at the throne of grace, at his table, and so on. Highlighted here, in a practical manner, is the benefit of mutual conference among believers upon spiritual things, that both the common and the personal nature of Christian experience may be understood all the better.

This leads into two of the best known verses in the Song, as the Shulamite, leaning upon her beloved, continues speaking to him. The choice subject of verses 6-7 as a whole is the unchanging love of Christ towards his bride, set forth in a series of vivid word pictures.

Set me as a seal upon your heart, as a seal upon your arm (8:6), is how she begins here. The reference is to the ancient near eastern practice of wearing signet rings, stones, metal seals or cords on hands, wrists or as pendants around the neck and hanging over the heart. Frequently these would have the name or even the portrait of the beloved person engraved on them and would serve as an indication of the wearer being loved, owned or possessed by the one who had given the item. The bride speaks of herself as such a seal (set/place me as a seal upon your heart and your arm), 'your heart' and 'your arm' having masculine endings and so referring to her husband. She desires to be acknowledged as belonging to him, and does not mind who knows. She craves a fresh and firm assurance of her permanent place in his heart and interest in his love. Such is the desire and craving of every true believer with regard to Christ, for herein does their blessedness and happiness abound. Deeply conscious of their utter unworthiness of his love, yet they cannot live without this assurance of it.

It is not that believers can ever have any reason to doubt the constancy of Christ's love to them; rather, knowing their own hearts, they fear the inconstancy of their own love to him, and so pray in this manner. The seal carries the sense of Christ's stamp and signature which cannot be revoked or removed, as the Christian/church is hidden in Christ's heart and held upon his arm, and so kept continually in his remembrance. Compare what is said concerning 'name' in Revelation 3:12, along with verses like Exodus 28:11-12 (the engravings in connection with the high priest's garments), Isaiah 49:14-16 (the Lord inscribing his people on the palms of his hands) and Haggai 2:23 (the signet ring). Observe also the teaching of Ephesians 1:13-14 and 4:30 on the sealing of the Holy Spirit.

An interpretative difficulty presents itself at this point. Commentators and preachers on the Song are divided over whether what now follows to the end of verse 7 is the bride's description of the nature of her own love to Christ which lies behind and compels the plea just issued, or whether the words are her declaration (from experience) of how the Lord Jesus loves her. The Shulamite does not say either 'my love' or 'your love'; just 'love'. As was remarked on 6:11-13, when something of a similar problem was faced, there is an important sense in which it does not matter too much. The love of the church to Christ has been described as the child of Christ's love to the church. Christ's love to the church comes first and the church's love to Christ follows after (1 John 4:19); the former has been called the magnificent image and the latter the beautiful miniature. They are not on an equal footing, for the love which the church returns to Christ cannot begin to compare with the love which Christ bears to the church. Yet they share a certain likeness and, as has been observed throughout the commentary, are wholly and highly mutual. So there is an appropriateness in taking the present portion either way. On balance, however, the comments that follow take the words as referring to Christ's unchanging love towards his bride in its strength ('love ... as strong as death'), its intensity ('jealousy as cruel as the grave'), its passion ('flames of fire'), its unquenchableness ('many waters cannot quench love') and its preciousness ('all the wealth of his house ...'). They all dovetail together.

First to be mentioned is the strength of Christ's unchanging love: **for love is as strong as death.** There is no doubting the strength of death, which cannot be escaped and must be faced. The word for 'strong' makes its only appearance in the Song here, though often occurs elsewhere in the Old Testament. Who can beat back death or do battle with it? There is a fierceness about death's strength. The word here for strong, evidently, designates someone who (when being assailed) cannot be overcome and (when doing the assailing) cannot be withstood. Death is being viewed in these terms. Yet strong as death is, the love of Christ is as strong, and stronger. No matter how irresistible death is, Christ's love is far more so. His love for his bride caused him to taste death, to suffer death, to vanquish death and to rise from death, so that every believer can join with the apostle Paul in jubilation: 'Death is swallowed up in victory' (1 Cor. 15:54, drawing upon Isa. 25:8), and 'O Death, where is your sting? O Hades, where is your victory?' (1 Cor. 15:55, reflecting Hos. 13:14).

In no way can death overcome Christ's love. His salvation for his people (Matt. 1:21) is the proof of that, and the death of believers is the entrance into that eternal world of joy where Christ's love will be enjoyed more fully, more richly and more perfectly than ever before (Ps. 16:11). Love, like death, must have its object, and Christ, who 'loved the church and gave himself for it' (Eph. 5:25), must have his bride for himself. His love has a constraining power that cannot and will not be denied. This heavenly bridegroom preferred his bride to his own life, and chose death rather than to be without her. How much, then, his bride should love him.

Then there is the intensity of Christ's unchanging love: **jealousy as cruel as the grave**. Jealousy as one of the divine attributes needs to be understood carefully and given due weight. When giving the law at Sinai, Jehovah declared: 'For I, the LORD your God, am a jealous God' (Exod. 20:5), and the theme recurs throughout Scripture. He will not share his worship with anyone or anything, for he alone is the true, living and eternal God. In keeping with this, the love of Christ to his church is marked by a holy and pure jealousy. It is a possessive love. It will not stand for any rivals. It will not take second place. Recall how the risen, ascended, glorified Lord Jesus Christ addressed the church at Laodicea: 'I could wish you were cold or hot' (Rev. 3:15). The lukewarmness of his bride is a cause of deep offence to Christ.

There is nothing here of the darkness or sinfulness of human jealousy; there cannot be, since this is the love of Christ. Rather he would affirm his rightful claim over his bride, to have her entirely for himself, betrothed to him as her 'one husband', as 'a chaste virgin' (2 Cor. 11:2). He who is jealous for his own glory is jealous also for his own bride. In such a holy sense, this jealousy is the highest degree of love. It is related here to the cruelty of the grave. Just as the grave swallows up and carries off its prey, so does the love of Christ attain its object with a jealous determination and success. How magnificently this is seen in the manner in which he set about the salvation of his people, for his Father's glory, laying down his life and taking it up again (John 10:17-18). The word for 'jealous' is sometimes rendered 'zeal', which recalls such a reference to Christ as is found in Psalm 69:9, fulfilled in John 2:17 on the occasion of the cleansing of the temple.

'Cruel' is another word making its sole appearance in the Song, though it is often found elsewhere in the Old Testament. NIV translates it 'unyielding'; other renderings that have been offered include hard, inexorable, firm and severe. Grave is 'Sheol', a word used variously in the Old Testament for death, the grave, the abode of the dead and a place of punishment for the wicked. The linking here of the three words (jealousy, cruel, grave) emphasises how Christ takes complete hold and possession of his bride, keeps her safe for himself, and so absorbs her in an overwhelming manner with that love that she is entirely taken up with him. While believers need never suspect the reality and intensity of Christ's love towards them, it is a sad fact of Christian experience that we give him all too much reason to be jealous of our love to him, lest that love ever be given to another.

Next comes the passion of Christ's unchanging love: **its flames are flames of fire, a most vehement flame.** AV has 'the coals thereof are coals of fire', though flames is preferable; while NIV translates, 'It burns like blazing fire, like a mighty flame.' Those last words may be rendered 'a flame of Jehovah' (NIV footnote, 'like the very flame of the LORD'), which would mean this is the one occasion in the whole of the Song where the divine name is actually mentioned. Both the origin and the greatness of the divine love are thereby denoted. That should not cause any surprise, 'for God is love' (1 John 4:8) and 'love is of God' (1 John 4:7).

It is worth noting that when Hebrew would express a superlative, one or other of the names of God are sometimes employed. So 'the mountains of God' are the highest and most imposing mountains and 'the cedars of God' are the tallest and most magnificent cedars. The divine love is the most vehement love. Moreover, it may be observed further that this possible rendering, 'a flame of Jehovah', is a reminder that the Song is no mere love song but a song of divine loves – that of Jehovah-Jesus to his church and that of his church to him (kindled by the Holy Spirit).

The force of this whole statement cannot be missed. The love of Christ for his bride is no half-hearted, on and off, affair of 'he loves me, he loves me not'. It is a burning love, hot, ardent, flaming, passionate, sparkling, consuming. He cannot turn away or cease from it. This matchless love was given full vent upon the cross of Calvary and is a love whose flames of fire continue to burn and are never extinguished. Rightly does the apostle Paul ask, 'Who shall separate us from the love of Christ?', and then proceed to give the answer, 'For I am persuaded that neither death nor life, nor angels nor principalities nor powers, nor things present nor things to come, nor height nor depth, nor any other created thing, shall be able to separate us from the love of God which is in Christ Jesus our Lord' (Rom. 8:35, 38-39).

The fourth aspect of Christ's unchanging love to be mentioned is its unquenchableness: **Many waters cannot quench love, nor can the floods drown it** (8:7). The word picture being used here is not hard to understand. The love of Christ cannot be quenched, it cannot be washed away, it cannot be extinguished. It is constant, it is tenacious. No waters, floods, tides or any such thing could have any damaging or lessening effect upon it – not even all the oceans of his people's sins and corruptions, not even all the depths of his own humiliations and sufferings. His love, supremely, 'suffers long and is kind ... bears all things ... endures all things ... never fails' (1 Cor. 13:4, 7, 8). In other words, Christ loves his own and he loves them for ever. This, of course, is the very essence of divine covenant love. God announces, 'I have loved you with an everlasting love' (Jer. 31:3), and what is everlasting in its origin is everlasting also in its continuance. Recall John 10:27-30 on the Christian's security in Christ's love.

Finally, in this grand sequence, attention is drawn to the preciousness of Christ's unchanging love: **If a man would give for love all the wealth of his house, it would be utterly despised** (literally, 'despising they despise it/him', or 'they surely would despise it/him'). The love of Christ is most precious, inestimable, beyond any possibility of assessing or stating its value. It cannot be bought or sold. It is bestowed freely and graciously. Love begets love, but it cannot be purchased. Even if all the worldly riches that can be imagined were offered in exchange for it, 'it' (the wealth), or 'he' (the offerer), would be worthy only of scorn. The very thought is unthinkable! There is a reminder in this of Paul's testimony in Philippians 3:7-11, concerning counting 'all things loss for the excellence of the knowledge of Christ Jesus my Lord ... that I may know him.' The love of Christ is absolutely beyond compare, as every true believer knows and every true church proclaims. His loving-kindness is better than life (Ps. 63:3).

Before passing on to the final section of the Song, two comments need to be made. The first is this: how needful it is that the Christian's/church's love to Christ really should mirror or reflect Christ's own love far more than it does. His love is to be the model for the response of love which is due to him. So his bride needs to seek, with all seriousness and importunity, such supplies of grace as will enable her to render to Christ a love which (like his own) is strong, intense, passionate, unquenchable and precious (and so unable to be bribed or seduced away in any other direction).

As for the second matter, it should now be clearer why the bride prayed the opening words of verse 6. That desire expressed a longing for a greater nearness to Christ, a deeper abiding in him, a closer communion with him. Why? Because of the glory, the vastness, the delightfulness and the sheer enjoyment of his unchanging love which was then described in the rest of the section. Once a believer has been enabled, by grace through faith, to begin with Christ's love, no amount of that love can ever be enough. There is to be about every Christian that blessed tension of being absolutely satisfied in and with Christ, yet experiencing daily what can only be termed a holy dissatisfaction borne out of a sense of never being able to get enough of him, because there is so much fulness in him. This very tension is at the heart of the Song.

8:8-12. A sister and a vineyard

At first glance this section looks most puzzling, with its apparently mysterious references to 'a little sister' and Solomon's vineyard. The priority must be to establish clearly who is speaking at each point. NKJV ascribes verses 8-9 to the Shulamite's brothers, NIV to friends. The whole section is kept much simpler, however, if we restrict the speakers to the bride and the bridegroom: the bride (v.8) and the bridegroom (v.9), each speaking for one another; or the bride in both verses speaking for them both; or the bride and bridegroom speaking together in the two verses (that is, thinking and speaking as one); then it is the bride herself (vs.10-12). This is not intended to be a confused arrangement which leaves all options open. Rather, as has been noted earlier in the Song, one of the reasons why it is extremely difficult to discern who is speaking at certain points is because it could quite literally be either Christ or the believer/ church, on account of the covenantal marriage union that exists between them. Those whom God has joined together (in this case, Christ and his bride) cannot be separated.

We have a little sister, and she has no breasts (8:8). The 'we' is highly significant. It refers to both the bride and the bridegroom together, to Christ and his people as one. Maybe the bride alone is speaking for the two of them, or maybe they are speaking together.

Who is the 'little sister'? The answer is an either/or or a both/ and. The reference may be to the Gentiles, as opposed to the Jews, in which case there is a parallel here with the language of Ephesians 2:11-13, which speaks of those being 'at that time without Christ, being aliens from the commonwealth of Israel and strangers from the covenants of promise, having no hope and without God in the world', and so 'far off' until 'made near by the blood of Christ'. Along not dissimilar lines, but taking the reference a little more widely, the 'little sister' may refer to the elect of God not yet called by grace through faith, the 'other sheep I have', of whom the Lord Jesus says 'them also I must bring' (John 10:16). There may also be included here a reference to those who have already been brought into a saving relationship with the Lord Jesus Christ but who are still very much babes in Christ, still taking milk rather than meat (along the lines of how, throughout this commentary, we have understood the daughters of Jerusalem).

The adjective 'little' (NIV, younger) makes sense here, whether in terms of their lack of saving knowledge as yet or the early days still of their belonging to Christ and his church. The term 'sister', being a relationship word, is also very fitting, whether in respect of the saving relationship that was purposed in eternity that is yet to come to pass in actuality or of the relationship already entered into in real experience. As for the remark 'she has no breasts', this points to the absence (necessarily at present, from those who are not saved) of love and affection to Christ or to the immature development and expression of the same so far in the lives of young believers. All of these expressions are of real sympathy, affection and compassion.

A question is posed immediately. **What shall we do for our sister in the day when she is spoken for?** Again the 'we' is very striking, as is the 'our'. Here is the mutual concern, regard and compassion of Christ and his church for those given to Christ by the Father in the eternal purposes: the salvation of the elect, the gathering in of the lost, the adding to the church of all those who believe, the sanctifying of them all. Jesus' words in John 6:37 are important here: 'All that the Father gives me will come to me, and the one who comes to me I will by no means cast out.' This mention of 'the day she is spoken for' is surely that very day of the calling of the chosen, the bringing to repentance and faith of the sinner. What a blessed day that always is, one of rejoicing both in heaven and upon earth, one when the entire Godhead is glorified. Compare verses like Luke 15:10, 2 Corinthians 6:2 and Hebrews 4:7. The gospel, faithfully preached, is the glorious and free offer to the sinner of Christ as Saviour and Husband. It is the invitation of needy, helpless, perishing sinners to a wedding (Matt. 22:1-14).

The salvation and sanctification of his people is ever upon Christ's heart and it is a mark of true Christ-likeness that it should be upon his church's heart as well. While sin makes the sinner selfish, grace makes the Christian gracious, ever watchful for souls and earnestly desirous that others also should 'taste and see that the LORD is good' and discover that 'blessed is the man who trusts in him!' (Ps. 34:8). The true Christian reaches out to embrace Christ and reaches out also to bring others into Christ's embrace.

If she is a wall, we will build upon her a battlement of silver; and if she is a door, we will enclose her with boards of cedar (8:9). As in the previous verse, it may be that the bride is speaking for herself and the bridegroom, or both are continuing to speak together; it is more likely, however, that the bridegroom himself now speaks, though still for them both. Continuing to come through very strongly here is the concern shared by both Christ and his church for the prospering of the great eternal design of the gospel in providing a bride for Christ by the saving of sinners and uniting them to him, and the church being 'holy and without blame' (Eph. 1:4). The Lord is never unmindful of his people's intercessions upon these things and readily and abundantly grants a response.

This ninth verse is an answer to the question that was proposed in the second part of the eighth: 'what shall we do for our sister?' The answer is given in two ways, the first using the imagery of a wall, the second that of a door. Both of these pictures set forth the glorious and gracious transformation which God works by his Holy Spirit in the conversion of a sinner and then in the sanctification of a Christian. That this is a thorough transformation and not a mere surface change is made plain in Scripture. Conversion is described as being turned 'from darkness to light, and from the power of Satan to God' (Acts 26:18), while sanctification is presented in these grand terms: 'But we all, with unveiled face, beholding as in a mirror the glory of the Lord, are being transformed into the same image from glory to glory, just as by the Spirit of the Lord' (2 Cor. 3:18).

The sinner, to begin with, is an ordinary wall, or a plain door. Yet when grace begins to do its work and continues to do its work, what a change is undergone. This is no temporary human makeover but a permanent divine change. That unornamented wall has 'a battlement (or turret) of silver' built upon it and is changed and beautified out of all recognition. That unremarkable door is encased 'with boards of cedar', the most costly, polished and exquisite wood, and becomes a sight and object of great beauty and admiration. The Solomonic background to the Song is in evidence once again: the walls around Jerusalem on which were raised turrets of silver, and the magnificently overlaid doors made for the temple.

Ultimately, then, the wonders of salvation and the beauties of holiness are the things in view here, altogether surpassing the material things created out of the choicest silver and cedar. All of this is 'the LORD's doing; it is marvellous in our eyes' (Ps. 118:23). It is reminiscent of Paul's words to the Ephesians: 'the whole building, being joined together, grows into a holy temple in the Lord, in whom you also are being built together for a habitation of God in the Spirit' (Eph. 2:21-22). Here is God saving, God sanctifying and God keeping and protecting (surrounding and enclosing) all whom he saves and sanctifies. The triune God promises to give to his people 'grace and glory' (Ps. 84:11). Consequently, if right from the start a believer being 'in Christ ... a new creation' (2 Cor. 5:17) is a wonder to behold, how will Christ's bride appear when she is 'like him' and 'shall see him as he is' (1 John 3:2)?

The Shulamite speaks throughout verses 10-12. **I am a wall, and my breasts like towers** (8:10). The language is very much that of the two verses just considered, with the occurrence again of 'wall' and 'breasts'. This is the believer's personal testimony to and glad rejoicing in the very work of God in his/her own life which the Lord has been promising to do for the 'little sister'. The Shulamite, too, once was not a wall and had no breasts. Now she has been made a wall and has been given breasts. She has been saved by grace and united to Christ by faith. She stands on a firm foundation. She has been sealed with the Spirit and is being enabled to bring forth his fruit. She is Christ's and Christ is hers. She is being kept firm and made holy. She desires him to have all the praise and glory.

There is a most important principle here. One Christian's experience of the grace and power and Spirit of God furnishes two things: a welcome assurance that what the Lord has done for one unworthy sinner he would be pleased (and able) to do for another, and a stirring incentive to pray on and work on to that very end, sparing no effort or labour. Such assurance and incentive, of course, should come from the word of God itself, and not rest on the necessity of experience to back up or confirm the word. Nevertheless, it is a great encouragement to behold the word of God coming to pass both under our very eyes and in our own hearts.

This testimony continues: **then I became in his eyes as one who found peace.** The 'then' may also be translated 'thus'. This experience has been likened to the promise of God pronounced through Moses upon Naphtali in Deuteronomy 33:23: 'satisfied with favour, and full of the blessing of the LORD.' The bride owes everything to her bridegroom, and is glad to acknowledge it. This is in no way a display of pride in personal achievement (look at me, look at what I have done for myself!) but is in every way a tribute to the loving kindness of the Lord (look at me, for this is what he has done for me!) He it is who has made her what she is. Note the root of it: the divine favour, 'as one who found peace', and the tender and delicate 'in his eyes'. The heavenly bridegroom does not lay hold upon his bride violently but with his eyes of love fixed upon her draws her graciously, persuasively and willingly to himself. This, truly, is irresistible grace! 'But by the grace of God I am what I am, and his grace towards me was not in vain' (1 Cor. 15:10). It is the delightful obligation of the Christian to keep in review continually this grace of God in salvation, in spiritual growth and in every realm and department of life.

It is worthy of note that there is to be found here (and running into the next verse) in the Hebrew a delightful sequence of words from the one root 'peace', which may be expressed in English as follows: 'I (Shulamite) found peace (shalom) with Solomon (in his character here as a type of Christ). 'This is every believer's sweet experience.

In the next two verses the picture of Solomon's vineyard comes into view, the Shulamite still speaking. To understand the sense, these verses need to be held together. **Solomon had a vineyard at Baal Hamon; he leased the vineyard to keepers; everyone was to bring for its fruit a thousand pieces of silver** (8:11). No firm location can be given for Baal Hamon and it is useless to speculate. It may even be fictitious or poetic. The meaning of the name is 'master or lord of the multitude'. A situation is envisaged as follows: Solomon had a vineyard which he leased to keepers (tenants) whose responsibility it was to bring to him a thousand pieces/shekels of silver as an annual rent, while themselves being free to keep the fruit of the vineyard. The words 'pieces/shekels' do not appear in the Hebrew, which reads 'a thousand of silver', but the shekel is probably intended. It was evidently the common measure of weight, as well as (after about 500 BC) of coinage also.

However, something different obtains where the Shulamite herself is concerned. She actually is a vineyard and desires that all that she has and is be given to Solomon, not under constraint or out of mere obligation, but willingly and freely. **My own vineyard is before me. You, O Solomon, may have a thousand, and those who keep its fruit two hundred** (8:12). The 'thousand' (which has a definite article with it) represents the entire produce of this vineyard and it will all be given to Solomon, with nothing held back by the Shulamite for herself. The reference to the 'two hundred' for 'those who keep its fruit' does not contradict that, as will be explained below.

The application of this in spiritual terms is not difficult to see. Since the Lord Jesus Christ (the one greater than Solomon) is everything to the church and to each believer, his bride's desire is to be his, his alone and his completely, without any reservation whatsoever, and to be fruitful for him. This is not a new thought or theme in the Song. Moreover, this devotion and dedication arises not from any legalistic view of works rendered, but is the fruit of grace in the heart and life. The bride has not earned favour but has been given it, and desires in response to demonstrate her exclusive belonging and absolute allegiance to her beloved bridegroom, Christ. She would not wish there to be any question about this. The 'You, O Solomon', speaking in the second person, is very striking.

The church is Christ's vineyard. This is very familiar Bible teaching (compare, for example, Isa. 5:1-7 and 27:2-3, as well as Matt. 21:33-46). He takes great delight in and care of his vineyard and would have his people to be of the same mind. Consequently everyone who belongs to Christ's church has a responsibility for keeping the vineyard (the vineyard of their own heart – think back to 1:6, and the vineyard as a whole, guarding and cultivating it). This needs constant attention and affection and a holy jealousy. Note the 'before me' in the bride's words. It is both sacred and solemn work. Vineyards need watering, pruning and propping up; the stones have to be cleared away from the ground round about and the area needs to be fenced and protected. So it is in the spiritual realm. For this stewardship Christ will require an account. Love to Christ must issue in love for one another (love for the church) if that love to Christ is genuine. Consider such verses as Philippians 2:3-4 and 1 John 4:20-21. This is part of what might be termed 'the gospel rent' that is due to Christ, who comes seeking fruit for his glory.

Yet the Lord Jesus Christ is exceedingly generous, and so orders matters that when all is done for him by his church she herself receives much by way of blessing, comfort and joy. Hence the words at the end of verse 12 about the keeping of the fruit. This is not Christians holding back something of themselves for themselves, but expresses the rich blessings and benefits from Christ that he loads upon those who serve him faithfully and wholeheartedly. Putting it in very basic terms, there are never any losers in true Christian service; it is not a risky business. Observe Matthew 13:23, Mark 10:28-31 and John 15:8,16 in

215

this connection; compare also verses such as Proverbs 3:9-10 and 2 Corinthians 9:6. Where the owner of the vineyard himself (Christ) gets the thousand, his people will not be lacking for the two hundred.

Built in here, too, is the regular Scriptural insistence that 'the labourer is worthy of his hire', worked out in detail in a chapter like 1 Corinthians 9. It has application to the support and remuneration of Christ's ministers, the honour and esteem in which they are to be held in his church and the commendation that those who have been faithful will receive in person from the Lord Jesus Christ at his appearing. Their being designated here as keepers fits well with such other names for them in Scripture as watchmen, overseers, stewards, builders, husbandmen, shepherds, pastors and the like. Where the head and bridegroom is rightly honoured in his church, so will his spiritual ministers receive their proper due.

All of this now brings us to the closing verses of the Song.

8:13-14. A final word each

It is highly appropriate, given the whole nature and theme of the Song, that it should end with a word from each of its main characters: first the bridegroom addressing his bride (v.13), followed by the bride addressing her bridegroom (v.14). What they say to one another really amounts to the same thing in each case: come to me! Each desires more of the other, with deep and heartfelt longing.

There is something very significant to be noted however, before proceeding to the details of the two verses. Usually, love stories with a happy ending would close on the note of the two lovers being together (hand in hand, or arm in arm, perhaps strolling along some sandy beach at sunset, with the waves gently lapping on the shore and some palm trees swaying in the evening breeze). That, or something like it, is the picture that would be painted in a classic romance. The Song, however, ends with the two lovers apart, hence their mutual desire for hearing one another's voice and enjoying one another's company. They are apart and desiring to be together again.

This is not strange, though. It is realistic. It is true to the facts of spiritual experience. For although the bride belongs to the bridegroom, although the church is married to Christ, although the believer is united to him, and although it is possible (as the Song has shown) to enjoy rich and precious communion and fellowship with Christ here and now, there is no escaping the fact that in one sense Christ and the church, Christ and the believer, are apart. For Christ is in heaven, 'sitting at the right hand of God' (Col. 3:1), while his church is upon the earth, 'at home in the body' while 'absent from the Lord' (2 Cor. 5:6). Both of those Scriptures look forward to the time when this separation will be ended (see Col. 3:2-4 and 2 Cor. 5:8, as well as John 14:1-3), and that once and for all, but for now it obtains. This explains the language of the bridegroom and the bride here at the end of the Song, as they each recognise this situation, but also as they each look beyond it and strain forward to that time when they will be together for ever in heaven's glory and fellowship.

You who dwell in the gardens, the companions listen for your voice – let me hear it! (8:13). In the previous verse the bride has assured the Lord Jesus Christ of her absolute devotion and consecration to him, which now moves him to speak to her as he does (recall 2:14). The dwelling in the gardens is a familiar Song picture. The church herself, as a whole, is Christ's garden, and thereby an object of great beauty and intense delight to him and in which he loves to dwell. The various congregations of the Lord's people are, individually, gardens. There is much work for the church on earth still to do – kingdom work, work that will last, work for the glory of God. So she dwells (for now, for the time being, at present) 'in the gardens'. There is a throwback here all the way to the garden of Eden where, in the beginning, 'the LORD God' put Adam 'to tend and keep it' (Gen. 2:15). The church may be described as the Lord's spiritual Eden. Moreover, the two words vineyard (v.12) and garden (v.13) were evidently often used interchangeably among the Jews.

The reference to 'the companions' is to fellow believers together in spiritual fellowship. The psalmist testifies to the Lord, 'I am a companion of all those who fear you, and of those who keep your precepts' (Ps. 119:63). Believers are to be good companions and not false ones. It is a choice description of Christians and intimates such things as having a mutual interest in the covenant of grace, having the same heavenly Father, belonging to the same glorious Saviour and Husband, being indwelt by the same Holy Spirit, partaking of the same grace, inheriting the same promises, facing the same trials and heading for the same heavenly home. If such companions listen for (or 'to'?) one another's voice (remember Malachi 3:16: seeking to edify, encourage and engage one another all the more in the things of Christ), how much more is Christ himself pleased to hear it!

This is a strong and striking note for Christ to end on and should leave his church in no doubt of his affection towards her, his delight in her and his listening out for her, glorious themes which have run throughout the whole of the Song. He desires to hear from us often, in praise and prayer. Would we neglect him or disappoint him? Would we be much with one another yet little with him? Would we say all manner of things to our spiritual brethren, yet fail to pour out our hearts before him? Where do our priorities really lie? Who is most important to us? Would we take no notice of his invitations or think nothing of his encouragements? Whom do we love and desire most? Christ's words, 'let me hear (it)', with regard to the church's voice, have been translated 'cause me to hear (it)'. This emphasises further the primacy of seeking Christ continually, and not allowing anyone or anything else to get in the way or to deflect us from this. 'Therefore by him (Christ) let us continually offer the sacrifice of praise to God, that is, the fruit of our lips, giving thanks to his name' (Heb. 13:15). We are to 'pray without ceasing' (1 Thess. 5:17). Such communications are most welcome and pleasing to Christ. The bridegroom must hear from his bride.

Make haste, my beloved, and be like a gazelle or a young stag on the mountains of spices (8:14). With these words the bride responds immediately to Christ, and the Song itself comes to an end. Very noticeable is the name by which the bride calls the Lord Jesus Christ, just as has been the case all the way through: 'my beloved'. How it speaks of tender love to Christ, deep affection for him, and the complete absence of any sense of embarrassment or shame over feeling this way about him, and not worrying who knows. It is also a most suitable title with which to press upon him her suit in this verse. There is a sense in which all the desires and longings that she has ever expressed to Christ in the Song are here gathered up and compressed together in these few words. 'Christ is all and in all' (Col. 3:11).

The opening verb, 'make haste', may be rendered 'come away' (with NIV), 'flee' or even 'hurry'. This is its only occurrence in the Song, though it appears many times elsewhere in the Old Testament. On those other occasions it often signifies flight from enemies, though not here; here it is the rapid, not delayed one moment longer than necessary, flight of Christ and his church to one another. The figure of 'a gazelle or a young stag' (recall 2:17) underscores the sense of speed and urgency. To know, serve and enjoy Christ here on earth is itself a remarkable thing, but 'to depart and be with Christ ... is far better' (Phil. 1:23). Then 'we shall always be with the Lord' (1 Thess. 4:17). Then indeed the day will break and the shadows will flee away. Just as the Song opens with the church's strong desire for the enjoyment of the love (loves) of Christ (1:2), so now it ends with the focus being upon the perfection of that enjoyment in the closest and most holy fellowship imaginable. Since his love and his company is so delightful here below, how much more so will it be above.

Of particular interest is where the Lord Jesus Christ is viewed by his bride as coming from like these fleet-footed animals: 'on the mountains of spices'. Mountains have already occurred in 2:17, 4:6 and 4:8. It was observed in the preliminary remarks upon these last two verses of the Song that Christ and the church are apart, for he is in heaven. So it must be from heaven that he comes, and so it is. These 'mountains of spices' must be understood as referring to heaven. The reference is entirely appropriate, for in heaven the fragrant spices of Christ's beauty, his merits, his intercessions and his praises abound. All heaven is perfumed with his presence and his glory. Think of Psalm 45:8: 'All your garments are scented with myrrh and aloes and cassia, out of the ivory palaces, by which they have made you glad.'

The heavenly bridegroom is continually coming to his church while she continues upon the earth, pouring out his heavenly blessings, granting his Holy Spirit and performing great and mighty deeds in the accomplishment of the eternal divine purposes. But (as was also remarked above) in these concluding expressions in verses 13-14 both parties are looking beyond the various 'comings' of Christ to his church in the meantime and have their ultimate gaze fixed upon his return at the end of the age. This is the return that he himself has promised (in, for example, Matt. 24:29-31 and Rev. 22:7, and in the latter he uses the word 'quickly' – NIV, soon), and the return which is promised in other Scriptures as well (such as Acts 1:11 and Rev. 1:7). While for those who do not love Christ his appearing will be a time of grief and woe, yet to those who are his own it will be their glory and their joy (2 Thess. 1:7-10). True believers are those who are 'looking for the blessed hope and glorious appearing of our great God and Saviour Jesus Christ' (Tit. 2:13). To love him and to long for him is to love and long too for his appearing.

It is the consistent testimony of Scripture that the Lord Jesus Christ will come again (at his parousia, the second advent) personally, visibly and gloriously. He will come in his Father's glory, on the clouds of heaven, in the company of the angels and at the sound of a trumpet. Here at the end of the Song, this is what Christ looks forward to as his joyous prospect and this is what his church looks forward to as her spiritual horizon, bridegroom and bride together. Yet this is not only how the Song of Songs ends. For how does the whole of Scripture end? In exactly the same way (Rev. 22:20), where the Lord Jesus Christ utters the precious words, 'Surely I am coming quickly', and his bride responds (how else?) 'Amen. Even so, come, Lord Jesus!'

Christian Focus Publications publishes biblically-accurate books for adults and children. The books in the adult range are published in three imprints.

Christian Heritage contains classic writings from the past.

Christian Focus contains popular works including biographies, commentaries, doctrine, and Christian living.

Mentor focuses on books written at a level suitable for Bible College and seminary students, pastors, and others; the imprint includes commentaries, doctrinal studies, examination of current issues, and church history.

For a free catalogue of all our titles, please write to
Christian Focus Publications,
Geanies House, Fearn,
Ross-shire, IV20 1TW, Great Britain

For details of our titles visit us on our web site
http://www.christianfocus.com

Focus on the Bible Commentaries

Genesis – John Currid*
Exodus – John L. Mackay*
Deuteronomy – Alan Harman*
Judges and Ruth – Stephen Dray
1 Samuel – Dale Ralph Davis (2000)
2 Samuel – Dale Ralph Davis (1999)
1 and 2 Kings – Robert Fyall*
Ezra, Nehemiah and Esther – Robin Dowling*
Job – Bill Cotton (1999)
Proverbs – Eric Lane (1999)
Song of Songs – Richard Brooks
Isaiah – Paul House*
Jeremiah – George Martin*
Ezekiel – Anthony Billington*
Daniel – Robert Fyall
Hosea – Michael Eaton
Amos – O Palmer Robertson*
Jonah-Zephaniah – John L. Mackay
Haggai-Malachi – John L. Mackay
Matthew – Charles Price
Mark – Geoffrey Grogan
John – Robert Peterson*
Romans – R. C. Sproul
1 Corinthians – Paul Barnett*
2 Corinthians – Geoffrey Grogan
Galatians – Joseph Pipa*
Ephesians – R. C. Sproul
Philippians – Hywel Jones
Colossians – Robert Willoughby
1 and 2 Thessalonians – Richard Mayhue (1999)
The Pastoral Epistles – Douglas Milne
Hebrews – Walter Riggans
James – Derek Prime
1 Peter – Derek Cleave
2 Peter and Jude – Paul Gardner
Revelation – Steve Motyer*

Journey Through the Old Testament – Bill Cotton
How To Interpret the Bible – Richard Mayhue

Those marked with an * are currently being written.

Richard Brooks is pastor of York Evangelical Church in York, England. For Christian Focus he has also written *The Doors of Heaven*, a study of various pictures of heaven found in the Book of Revelation. For other publishers he has written *Great is Your Faithfulness* (a commentary on Lamentations), *The Lamb is All the Glory* (a commentary on the Book of Revelation), and *String of Pearls* (a study of Psalm 119).